1 Dead in Attic

AFTER KATRINA

Chris Rose

SIMON & SCHUSTER PAPERBACKS

NEW YORK LONDON TORONTO SYDNEY NEW DELHI

Simon & Schuster Paperbacks
An Imprint of Simon & Schuster, Inc.
1230 Avenue of the Americas
New York, NY 10020

This Simon & Schuster trade paperback edition August 2015

SIMON & SCHUSTER PAPERBACKS and colophon are registered
trademarks of Simon & Schuster, Inc.

For information about special discounts for bulk purchases,
please contact Simon & Schuster Special Sales at
1-800-456-6798 or business@simonandschuster.com

Designed by C. Linda Dingler

Manufactured in the United States of America

10 9 8 7 6 5 4

Library of Congress Cataloging-in-Publication Data
Rose, Chris
  1 dead in attic : after Katrina / Chris Rose.
      p. cm.
    Originally published: New Orleans, LA. : Chris Rose Books, c2005.
   1. Hurricane Katrina, 2005. 2. Hurricanes—Louisiana—New Orleans.
  3. Natural disasters—Louisiana—New Orleans. 4. Disaster victims—
  Louisiana—New Orleans. I. Title. II. Title: One dead in attic.
  HV6362005.L8 R67 2007
  976.3'35064—dc22   2007019365

ISBN 978-1-5011-2537-9 (pbk)
ISBN 978-1-4391-2624-0 (ebook)

This book is dedicated to Thomas Coleman, a retired longshoreman, who died in his attic at 2214 St. Roch Avenue in New Orleans' 8th Ward on or about August 29, 2005. He had a can of juice and a bedspread at his side when the waters rose.

There were more than a thousand like him.

Contents

Foreword   xi

Introduction   xvii

Who We Are   1

Early Days

Facing the Unknown   7
The First Time Back   10
Survivors   13
Life in the Surreal City   16
Hope   19
Rita Takes Aim   22
The Empty City   25
God and Strippers   28
The More Things Change   31
Enough to Feed an Army   34

Tough Times in the Blue Tarp Town

Blue Roof Blues   41
The Smell   44
The Elephant Men   48
Mad City   51
1 Dead in Attic   56
Despair   61

The Ties That Bind

My Introduction to New Orleans   67
The Funky Butt   72
The Hurricane Kids   75
Traveling Man   78
Have Barbie, Will Travel   81
Prep Boys and Jesuits   84
Good-bye   89
Groundhog Day   92
Coming Home   95

Life in the Refrigerator City

Civil Unrest   101
Refrigerator Town   105
Lurching Toward Babylon   107
The Cat Lady   110
Caving In   113
The Magnet Man   116
The Last Ride   119
Lights in the City   123
Let the Good Times Roll   127
Our Katrina Christmas   131
Tears, Fears, and a New Year   134

Misadventures in the Chocolate City

Chocolate City   141
Tutti-Frutti   145
He Had a Dream   147
He's Picking the Pairs for Nola's Ark   150
Rider on the Storm   153
Car 54, Where Are You?   156

Not in My Pothole   160
Survive This   163

Love Among the Ruins

September Never Ends   169
The Muddy Middle Ground   172
Misery in the Melting Pot   176
The End of the World   181
A Huck Finn Kind of Life   187
Our Very Scary Summer   192
Songs in the Key of Strife   196
The End of the Line   200
We Raze, and Raise, and Keep Pushing Forward   210
Echoes of Katrina in the Country   215

The Purple Upside-Down Car

Second Line, Same Verse   221
Don't Mess with Mrs. Rose   226
Shooting the Rock   229
The City That Hair Forgot   233
A Rapturous Day in the Real World   238
Big Daddy No Fun   243
Peace Among the Ruins   247
Artful Practicality   250
"She Rescued My Heart"   253
Miss Ellen Deserved Better   257

Things Worth Fighting For

Rebirth at the Maple Leaf   267
Melancholy Reveler   270
They Don't Get Mardi Gras, and They Never Will   274

Reality Fest   278
Love Fest   281
O Brothers, Where Be Y'all?   285
Funeral for a Friend   289
Thanks, We Needed That   292
Say What's So, Joe   296
A Night to Remember   301
Eternal Dome Nation   308

Falling Down

On the Inside Looking Out   317
A City on Hold   320
A Tough Nut to Crack   323
Hell and Back   327
Letters from the Edge   340

Where We Go From Here

Children of the Storm, It's Time to Represent   347
Thank You, Whoever You Are   353
A New Dawn   358

Acknowledgments   363

TEN YEARS LATER
A Foreword by Chris Rose

Hard to believe it's been ten years.

Sometimes it seems like a million years ago, sometimes like it was yesterday. But it never seems like it didn't happen.

Even ten years after—with so much rebuilt, restored, resettled, reconfigured, and entirely reimagined—the specter of Katrina still colors life here, in some small way, even if just a muted gray.

In casual conversations or social settings, it comes up. Might take a while, but it *will* come up eventually.

That's not to suggest that the stranger sitting next to you is ready to collapse into a fit of despair, rail against the injustice, and then itemize everything he lost.

It's not like *that* anymore, thank God.

It was for a really long time, though.

And that time sucked.

Looking back, the hardest thing to wrap your head around is remembering how many people said: Let it go. Let New Orleans wash into the sea.

This was not just the discontented grumblings from America's online lunatic fringe, but from established members of the media, the clergy, and Congress, most of whom made such vulgar pronouncements far away from the stink, the misery, and the wreckage.

The prevailing sentiment among such folks was that New Orleans—bless her charming, offbeat little powdered-sugar heart—was not worth fixing.

Because not just the levees needed fixing. The roads needed fixing, the parks needed fixing, the schools needed fixing.

The jails, which needed fixing, were being jammed by the judiciary, which needed fixing. They were stressed to the breaking point handling the massive caseloads delivered by the NOPD, which needed a *lot* of fixing, and who were not fit or equipped to handle this city's crime situation—which needed the most fixing of all.

You wonder: How could anyone have thought New Orleans was broken beyond repair?

(That was sarcasm.)

I acknowledge, looking back now from this side of the rubble and the flood—looking back from this side of history—that even a conservative estimate of the projected cost of rebuilding this city, coupled with the dubious integrity and doubtful competence of City Hall at the time . . . it was not a sure bet.

But still: Let New Orleans die?

When destiny calls you home, when it's time to exit the stage, when your number is called (insert any other number of overused clichés for dying): There's not a damn thing you can do about it. Money and politics can't fix dead.

But we weren't dead. Or if we were, we didn't know it.

Here, in arguably the most death-obsessed city in the world, the natives are by turns unaware, unconcerned, and often unconvinced of our own mortality.

And whereas our geographical positioning might have seemed like a great idea at the time—say, 1718—it's now a challenge, perhaps even a risk.

And it's true, we are neither the most logical nor efficient municipality in this great land.

But still.

We're also not the most educated folks you'll ever meet, but one thing we *did* know: We were not going gently into that good night. We were not giving up on New Orleans.

And with the help of 500,000 of our closest friends around the country—or hell, maybe a million—we put on some boots, pulled on some gloves, and got busy.

If what the magazines and websites have been saying—if what the analysts and futurists are predicting—is true, then New Orleans is the destination for America's next generation of young artists, entrepreneurs, and designers. Millennials, dreamers, and visionaries are here creating the next new business model, designing the next great app, fusing the next landmark technology, mixing the next banging cocktail.

We're the new Austin. The new Portland. The new Brooklyn. Hollywood South. Hipster City, USA. The New New Orleans, the bright new shining city on the hill. Except, well, without the hill.

We don't have any hills.

But you get the point.

And maybe that's all a load of piffle, I don't know. I reckon time will tell.

But I do know this: The more New Orleans changes, the more she remains the same. That is the nature of a place where irony is a birthright and contradiction is the dominant hand of fate.

It's hard to envision the day when the Thinking Class outnumbers the Drinking Class in this city, but we are approaching a necessary equilibrium between the old and new, the practical and the frivolous, the digital and the sensual.

We are innovation and tradition, high-tech and antique, fiber optics and gas lamps, new urbanism and the Vieux Carré, Uber cabs and streetcar lines, Airbnb and the Hotel Monteleone.

We're Dixieland jazz and sissy bounce.

New Orleans is today, as it was before, a place suspended between the physical world and the realm of imagination. The experience of everyday life here is magnified by emotional intensity and creative reverie, yet also reduced by the heat, humidity, and altitude to its most basic and primal elements: Food, shelter, and the Saints.

You can regulate our smoking and regulate our music and—hard to believe this day has come—you can even regulate our go-cups.

But you cannot regulate soul. You cannot legislate funk. And you cannot pass an ordinance that makes us ordinary.

The best things about us will never change.

And one final word: Thank you, America. Thank you, from me and my city—you 500,000 (or hell, maybe a million) of our closest friends—who came down here over the past ten years and helped us rebuild this crazy, shambling, loveable hot mess of a city.

Because without New Orleans, where would all the Wild Things go in the night?

There's a bunch of old nicknames for this city and a whole bunch more now, but taking stock of this past decade of transformation—from our despair to our triumph, from our shame to our redemption—I know where I live now.

Welcome to Lucky Town.

—June 2015

"If there was no New Orleans, America would just be a bunch of free people dying of boredom."

—JUDY DECK

Introduction

Writing an introduction for a book like this is tricky business.

Intros I have read over the years are generally composed of personal anecdotes and references to the body of work that follows. But, in this case, what follows *is* the personal work, the veil pulled away, the soul of a city—and a writer—laid bare.

Newspaper reporters are used to covering death and disaster—it's our bread and butter—but nothing prepares you to do it in your own town. Usually, we parachute into trouble, fill our notebooks, and then hightail it back to the comfort of our homes and offices.

Katrina changed all that.

Our comfort zones disappeared, turned into rubble, wastelands, and ghost towns. I went from being a detached entertainment columnist to a soldier on the front line of a battle to save a city, a culture, a newspaper, my job, my home.

Whether we won or lost the war remains to be seen. New Orleans is still a work in progress. The observations, lamentations, and ruminations that follow are the story so far, as it unfolded to me in the first sixteen months after the flood.

It's probably too emotional for conventional newspaper work. Too sentimental. Too angry. And way too self-absorbed, particularly for someone who weathered the storm remarkably well—in a material sense, at least (I suffered a broken screen door and a loose gutter)—and whose career not only survived the storm, but actually thrived in the aftermath.

I got a book deal, a movie deal, a Pulitzer Prize, dinner with Ted Koppel, and a mention in the social column of *The Washington Times*. If that ain't Making The Grade, then I don't know what is.

Natural disasters are a good career move for a man in my line of work.

But you didn't have to lose your house, your car, your dog, your job, your marriage, or your grandparents in an attic to suffer the impact of this storm. Unfortunately, most folks around south Louisiana and Mississippi did lose some or all of this.

Others lost less tangible assets: their peace of mind, security, serenity, ability to concentrate, notions of romance, sobriety, sanity, and hope.

The toll it took on me is in the book; I'll not belabor it here other than to say Katrina beat the shit out of me. It beat the shit out of everyone I know. This is our story.

In the winter of 2006, I self-published a collection of my post-Katrina columns from *The Times-Picayune*, a slim volume of love letters to New Orleans, howls of protest, cries for help, and general musings on the surrealistic absurdities of life in a post-Apocalyptic landscape.

I called it *1 Dead in Attic*, a phrase I saw painted on the front of a house in the city's 8th Ward; words that haunted me then, and haunt me still.

Within six months, I ran through five printings of the book, collected great reviews from publications large and small, and sold 65,000 copies. I'm a neophyte in the world of independent publishing, but I'm told that's a real good number for a self-published volume. In fact, it's a good number for any volume.

And that's how the book came to attention of Simon & Schuster. I was preparing a follow-up to *1 Dead in Attic*, another collection of stories that I was going to call *The Purple Upside-Down Car*, a declarative observation my four-year-old son made from our car during a tour of the Lower 9th Ward that I clung to as the perfect metaphor for the whole of New Orleans and not just some wasted, toppled vehicle lying in a field of debris down on — get this — Flood Street.

The irony in this place could kill you.

Simon & Schuster bought the rights to *1 Dead in Attic* and the as-yet-unpublished *Purple Upside-Down Car* and we put them together and that's what you're holding in your hands. Faced with two titles but only one book, we went with the former because it already has brand recognition and because, well . . . the other one kind of sounds precariously like a Dr. Suess book.

This book takes the reader up to New Year's Day, 2007. A lot has happened since then, to the city, to me. On the eve of publication, I split with my wife of eleven years and went to rehab for an addiction to prescription painkillers, which I turned to in my ongoing struggles with anxiety and depression.

It would be easy to lay this blood on the hands of Katrina, though there is more, much more, to the story.

There always is.

But I guess that's the next chapter, the next story. The next book.

— Chris Rose
New Orleans, June, 2007

Who We Are

Dear America,

I suppose we should introduce ourselves: we're South Louisiana.

We have arrived on your doorstep on short notice and we apologize for that, but we were never much for waiting around for invitations. We're not much on formalities like that.

And we might be staying around your town for a while, enrolling in your schools and looking for jobs, so we wanted to tell you a few things about us. We know you didn't ask for this and neither did we, so we're just going to have to make the best of it.

First of all, we thank you. For your money, your water, your food, your prayers, your boats and buses, and the men and women of your National Guards, fire departments, hospitals, and everyone else who has come to our rescue.

We're a fiercely proud and independent people, and we don't cotton much to outside interference, but we're not ashamed to accept help when we need it. And right now, we need it.

Just don't get carried away. For instance, once we get around to fishing again, don't try to tell us what kind of lures work best in your waters.

We're not going to listen. We're stubborn that way.

You probably already know that we talk funny and listen to strange music and eat things you'd probably hire an exterminator to get out of your yard.

We dance even if there's no radio. We drink at funerals. We talk too much and laugh too loud and live too large, and, frankly, we're suspicious of others who don't.

But we'll try not to judge you while we're in your town.

Everybody loves their home, we know that. But we love south Louisiana with a ferocity that borders on the pathological. Sometimes we bury our dead in LSU sweatshirts.

Often we don't make sense. You may wonder why, for instance, if we could carry only one small bag of belongings with us on our journey to your state—why in God's name did we bring a pair of shrimp boots?

We can't really explain that. It is what it is.

You've probably heard that many of us stayed behind. As bad as it is, many of us cannot fathom a life outside our border, out in that place we call Elsewhere.

The only way you could understand that is if you have been there, and so many of you have. So you realize that when you strip away all the craziness and bars and parades and music and architecture and all that hooey, really, the best thing about where we come from is us.

We are what made this place a national treasure. We're good people. And don't be afraid to ask us how to pronounce our names. It happens all the time.

When you meet us now and you look into our eyes, you will see the saddest story ever told. Our hearts are broken into a thousand pieces.

But don't pity us. We're gonna make it. We're resilient. After all, we've been rooting for the Saints for thirty-five years. That's got to count for something.

Okay, maybe something else you should know is that we make jokes at inappropriate times.

But what the hell.

And one more thing: In our part of the country, we're used to having visitors. It's our way of life.

So when all this is over and we move back home, we will repay you the hospitality and generosity of spirit you offer us in this season of our despair.

That is our promise. That is our faith.

Early Days

Facing the Unknown

I got out.

I'm mystified by the notion that so many people didn't even try; but that's another story for another time.

We left Saturday, my wife, kids, and me. We went first to Picayune, Mississippi, thinking that a Category 3 storm would flood New Orleans and knock out power, but that we'd be dry and relatively comfortable in the piney woods while the city dried out.

Sunday morning, of course, Katrina was a massive red blob on our TV screens—now a Cat 5—so we packed up and left again.

We left my in-laws behind in Picayune. They wouldn't come with us. Self-sufficient country folk; sometimes you can't tell 'em nothing.

We don't know what happened to them. My wife's dad and her brother and their families: No word. Only hope.

Like so many people around the country wondering what happened to those still unaccounted for, we just don't know. That's the hardest part.

If you take the images you've seen on TV and picked up off the radio and Internet, and you try to apply what you know to the people and places you don't know about, well, the mind starts racing, assumptions are made, and, well . . . it consumes you.

The kids ask you questions. You don't have answers. Sometimes they look at me, and though they don't say it, I can see they're wondering: Daddy, where are you?

My six-year-old daughter, she's onto this thing. What is she thinking?

We spent Sunday night in a no-tell motel in a forgotten part of downtown Vicksburg; a neighborhood teetering between a familiar antiquated charm and hopeless decay. Truth is, it called to mind my beloved New Orleans.

Most of the folks in the hotel seemed to live there permanently, and it had a hard-luck feel to it. It was the kind of place where your legs start itching in the bed and you think the worst and you don't want your kids to touch the carpet or the tub and we huddled together and I read them to sleep.

Monday morning, my wife's aunt told us they had a generator in Baton Rouge. As Katrina marched north and east, we bailed on our sullen little hotel and drove down along the western ridge of the storm, mostly alone on the road.

Gas was no problem. We had catfish and pulled pork in a barbecue joint in Natchez, and the folks there—everyone we have met along our three-day journey—said the same thing: Good luck, folks. We love your city. Take care of it for us.

Oh, my city. We have spent hours and hours listening to the radio. Image upon image piling up in your head.

What about school? What about everyone's jobs? Did all our friends get out? Are there still trees on the streetcar line? What will our economy be like with no visitors? How many are dead? Do I have a roof? Have the looters found me yet? When can we go home?

As I said, it consumes you as you sit helplessly miles from home, unable to help anyone, unable to do anything.

If I could, what I'd do first is hurt the looters. I'd hurt them bad.

But you have to forget all that. You have to focus on what is at hand, what you can reach, and when you have three little kids lost at sea, they are what's at hand and what you can reach.

I took them to a playground in Baton Rouge Tuesday afternoon. They'd been bottled up for days.

Finally unleashed, they ran, they climbed, they fell down, they fought, they cried, they made me laugh, they drove me crazy; they did the things that make them kids.

It grounds you. You take a breath. You count to ten. Maybe— under the circumstances—you go to twenty or thirty this time.

And tonight, we'll just read them to sleep again.

We have several books with us because—and this is rich—we brought on our evacuation all the clothes and things we planned to bring on a long-weekend trip that we were going to take over Labor Day weekend.

To the beach. To Fort Morgan, right at the mouth of Mobile Bay.

Man.

Instead of that, I put on my suntan lotion and went out in the yard of the house where we're staying in Baton Rouge and I raked a massive pile of leaves and limbs from the yard and swept the driveway.

Doing yard work and hitting the jungle gym on the Day After. Pretending life goes on. Just trying to stay busy. Just trying not to think. Just trying not to fail, really.

Gotta keep moving.

The First Time Back
9/7/05

The first time you see it . . . I don't know. Where are the words?

I got to town Monday afternoon. I braced myself, not knowing how it would make me feel, not knowing how much it would make me hurt.

I found out that I am one of the lucky ones. High ground. With that come gratitude and wonder and guilt. The Higher Powers have handed me my house and all my stuff, and now what? What is there?

I live Uptown, where all the fancy-pants houses are, and they're all still here. Amid the devastation, they never looked so beautiful. They never looked more like hope. This swath of land is where this city will begin its recovery.

There are still homes and schools, playgrounds, stores, bars, and restaurants. Not so many trees, I'm afraid. We'll have to do something about that.

The Circle K near my house was looted, but there are still ample supplies of cigarettes and booze. They just took what they needed. The hardware store and Perlis—the preppy clothing store—same thing.

Someone kicked in the window at Shoefty, a high-end shoe boutique, and what good a pair of Manolo Blahnik stilettos is going to do you right now, I don't know.

Idiots.

I myself was escorted out of the local Winn-Dixie by narcotics officers from Rusk County, Texas.

I told them I thought it was okay to take what we need. "And what do you need?" the supervisor asked me. I reached into my bag and held up a bottle of mouthwash.

I told him I will come back to this Winn-Dixie one day and pay for this bottle, and I will. I swear it.

Right by the entrance to the store, there is a huge pile of unsold newspapers stacked up from the last day they were delivered, Sunday, August 28.

The Times-Picayune headline screams: KATRINA TAKES AIM.

Ain't that the truth? Funny, though: The people you see here—and there are many who stayed behind—they never speak her name. She is the woman who done us wrong.

I had the strangest dream last night, and this is true: I dreamt I was reading an ad in the paper for a hurricane-relief benefit concert at Zephyr Field and the headliner act was Katrina and the Waves.

They had that peppy monster hit back in the '80s, "Walking on Sunshine," the one they play on Claritin ads on TV and that almost seems funny in light of what happened.

Almost.

Riding my bike, I searched out my favorite places, my comfort zones. I found that Tipitina's is still there, and that counts for something. Miss Mae's and Dick & Jenny's, ditto.

Domilise's po-boy shop is intact, although the sign fell and shattered, but the truth is, that sign needed to be replaced a long time ago.

I saw a dead guy on the front porch of a shotgun double on a working-class street, and the only sound was wind chimes.

Everybody here has a dead-guy story now. Everybody here will always be different.

I passed by the Valence Street Baptist Church and the facade was ripped away and I walked in and stared at the altar amid broken stained glass and strewn Bibles and I got down on my knees and said Thank you but why? why? why? and I'm not even anything close to Baptist.

It just seemed like a place to take shelter from the storm in my head.

The rockers on my neighbors' front porch are undisturbed, as if nothing ever happened. At my other neighbors' house—the ones who never take out their trash—a million kitchen bags are still piled in the mound that's always there and I never thought I'd be happy to see garbage, but I am.

Because it reminds me of my home.

I haven't been down in the kill zone yet. I haven't seen the waters. I haven't been where all hope, life, and property are lost.

I have only seen what I have seen, and we took the hit and it is still here. This is where we'll make our start. This is where we'll make our stand.

And when everything gets back to normal—whenever that may be—I'm going to do what I've been putting off for a very long time. I'm going to walk next door and tell my neighbors that they really do need to start taking out their trash.

Survivors
9/8/05

They're telling the people they have to go. They're going door to door with rifles now.

They came to our little hovel on Laurel Street Uptown—a dozen heavily armed members of the California National Guard—they pounded on our door and wanted to know who we were.

We told them we were the newspaper, the Big City Daily. I admit, it doesn't look like the newsrooms you see on TV. I suppose if we wore shirts, we'd look more professional.

The Guard moved on, next door, next block. They're telling people they have to go.

It won't be easy. The people who stayed here have weathered ten days of unfathomable stench and fear, and if they haven't left yet, it seems unlikely that they're going to be willing now.

In a strange way, life just goes on for the remaining. In the dark and fetid Winn-Dixie on Tchoupitoulas, an old woman I passed in the pet food aisle was wearing a house frock and puffy slippers and she just looked at me as she pushed her cart by and said, "How you doin', baby?"

As if it were just another afternoon buying groceries. I love the way strangers call you "baby" in this town.

Outside the store, there's an old guy who parks his old groaning car by the front door from sunup to sundown. There are extension cords running from his trunk into the store, which still has power—don't ask me how; I have no idea—and he watches TV in his front seat and drinks juice.

That is what he does, all day, every day.

At this point, I just can't see this guy leaving. I don't imagine he has any place else in the world but this.

And life goes on. Down on St. Claude Avenue, a tribe of survivors has blossomed at Kajun's Pub, where, incredibly, they have cold beer and cigarettes and a stereo playing Elvis and you'd think everything was in standard operating procedure but it is not: the Saturday-night karaoke has been suspended indefinitely.

The people here have a touch of Mad Max syndrome; they're using an old blue Cadillac for errands, and when parts fall off of it—and many parts have fallen off—they just throw them in the trunk.

Melvin, a bar owner from down the block, had the thing up for sale for $895, but he'll probably take the best offer now.

Melvin's Bar and Kajun's Pub have pooled their inventories to stay in business.

"We've blended our fortunes together," said Renee dePonthieux, a bartender at Melvin's. "We carried everything we could down here, and we'll make the accounting later. What else are you gonna do? In case you haven't heard, Budweiser ain't delivering."

A guy with a long goatee and multiple tattoos was covering a couple of aluminum foil pans of lasagna and carrying them up to the roof to cook them in the sun on the hot slate shingles.

Joann Guidos, the proprietor at Kajun's, called out for a game of bourré and they all dumped their money on a table and sat down and let the cards and liquor flow.

A National Guard truck pulled up and asked if they were ready to leave yet. Two guys standing out on the sidewalk in the company of pit bulls said, "Hell no."

DePonthieux said, "We're the last fort on the edge of the wilderness. My family's been in exile for three hundred years; this ain't shit."

I just don't see these people leaving.

Uptown, on what was once a shady street, a tribe is living in a beautiful home owned by a guy named Peanut. There are a seaplane in his driveway, a bass boat in the front yard, and generators running the power.

Let's just say they were prepared.

All the men wear pistols in visible holsters. They have the only manicured lawn in the city. What else is there to do all afternoon, really?

Christine Paternostro is a member of this tribe, an out-of-work hairstylist from Supercuts in a city where no one shaves or bathes. Not many prospects for her at this point.

"Everyone will need a haircut when this is over," I offered.

While members of this tribe stood talking on their street, a woman came running out of the house, yelling, "Y'all, come quick. We on WWL! We on WWL!"

Everyone ran in the house and watched a segment about how people are surviving in the city. And these guys are doing just that. (Although I think the airplane in the driveway is a little over the top.)

As I was leaving, the WWL woman asked me, "Are you staying for dinner?"

I was not, but I asked what they were having. "Tuna steaks," she said. "Grilled."

If and when they rebuild this city and we all get to come home, I want to live near people like this. I just can't imagine them ever leaving.

They make me wonder if I ever could.

Life in the Surreal City
9/10/05

You hear the word "surreal" in every report from this city now. There is no better word for it.

If Salvador Dalí showed up here, he wouldn't be able to make heads or tails of it. Nobody could paint this.

He did that famous painting of the melting clock, and our clocks melted at 6:45 the morning of August 29. That's what the clocks in the French Quarter still say. That's when time stood still.

The Quarter survived all this; you've probably heard that much. Most of what remains unscathed—and I'm using a very relative term here—is a swath of dry land from the Riverbend through Audubon Park, down St. Charles and Tchoupitoulas to the Quarter and into the Bywater.

It's like a landmass the size of Bermuda, maybe, but with not so many golf courses.

There are other dry outposts in the great beyond—little Key Wests across the city—but I haven't seen them.

The weather is beautiful, I don't mind telling you. But if I wrote you a postcard, it wouldn't say, "Wish you were here."

There are still hearty rosebushes blooming on front porches, and there are still birds singing in the park. But the park is a huge National Guard encampment.

There are men and women from other towns living there in tents who have left their families to come help us, and they are in the park clearing out the fallen timber. My fellow Americans.

Every damn one of them tells you they're happy to be here (despite what you've heard, it still beats the hell out of Fallujah), and every time I try to thank them, on behalf of all of us, I just lose it. I absolutely melt down.

There is nothing quite as ignominious as weeping in front of a soldier.

This is no environment for a wuss like me. We reporters go to other places to cover wars and disasters and pestilence and famine. There's no manual to tell you how to do this when it's your own city.

And I'm telling you: it's hard.

It's hard not to get crispy around the edges. It's hard not to cry. It's hard not to be very, very afraid.

My colleagues who are down here are warriors. There are a half dozen of us living in a small house on a side street Uptown. Everyone else has been cleared out.

We have a generator and water and military food rations and Doritos and smokes and booze. After deadline, the call goes out: "Anyone for some warm brown liquor?" And we sit on the porch in the very, very still of the night and we try to laugh.

Some of these guys lost their houses—everything in them. But they're here, telling our city's story.

And they stink. We all stink. We stink together.

We have a bunch of guns, but it's not clear to me if anyone in this "news bureau" knows how to use them.

The California National Guard came by and wanted an accounting of every weapon in the building and they wrote the serial numbers down and apparently our guns are pretty rad because they were all cooing over the .38s.

I guess that's good to know.

The Guard wanted to know exactly what we had so they would be able to identify, apparently by sound, what guns were in whose hands if anything "went down" after dark here at this house.

That's not so good to know.

They took all our information and bid us a good day and then sauntered off to retrieve a dead guy from a front porch down the street.

Then the California Highway Patrol—the CHiPs!—came and demanded that we turn over our weapons.

What are you going to do? We were certainly outnumbered, so we turned over the guns. Then, an hour later, they brought them back. With no explanation.

Whatev. So here we are. Just another day at the office.

Maybe you've seen that *Times-Picayune* advertising slogan before: "News, Sports and More."

More indeed. You're getting your money's worth today.

Hope
9/11/05

Amid the devastation, you have to look for hope. Forward progress of any kind.

Even the smallest incidents of routine and normalcy become reassuring. For instance, I was driving down Prytania, and at the corner of Felicity, the light turned red.

Out of nowhere, in total desolation, there was a working stoplight. I would have been less surprised to find a Blockbuster Video on Mars.

And the funny thing is, I stopped. I waited for it to turn green, and then I drove slowly on my way, even though there were no other cars anywhere and the likelihood of getting a ticket for running the only traffic signal in town seems very unlikely right now.

Considering.

Also on Prytania, there was a gardener watering the plants on the porch of Nicolas Cage's mansion, and I guess that's a good sign. Life goes on. In very small ways.

The toilets flush now, and I never thought that would be a sound of reassurance. Even better was finding out that WWOZ is broadcasting on the Web—radio in exile—laying out its great New Orleans music.

That's important. I have no idea from where they're operating or which disc jockeys are spinning the discs, but I can tell you this: The first time I hear Billy Dell's *Records from the Crypt* on the radio again, I will kiss the dirty ground beneath my feet.

On Friday, you started to see guys with brooms cleaning Canal Street and Convention Center Boulevard. Up until then, any tidying up required a backhoe, a crane, or a Bobcat.

God only knows where they're going to put all this garbage, all this rubble, all these trees, but they're gathering it up all the same.

The streets of the French Quarter, absent the rubble of the CBD, basically look and smell the same as they do the day after Mardi Gras, except with no broken strands of beads in the gutter.

Okay, maybe it was a real windy Mardi Gras, but you get the point.

It just needs a little face-lift, a little sweeping up, and a good hard rain to wash away . . . all the bad stuff.

A counterpoint to that scene would be Uptown on Broadway—Fraternity Row—where the street is actually cleaner than usual, and that's because the fine young men and women of our universities had not yet settled into their early-semester routines of dragging living room furniture out onto their front yards and drinking Red Bull and vodka to while away their youth.

I wonder where all of them are. When this is over, who will go there and who will teach there?

What will happen to us?

One thing's for sure, our story is being told.

The satellite trucks stretch for eight blocks on Canal Street and call to mind an event like the Super Bowl or the Republican National Convention.

It's a strange place. Then again, anywhere that more than ten news reporters gather becomes a strange place by default.

I saw Anderson Cooper interviewing Dr. Phil. And while Cooper's CNN camera crew filmed Dr. Phil, Dr. Phil's camera crew filmed Cooper, and about five or six other camera crews from other shows and networks stood to the side and filmed all of that.

By reporting this scene, I have become the media covering the media covering the media.

It all has the surrealistic air of a Big Event, what with Koppel and Geraldo and all those guys wandering around in their Eddie Bauer hunting vests, and impossibly tall and thin anchorwomen from around the region powdering their faces and teasing their hair so they look good when they file their latest report from Hell.

"And today in New Orleans . . . blah blah blah."

Today in New Orleans, a traffic light worked. Someone watered flowers. And anyone with the means to get online could have heard Dr. John's voice wafting in the dry wind, a sound of grace, comfort, and familiarity here in the saddest, loneliest place in the world.

It's a start.

Rita Takes Aim
9/23/05

The slightest rain fell here Thursday morning.

You know, the kind of New Orleans rain that just gives everything a light coat and sheen, that tamps down the dust of the old shell roads and washes down the oyster stink in the French Quarter gutters and slicks up all the playground equipment and makes New Orleans smell—is it possible?—so fresh. So southern.

The kind of rain that falls even though the sun is shining. Does that happen in other places?

New Orleans rain has always been like drops of clarity in an otherwise murky habitat, sometimes too much, sometimes too little, but always a marvel to behold. There's always something that needs to be washed down here.

In *A Streetcar Named Desire*, Blanche DuBois said it best: "Don't you just love those long rainy afternoons in New Orleans when an hour isn't just an hour, but a little piece of eternity dropped into our hands—and who knows what to do with it?"

Indeed, what to do?

That was the rain that fell Thursday. And we needed it. Because the oyster stink is at noxious levels and the city is stacked with an apocalyptic vision of dry kindling that requires only one dummy with a discarded cigarette to torch an entire block.

Which raises one of the things that most catches the eye here: the trees. Or the lack thereof. I don't know that anyone will ever be able to count how many trees fell or just plain withered and died under Katrina's fierce hot breath, but I'm sure some expert will tell us in due time. Whatever the raw number, it won't match the impact on the senses.

I can't remember where I read it, but someone interviewed a New Orleans artist who had returned home last week, and this guy—whose very living hinges upon his interpretations of shadow, nuance, and color—said the problem with New Orleans now is that there is too much sunlight on the ground.

That changes everything. Because if there were ever a town that couldn't afford to surrender shade, it is this one, where a walk on a summer afternoon can be like sauntering through a blast furnace.

Maybe only the bad golfers will be happy about this development, for their way from tee to green is now so much more accessible.

It had been three weeks since it rained—since you know when—and that's as unfathomable a notion here as a September without fresh oysters.

Of course, by the time you read this, Friday, rain might not be such a charming enterprise here. And Blanche DuBois's notion of eternity may not be so romantic.

Rita swirls out in the Gulf of Mexico, capriciously choosing its path of destruction, and even the slightest brush of wind could take out so many more trees and the slightest rain—the kind that tourists with their Big Ass Beers in hand used to stand under French Quarter balconies and watch with a sense of comic wonder—could wind the clock back three weeks to that piece of eternity we don't ever want to live again.

Under one of those French Quarter balconies, those famous mannequin legs at Big Daddy's strip club improbably swing in and out of a window, an alluring, optimistic, or delusional signal that the libertine times will once again return to the Old City. That *les bons temps* will *rouler* again someday.

There is no power on that block of Bourbon Street where the

legs swing; the owner just thought that the best use of portable power would be to swing those legs.

Swinging in the rain. Drinking a hurricane instead of dodging one. Living in a place where the past and present and future have never collided so chaotically and without rational analysis.

There is no one who can tell us what tomorrow will bring. But, personally, I consider it a very bad sign that the killer hurricane that is dancing on our television screens and toying with our collective psyche is named after a meter maid.

That can't be good.

The Empty City
9/24/05

It's hard to imagine that it could have felt any lonelier in New Orleans than it has for the past three weeks. But Friday, everything just disappeared.

What little life there was seemed to dissipate into the not-so-thin air of a colossal barometer drop. The Furies, it seems, are aroused.

The wind buffeted cars and put the heavy hand on already weakened trees. Magazine Street boutique signs—most hanging askew by only one chain after Katrina—spun in place like pinwheels. Loose power lines whipped and flapped across Uptown and Lakeview streets like fly-fishing rods.

The rain came, misting one minute, blinding the next. Outside the CBD emergency operations center, anywhere you drove, you saw . . . nobody.

The folks who had been trickling into town for the past week or so, checking on homes and businesses, simply disappeared. Police on the outskirts of town blocked all entry. The big National Guard camps in Audubon Park disappeared overnight without a sign that they had ever been there.

So much for the repopulation plan. A TV station reported that there were only five hundred civilians left in the city as Hurricane Rita set aim on the Cajun Riviera, all those miles away to the west, and you were hard-pressed to find any of them.

A passing truck stopped me, and the guys inside asked for directions to the Nashville Wharf, and it was good just to talk to someone.

The isolation can be maddening. The car radio just tells you bad things. You just want to find someone, anyone, and ask, "How 'bout dem Saints?"

You know those classic New Orleans characters—the cab drivers, bartenders, and bitter poets—who buttonhole you and natter on and on forever about tedious and mundane topics that date back to Mayor Schiro's term and when the Pelicans played out on Tulane Avenue? Usually when you're in a hurry somewhere?

I'd give anything to run into one of those guys right now. Go ahead and tell me about the fishing in Crown Point; I'll listen to just about anything you have to say.

I went to Walgreens on Tchoupitoulas, which had been open most of the week, figuring there would be life there, but it had shuttered at noon. There was a sign on the door that said "Now Hiring," and that's funny.

I guess.

The day before, the store's public address system was stuck in a time warp, a perky female voice reminding shoppers (both of them): "Don't let Halloween sneak up on you; stock up on candy early. You'll find great savings now . . . at Walgreens!"

Truth is, there sure was a hell of a lot of candy there. Trick or treat.

As I drove around, the gray sheets of rain pushed around all the stuff in the street, and, trust me, there's a lot of stuff in the street. For as far as you looked up and down every avenue, the same blank vistas.

Across town, the water was rising. Again. I suppose there were people there, trying to save our city again, though the cynical might ask: What's to save?

On dry land, the only place I found people gathered was at the fire station on Magazine Street in the Garden District. I went by to drop off some copies of the newspaper for the local guys and found about sixty firefighters from all over the country hanging out in a rec room watching TV and frying burgers.

That was perhaps the strangest sight of all, these guys just sitting around. Stranger in some ways than the desolation.

Because for once, with all this rain soaking the downed trees and rooftops and nobody around to do something stupid like start a fire, they had nothing to do.

Just sit and watch TV in a haunted city.

God and Strippers
9/27/05

Even at the End of Days, there will be lap dancing.

Over the weekend, while a desolate, desperate city plunged into darkness and the waters rose again in the Rita Aftermath, and while a population spread across the nation watched new horrors on TV with churning guts, a strip club opened on Bourbon Street.

The symbolism of this event can hardly be overstated.

The Saints are gone. The Hornets are gone. Zephyr Field is a staging area for choppers to go find dead people.

No college hoops. No movie theaters, no Swamp Fest, no Voodoo Fest. No horses running at the Fairgrounds. No line for Friday lunch at Galatoire's.

But there are topless women hanging upside down from brass poles at a place called Déjà Vu. Gaudiness, flesh, neon, and bad recorded music have returned to one small outpost on the Boulevard of Broken Dreams, and if that's not one small step towards normalcy—at least as that term is defined in the Big Uneasy—then I don't know what is.

There were about a hundred guys in there Saturday night, all of them with very, very short hair, which is basically what everyone around here who's not a journalist has these days.

Exactly how a posse of exotic dancers were smuggled into

town during the most severe lockdown in this city since the hurricane crises began, well, I don't know.

Inexplicable things seem to be the norm around here these days.

When I walk down the street one day and some rumpled grifter tells me he knows where I got my shoes, I guess I'll know we're fully on our way home. (Of course, I could be cynical and tasteless and tell the guy I got them at Wal-Mart on Tchoupitoulas like everyone else, but that would be cynical and tasteless.)

And speaking of tasteless: this is not a topic I want to delve too deeply into, but someone has to call out the demagogic ministers who have used Katrina's destruction to preach the message that God was tired of this city's libertine ways and decided to clean house.

Let me roll at you some snippets of wisdom that have been widely distributed on the Internet from Reverend Bill Shanks, pastor of New Covenant Fellowship in Metairie: "New Orleans now is Mardi Gras free. New Orleans now is free of Southern Decadence and the sodomites, the witchcraft workers, false religion—it's free of all of those things now. God simply, I believe, in His mercy purged all of that stuff out of there—and now we're going to start over again."

Well, almost. It's an interesting interpretation, to be sure, and Shanks is not the only man of the cloth to make such claims. No doubt it's a good message for the evangelical business.

Of course, try telling some poor sap down in St. Bernard Parish who has never heard of Southern Decadence and who goes to Bible study every Wednesday night that he lost his house and his job and his grandmother died in a flooded nursing home because God was angry at a bunch of bearded guys in dresses over on Dumaine Street.

Collateral damage, I guess. The question that arises, of course, is that if Shanks's prophecy is true, how come Plaquemines, St. Bernard, the East, and Lakeview are gone but the French Quarter is still standing?

I'd suggest that there are those who have confused meteorology with mythology, global warming with just plain hot air, but that might be cynical and tasteless. Might be crass and gaudy.

And I'll try to leave that stuff where it belongs—in the French Quarter, where the craziest patchwork of people ever gathered on this planet are cobbling back together a strange and mind-boggling Twilight Zone of what it once was.

File that one under: Only in New Orleans.

The More Things Change
10/8/05

You hang around New Orleans long enough these days, and you begin to absorb what is new and what is different.

For instance, I was sitting on my front stoop and an RTA bus marked MAGAZINE zoomed by. I thought: Well, how about that! That's a good sign.

Never mind that the bus was empty; at least it was running, and that's a sign of normalcy. And it was going way too fast, and therein was another harbinger of the same-ol', same-ol'.

Then, about ninety seconds later, another RTA bus marked MAGAZINE whizzed by, shaking my house to its foundation. It, too, was empty, but it was the realization that there were probably only two buses running the entire Magazine Street route and here they were, one right after the other and I thought: We're back!

What could be a better indication of a return to the old ways than the colossal inefficiency of our public transportation system? I don't know about you, but I will sleep better tonight; at least, that is, until an RTA bus blows by the house at midnight at Category 5 speed and does more damage to my plaster ceilings than Katrina did.

Of course, a common joke around here—dire times make for dire humor—is that when the mayor announced that he was laying off three thousand workers this week, who would notice? I believe he, or some other public official, called them "nonessential employees," and I'll let you fill in your own punch line.

I just hope it's not the two guys who've been assigned to cut the grass on the neutral grounds for the past ten years; man, things would really be different around here without them.

I have a feeling I just really ticked off three thousand people, maybe more. But then, that would be another sign of normalcy, wouldn't it? People being angry at the local newspaper: a comfort zone if ever there was one.

A casual drive around town — or at least what remains of it — is also a compelling reminder of the old days. It reminds you how much a simple afternoon drive can involve facing danger to its core.

First of all, at least half the city's one-way signs were turned sideways by the wind and now point in the wrong direction. And half the people driving around here are guys from out of state in massive pickup trucks and the National Guard put up temporary stop signs at intersections where traffic lights are now working, so it's all a game of Russian roulette. Or maybe chicken.

A run to the local drug store/gas station/strip club has turned into a not-so-virtual game of Grand Theft Auto.

Every now and then I see some church lady tooling down the road at 7 mph in her cream-colored, four-door Grand Marquis, and I can only wonder: Why are you here?

I know it's probably bad taste to kick the city while it's down, but it is interesting/fun/mind-boggling to watch some of the old New Orleans civic quirks work their way back into operation.

For instance, the mayor has urged business owners to come back into town and open up and we residents have been encouraged to patronize them, but neighborhood restaurants and bars are bum-rushed by the authorities every night at 8 p.m. and told to close for curfew.

I'm no restaurateur, but I can imagine it must be hard to build up a steady dinner clientele when you have to close at sunset. Oddly — maybe not so oddly, when I think about it — the strip clubs on Bourbon Street are somehow exempt from this rule and there are tons of big, beefy guys in town (who drive really big pickup trucks) with disposable cash who are all too happy to stuff garter belts full of fivers until the sun comes up and they have to report to work and operate heavy machinery on a one-way street.

Yes, indeed, all is returning to normal. I think there is no better indication of this than the running commentary that has been taking place on the plywood boards mounted over the windows of Sarouk Shop Oriental Rugs down on St. Charles Avenue near Lee Circle.

Early on, in the hairy days of Aftermath, the owner/proprietor/squatter who was living there spray-painted (I'm no handwriting analyst, but I'd say it was with some urgency), "Don't try: I am sleeping inside with a big dog, an ugly woman, two shotguns and a claw hammer."

Claw hammer. Nice touch.

Then, in a spray-paint posting dated 9/4/05 (talk about meticulous graffiti!), it says, "Still here. Woman left. Cooking a pot of dog gumbo."

As I said, dire times call for dire humor. Or maybe it wasn't a joke; some strange things have happened around here lately.

Anyway, in a spray-painted update dated 9/24, it says, "Welcome back, y'all. Grin & bear it."

Ain't that the truth? I mean, what are the other choices?

Enough to Feed an Army
9/15/05

I was walking around the French Quarter Saturday, surveying the hurricane cleanup efforts twelve days after the storm, when I came upon Finis Shellnut, who possesses one of the best names I've ever known.

"Come here," he told me. "I'm going to show you something you will never believe."

Shellnut is a real estate wheeler-dealer in the Quarter but is perhaps better known as the (now ex-)husband of Gennifer Flowers. They're originally from the Arkansas power network: he takes credit for introducing the Clintons into the Whitewater deal; she conducted more personalized business with the ex-president.

Together, they opened the Kelsto Club on St. Louis a few years ago and he held court behind the bar while she sang torch songs in the front of the windows that open across the street from the legendary Antoine's restaurant.

But they divorced just weeks before Katrina, which he weathered in the French Quarter. And after the storm passed, he immediately established himself as the go-to guy for goods and services on the street. Lumber, gas, cash, ice, backhoes, cleanup crews, cold champagne: Finis Shellnut can get it all. Within the hour, generally.

"I'm like Mr. Haney from Green Acres," he said. "I can get anything anybody needs." And then he proved it.

He led me around the corner, to an unmarked delivery entrance for Antoine's, where a guy named Wilbert has been reporting to work every day, trying to keep on top of the food situation before it all rots and stinks—and then trudging "back over to the projects," as he says, to sleep in a tenement with no tenants and no power.

So Wilbert deals with rancid butter and tomatoes that have gone to black. But there's one thing he hasn't had to deal with, and that's what Shellnut wanted to show me.

He positioned me in front of a big storage cooler that is probably about forty years old, and then he pulled the door open and a cloud of frost blew out. Inside, it was cold. Real cold. Not only had the ice inside Antoine's meat and seafood locker not completely melted—it hadn't even started to melt.

Don't ask me how this is possible. I do not know. And I did not take down the name of the ice company nor the refrigerator manufacturer, but I should have, because they've got a good bit of PR to capitalize on.

Because together they had saved shelves and shelves of lobster tails and soft-shell crabs and tubs of lump crabmeat and fillets and New York strips and tenderloin tips. Thousands of them.

This wasn't just a big pile of food. This was the overabundant but abandoned inventory of the city's glorious tradition of overconsumption. It was like looking at a small piece of New Orleans history.

And twelve days after the storm, when the city's survivors had long since acclimated to diets of looted Doritos, Salvation Army cheeseburgers, and prepackaged MREs from the National Guard . . . it made me hungry.

And speaking of the National Guard: We're standing there looking at all this food, and Shellnut asks me, "What are we going to do with this?"

He told me he'd been trying to give it to NOPD officers, but they were all too individually stressed out to embrace the concept of fine dining and there was no discernible central command to alert to this situation. And this was one hell of a situation.

I asked Shellnut if he was sure—*if he was positive*—that this was what it looked like: fresh food. I mean, how could it be?

He shrugged. He said this was how they had found it, he and Wilbert. So we cut open a fillet and we popped a lid on the lump crabmeat and smelled them and they smelled . . . beautiful.

So I proposed this: Uptown, where we have been operating an ad hoc "news bureau" by generator from inside a reporter's house, we are under the protective operations of the California National Guard.

They patrol our area and have given us their MREs (the beef ravioli is to die for), and they have generally treated us with more respect, grace, and kindness than one has a right to expect under martial law.

Fact is, every one that we have come in contact with—and there are plenty of them—has been a Good Joe.

Back home in California, these men and women are cops and teachers and businessmen who were given about twelve hours' notice to tie up any loose ends in their lives, say good-bye to their families, and come to New Orleans to bring some serious heat and restore order on our streets.

And they're doing a helluva job and that big pile of meat looked like a real good way to put into action what we've been putting into words for them for two weeks: Thank you.

But first, I figured we better test it. Despite its alluring physical appearance, if it was, in fact, rotten—as every other steak in this city most certainly was at this point—I did not want to be personally responsible for wiping out an entire unit of the California National Guard.

With all the bad headlines coming out of this town, that's not one I wanted to add to the pile.

So I tested it on my colleagues. I brought home about a dozen massive beef fillets and I seasoned and cooked them and they were excellent. (No one would try the crabmeat; despite appearances, the implications seemed daunting.)

In the morning, I polled my group of housemates and found no reports of constitutional distress—at least no more distress than usual, considering our fairly unhealthy living conditions. But enough about that.

So Sunday morning I went back to visit Shellnut. "Are you sure it's okay to take these?" I asked, and he assured me he had cleared it with the restaurant and I hope that is the case, and if it is not, Mr. or Mrs. Guste—or whoever currently runs that classic culinary landmark—we'll clear this up later. Somehow. I give you my word.

So we packed up 240 fillets and tenderloins and I dropped them off at Sophie B. Wright Middle School, where the California Guard unit is stationed.

Then I hustled a few grills off some front porches in my neighborhood—which is basically in preserved physical condition, so if the worst thing that happened to you in Katrina was losing your old Weber, then I don't want to hear about it.

It went to a good cause.

Then I called in a delivery of twenty bags of charcoal from a colleague in Baton Rouge and we set up at the corner of Prytania and Napoleon, under the oaks (they're still there!), and we had us a Sunday-afternoon barbecue.

And when I was informed that 240 steaks were not going to be nearly enough for the six hundred Guardsmen and -women based at the site, I dispatched a team of them to go down to the Quarter and find Shellnut—which is not hard to do—and they came back with him and also a few hundred more steaks.

The Guard, they went nuts. Absolutely nuts. As platoons came back from patrols, they were greeted by four grills going full steam, a much better smell than our city streets in these hard times.

At one point, several company cooks returned and were thrilled to have some real cooking to do, so they relieved me of duty. That was their prerogative. It is, after all, martial law.

So then I just watched. Shellnut and I leaned against my car and took in the scene, and all these guys, they just fell over us with gratitude, as if *we* were the heroes—an absurd notion. But maybe for one afternoon, we did a little bit of good on behalf of our city, our people, and particularly Antoine's world-famous restaurant.

And with my story told, I'd just like to add—gently, so as not to sound as though I'm complaining—but if we ever have a storm like Katrina headed this way again, if Wilbert or someone else down at Antoine's could toss a few hundred pounds of potato salad into that cooler before it hits, that would be great.

Because it would have been really nice to have some fresh sides with all that meat. Now, that would have been something.

Tough Times
in the
Blue Tarp Town

Blue Roof Blues
10/5/05

The first time I came back to New Orleans after Katrina, I'll admit that the whole specter shook me to my core. After spending eight days reporting in the city, my hands were shaking and I had lost about ten pounds. It was time to take a break.

As I drove to Baton Rouge to catch a flight, I pulled off at the first interstate exchange with any life to it—Laplace—and went to the McDonald's and got a Big Mac, a fish sandwich, large fries, and a large Coke.

I inhaled the stuff as I drove, and two exits later—Sorrento or somewhere like that—I pulled off and went to the McDonald's there and got a Big Mac and a large Coke to sustain me for the rest of the drive, my own personal take on *Super Size Me*.

Then, after a brief respite with my wife and kids in Maryland, I returned to New Orleans for more. Reporting, that is. Not McDonald's.

The second time I left New Orleans, Armstrong Airport was open. Again my hands shook as I drove away from town, but when I settled into my seat as we went aloft, my troubles, too, stayed behind on the ground.

I looked down over the region as we rose, and—maybe you've seen pictures of this—the sea of blue color beneath me was nothing less than awe-inspiring.

At first I had this vision that I was flying over Beverly Hills until I realized all that blue beneath me was not swimming pools but roof tarps and coverings. It is the color that bonds us in these times, maybe even more than that weird purple hue that Rex, LSU, and K&B seemed to conspire to make us love so many years ago.

The Blue Roof Town. Man, there's a great country song in there somewhere.

There are a lot of heartache songs in this whole ordeal, no doubt assisted by the syncopated double whammy of Katrina/Rita.

Somewhere, right now, someone is writing a song that will make Tim McGraw a million dollars; I just hope that someone is from New Orleans.

On my most recent trip back to New Orleans, earlier this week, I was waiting for my connection in Memphis and listened while the gate agent called the names of standby travelers to come forward: "Passenger Cheramie. Passenger Bettincourt . . ."

The gate agent's Tennessee drawl mauled these names, but it was a wondrous thing to hear these beautiful French names being called and to know that our people were coming home.

Settling into their seats, almost everyone turned to the stranger next to him or her and asked, "Have you seen it yet?"

It. Our home. Our place.

A haunting quietude consumed the plane as we descended over Lake Pontchartrain. You could tell that most of the people on the plane were coming home for the first time, and instead of the usual world-weary travelers burying their noses in paperbacks or trying to catch a last wink of sleep, everyone craned for looks out the windows to see what "it" looks like now.

It felt like a plane full of kids on their first flight, as if they had never seen such a vista from the air before. And, of course, they hadn't.

I wanted to pipe up: Man, you should have seen it a month ago; it was so much worse. Or maybe tell them all: It's not as bad as you think it's going to be.

Or, I thought, I could harness more practical advice from

recent experience and tell them: Whatever you do, *do not* open your refrigerator. Ever. Again.

But even though I have one of those profoundly annoying personal compulsions of talking to (at?) strangers all the time—particularly at inappropriate moments—I found myself lingering on some advice whose provenance I have long forgotten (and seldom followed) but that seemed so apt for this anguished moment: "If you cannot improve upon the silence, do not speak."

Words of wisdom, to be sure. At a time like this, a flow of platitudes from a self-absorbed dilettante veteran of the War of 2005—a dilettante with shaky hands, no less—is not what anybody needs to hear.

So I kept my mouth shut and let the passengers' heads wrap around what was about to happen to them when they got out of the plane and drove to their homes for the first time.

For some, it will be a foul-smelling but mildly comic discovery that they forgot to empty their Diaper Genie before they left. For a friend of mine who accompanied his mother to their home off Paris Avenue in St. Bernard Parish over the weekend, it was the discovery of two tenants in the rental side of her shotgun double—two tenants who had been dead for thirty-three days.

Wrap your head around that.

For those who return to the area and those who do not and those who never left, these are our collective memories now, our marks of distinction and suffering, small stuff like Aunt Ida's meat loaf sitting in your fridge for five weeks or big stuff like dead people on the other side of your living room wall.

Like our blue tarp rooftops, these are the bonds we will share forever. They are the bonds that will hold us together.

The Smell
10/7/05

New Orleans still unfolds itself to you in a sensual way. That was always her seductive forte, but it is different after the storm.

For instance, in the immediate days after the flood, it was sound: choppers, jets, boats, sirens, big trucks, bigger trucks, chain saws. And then at night, the damn scariest silence you never heard.

Then it was sight: the impenetrable darkness of the night, punctuated in the distance from time to time by a red or blue cherry top on a slow-rolling cruiser, and most likely the driver— a young state trooper from some town in the Midwest suddenly dropped into Fallujah—was as terrified as you.

There were lots of monsters under the bed in those early days.

Then came the blinding sunlight of morning—so much of it unfiltered by tree limbs after Katrina's indiscriminate and not-so-tidy pruning job—just slamming straight into your face and onto the ground.

Now the choppers are gone, and most of that other industrial noise, and at night you hear crickets. And the sunlight, so hellish weeks ago, is getting better with the approach of autumn, and the scary darkness is now sliced apart at night by streetlights and the yellow glow from occasional bedroom windows.

That leaves us the sense of smell. And, wow.

The Louisiana balladeer Randy Newman once wrote a song lamenting Baltimore's civic downfall many years ago with the line "Oh, Baltimore. Man, it's hard just to breathe."

That would be New Orleans now. It stinks here, just flat-out stinks. There are random piles of residential and commercial trash just everywhere, and even where there is no visible evidence, the slightest wind shift can take you to Puke City.

I mean it; it's rough. Even in places that are cleaned up and open for business, you can still smell the Aftermath. The CVS and Walgreens drugstores are open Uptown, and even though the air-conditioning is blasting and they've cleaned the hell out of those places, you can still sense it when you first walk in, just barely taste it.

A friend of mine e-mailed me recently that when she walked into a grocery store, her daughter said to her, "Mom, it smells like ass in here." I know that's not very appetizing terminology or imagery for a newspaper, but standard operating procedures have changed around here because New Orleans, it smells like, well . . . never mind.

I'm just trying to convey what it's like, and I can certainly muster no better description than that.

On many streets, refrigerators are duct-taped shut and lined up along the curbside, calling to mind nothing so much as the image of empty Mardi Gras parade ladders all in a row. All these structures, just waiting for something to happen.

Only problem is, there are no cleanup crews following these imaginary parades to remove the debris. So they stand, sturdy sentinels, fortress walls.

We should rename the streets around here Whirlpool Way, Amana Avenue, and Kenmore Court, because that's what it looks like. The streets are paved in appliances. Where trees once stood, they are sometimes the only shade on a block.

Where are they going to put all these things? I don't suppose they can be used to buttress our wetlands as they do with discarded Christmas trees every year, huh?

Do we even have any wetlands?

And, problem is, for every person who comes back here, either to reclaim residency or just to gather some valuables and clean up a bit, more garbage accumulates. Pity the folks who had been in the middle of home renovations when this hit, because their Dumpsters are now brimming with a primordial stew so nasty that even the rats abandoned it.

Very strange side note here: There are no rats. Everyone talks about this, says the same thing—they haven't seen a rat since Day One. Here on Dry Land, where I live, we thought they'd overrun us. But I don't know.

Anyway, I remember—until it was deemed injudicious by an image-conscious administration—when the city used to measure the success of Mardi Gras by announcing the accumulated tonnage of garbage collected during Carnival season. Well, by that measure, Katrina was a very successful hurricane.

Very.

Stink is a situation that TV and radio cannot successfully portray, olfactory being one of the senses not yet conquered by the airwaves or Internet. And until *The Times-Picayune* can successfully produce a scratch-'n'-sniff version of the daily newspaper—and this technology still seems to be at least three or four years down the road—we can only fail in our efforts to accurately capture the foulness of some of these street corners.

I don't mean to be complaining here, jumping on the gripe train and all that. Compared to losing a loved one, a home, or a job, this is civic kibbles and bits. But in terms of livability, it matters. There seem to be nine hundred guys from Texas who've been trucked into town to cut down trees and limbs; aren't there a dozen guys from River Parish Disposal who can cruise around New Orleans every day picking up stuff?

The whole idea of it makes me very nostalgic, the radio playing in my backyard on autumn Sunday afternoons in New Orleans, after a Saints game, listening to Buddy D pitching River Parish Disposal: "Our business stinks, but it's picking up."

What a great slogan that is.

Buddy D. The Saints. Garbage pickup. Ah, memories of my old New Orleans.

The Elephant Men
10/25/05

Every night, we gather on my front stoop. We are multiple combinations of jobless, homeless, familyless, and sometimes just plain listless.

We sit and some of us drink and some of us smoke and together we solve the problems of the city—since no one in any official capacity seems able or inclined to do so.

We're just one more committee howling at the moon. We are a civic life support system.

It began with close friends and neighbors, gathering as we trickled back into town, comparing notes and stories and hugs of comfort and welcome home. But the breadth of visitors has widened.

One night, while I was sitting with a couple of friends, a guy pulled up to the curb in an SUV and regarded us carefully. As the passenger-side window rolled down, I assumed it was an old friend stopping to say hello, so I stepped up to the door.

Turns out, it was a total stranger. He asked, "Displaced dads?" He had a six-pack of Corona on the front seat, and he was just driving around randomly, looking for someone to connect with, someone to talk to, something—God help us—something to do.

We nodded. Yeah, we are men without their women. Women without their men. Parents without their children.

But not without beer.

And he got out of the car and he sat with us for hours and we told our stories to each other and asked about each other's families, now spread across the planet, and when it was over we had a new friend. A displaced dad. Just looking for a place we used to call home.

We stoop sitters tend to get very wry and blend dark humor with our rants against the machine, but sometimes it gets very sad.

We often deal with First-Timer Syndrome. As my immediate neighbors trickle back into town, one by one—either just to clean up and move on or to move back in for good—they generally end up on my stoop. And they often cry.

It's the first time they've been back to town and they are shaken to their very core at what they've seen and smelled and we grizzled veterans of this war try to provide shelter from their storm.

They apologize for losing it, but we tell them that many tears have been shed here on this stoop and they are ours and it's okay. It happens to all First Timers. Hell, it happens still.

They're easy to spot, the First Timers. Either they sob or they sit silent and sullen, taking the occasional pull on a bottle of beer, with very little to add to the conversation of the night.

The next night, they usually come back, and they are a little better. One day at a time. Ain't that the way of life around here?

We sit around night after night because some of us are unable to sit still in a restaurant for ninety minutes or aren't ready to go back to the bar scene. Many can't concentrate on reading and television seems like an empty gesture, so we talk. We talk about the same damn thing over and over.

We talk about it. The elephant in the room.

I suspect many folks have sat with us and thought, upon going home: You guys need to get a grip. You need to talk about something else. You need to get a life.

That may be, but I, personally, have been unable to focus on anything but the elephant. I have tried to watch TV or read a magazine, but when I see or hear phrases like "Tom and Katie" or "World Series" or "Judge Miers," my mind just glazes over and all I hear is the buzz of a fluorescent light. That is the sound of my cerebral cortex now.

I can't hear what they're saying on TV. I don't know what they're talking about. I think: Why aren't they talking about the elephant?

Once, in an out-of-town airport, I searched desperately for something to read about the elephant, but we have been tossed off the front pages by other events. Finally I found a magazine with a blaring headline—"What Went Wrong?"—and I thought, finally, something about us.

It turns out, though, it was *People* magazine and "What Went Wrong" was not about FEMA or the levees or the flood, but about Renee Zellweger and Kenny Chesney.

And the fluorescent light goes zzzzzz.

One newcomer to the stoop one night said something along the lines of "Can you believe that call at the end of the White Sox game the other night?" And you would usually think that such a statement made in a group of drinking men would elicit an argument, at least—if not a bare-knuckle brawl—but the fact is, we all responded with silence.

We're a porch full of people who don't know who's playing in the World Series and don't know what movies opened this week and don't know how many died in Iraq today.

We are consumed. We would probably bore you to tears. But it is good therapy and we laugh more than we cry, and that's a start, that's a good thing, that's a sign of winning this war, of getting this damn elephant out of our city—out of our sight.

Mad City
11/6/05

It has been said to me almost a dozen times in exactly the same words: "Everyone here is mentally ill now."

Some who say this are health care professionals voicing the accumulated wisdom of their careers, and some are laymen venturing a psychological assessment that just happens to be correct.

With all due respect, we're living in Crazy Town.

The only lines at retail outlets longer than those for lumber and refrigerators are at the pharmacy windows, where fidgety, glassy-eyed neighbors greet one another with the casual inquiries one might expect at a restaurant: "What are you gonna have? The Valium here is good. But I'm going with the Paxil. Last week I had the Xanax and it didn't agree with me."

We talk about prescription medications now as if they were the soft-shell crabs at Clancy's. Suddenly, we've all developed a low-grade expertise in pharmacology.

Everybody's got it, this thing, this affliction, this affinity for forgetfulness, absentmindedness, confusion, laughing in inappropriate circumstances, crying when the wrong song comes on the radio, behaving in odd and contrary ways.

A friend recounts a recent conversation into which Murphy's Law was injected—the adage that if anything can go wrong, it will.

In perhaps the most succinct characterization of contemporary life in New Orleans I've heard yet, one said to the other, "Murphy's running this town now."

Ain't that the truth?

Here's one for you: Some friends of mine were clearing out their belongings from their home in the Fontainebleau area and were going through the muddle of despair that attends the realization that you were insured out the wazoo for a hurricane but all you got was flood damage and now you're going to get a check for $250,000 to rebuild your $500,000 house.

As they pondered this dismal circumstance in the street, their roof collapsed. Just like that. It must have suffered some sort of structural or rain-related stress from the storm, and then, two weeks later, it manifested itself in total collapse.

Now, I ask you: What would you do if you watched your home crumble to pieces before your eyes?

What they did was, realizing that their home now qualified for a homeowner's claim, they jumped up and down and high-fived each other and yelled, "The roof collapsed! The roof collapsed!"

Our home is destroyed. Oh, happy day. I submit that there's something not right there.

I also submit that if you don't have this affliction, if this whole thing hasn't sent you into a vicious spin of acute cognitive dissonance, then you must be crazy and—as I said—we're all whacked.

How could you not be? Consider the sights, sounds, and smells you encounter on a daily basis as you drive around a town that has a permanent bathtub ring around it. I mean, could somebody please erase that brown line?

Every day I drive past a building on Magazine Street where there's plywood over the windows with a huge spray-painted message that says: I AM HERE. I HAVE A GUN.

Okay, the storm was more than two months ago. You can take the sign down now. You can come out now.

Or maybe the guy's still inside there, in the dark with his canned food, water, and a gun, thinking that the whole thing is still going on, like those Japanese soldiers you used to hear about in the 1970s and '80s who just randomly wandered out of hiding in the forests on desolate islands in the South Pacific, thinking that World War II was still going on.

The visuals around here prey on you. Driving in from the east the other day, I saw a huge gray wild boar that had wandered onto the interstate and been shredded by traffic. Several people I know also saw this massive porcine carnage, all torn up and chunky on the side of the road.

It looked like five dead dogs. Directly across the interstate from it was an upside-down alligator.

I mean: What the hell? Since when did we have wild boars around here? And when did they decide to lumber out of the wilderness up to the interstate as if it were some sort of sacred dying ground for wildebeests?

Just farther up the road a bit are car dealerships with rows and rows and rows of new cars that will never be sold, all browned out as if they had been soaking in coffee for a week, which I guess they were.

All those lots need are some balloons on a Saturday afternoon and some guy in a bad suit saying "Let's make a deal!"

Welcome to the Outer Limits. Your hometown. Need a new car?

Speaking of car dealers, no one epitomizes the temporary insanity around here more than Saints owner Tom Benson, who said he feared for his life in a confrontation with a drunk fan and WWL sportscaster Lee Zurik at Tiger Stadium last Sunday.

Admittedly, the shape of Lee Zurik's eyebrows have an oddly discomfiting menace about them, but fearing for your life?

Just get a good set of tweezers and defend yourself, Tom. Get ahold of yourself, man.

Maybe I shouldn't make light of this phenomenon. Maybe I'm exhibiting a form of madness in thinking this is all slightly amusing. Maybe I'm not well, either.

But former city health director Brobson Lutz told me it's all part of healing. "It's a part of the human coping mechanism," he said. "Part of the recovery process. I have said from the beginning that the mental health concerns here are far greater than those we can expect from infectious diseases or household injuries."

The U.S. Army took Lutz onto the USS *Iwo Jima* a few weeks ago to talk to the troops about how to deal with people suffering from posttraumatic stress.

They were concerned, primarily, with the dazed-looking folks who wander around the French Quarter all day.

"I told them to leave those guys alone," Lutz said. "They may be crazy, but they survived this thing. They coped. If they were taken out of that environment, then they could really develop problems. Remember that in the immediate aftermath of all this, the primary psychiatric care in this city was being provided by the bartenders at Johnny White's and Molly's."

Interesting point. I mean, who needs a psychology degree? All anyone around here wants is someone to listen to their stories.

I thanked Lutz for his time and mentioned that our call sounded strange. It was around noon this past Thursday.

"Are you in the bathtub?" I asked him.

"Yes," he said. "And I'm having trouble coming up with sound bites."

Like I said, we're all a little touched by Katrina Fever.

My friend Glenn Collins is living in exile in Alabama, and one Sunday afternoon he went to a shopping mall in Birmingham. He went to the Gap and was greeted by a salesclerk with a name tag that said "Katrina."

He left immediately. He went next door to the Coach boutique, where he was greeted by a salesclerk with a name tag that said "Katrina."

He kinda freaked out. He asked the woman something along the lines of: What's with all the Katrinas? And she blurted out, "Oh, you know Katrina at the Gap? She's my friend!"

"I wish I was making this up," he told me. "I mean, what are the odds of this?"

He needed a drink, he said. So he went to a nearby Outback Steakhouse and ordered a beer, but the bartender told him they don't sell alcohol on Sundays.

"But I'm from New Orleans!" he pleaded. "Don't you have a special exemption for people from New Orleans? Please?"

They did not. So he drove across three counties to get a drink. He said to me, "The Twilight Zone, it just keeps going on and on and on."

1 Dead in Attic
11/15/05

I live on The Island, where much has the appearance of Life Goes On. Gas stations, bars, pizza joints, joggers, strollers, dogs, churches, shoppers, neighbors, even garage sales.

Sometimes trash and mail service, sometimes not.

It sets into mind a modicum of complacency that maybe everything is all right.

But I have this terrible habit of getting into my car every two or three days and driving into the Valley Down Below, that vast wasteland below sea level that was my city, and it's mind-blowing (A) how vast it is and (B) how wasted it is.

My wife questions the wisdom of my frequent forays into the massive expanse of blown-apart lives and property that local street maps used to call Gentilly, Lakeview, the East, and the Lower 9th. She fears that it contributes to my unhappiness and general instability, and I suspect she is right.

Perhaps I should just stay on the stretch of safe, dry land Uptown where we live and try to move on, focus on pleasant things, quit making myself miserable, quit reliving all those terrible things we saw on TV that first week.

That's advice I wish I could follow, but I can't. I am compelled for reasons that are not entirely clear to me. And so I drive.

I drive around and try to figure out those Byzantine markings and symbols that the cops and the National Guard spray-painted on all the houses around here, cryptic communications that tell the story of who or what was or wasn't inside the house when the floodwater rose to the ceiling.

In some cases, there's no interpretation needed. There's one I pass on St. Roch Avenue in the 8th Ward at least once a week. It says: 1 DEAD IN ATTIC.

That certainly sums up the situation. No mystery there.

It's spray-painted there on the front of the house, and it probably will remain spray-painted there for weeks, months, maybe years, a perpetual reminder of the untimely passing of a citizen, a resident, a New Orleanian.

One of us.

You'd think some numerical coding could have conveyed this information on this house, so that I—we all—wouldn't have to drive by places like this every day and be reminded: "1 Dead in Attic."

I have seen plenty of houses in worse shape than the one where 1 Dead in Attic used to live, houses in Gentilly and the Lower 9th that yield the most chilling visual displays in town: low-rider shotgun rooftops with holes that were hacked away from the inside with an ax, leaving small, splintered openings through which people sought escape.

Imagine if your life came to that point and remained there, on display, all over town, for us to see, day after day.

Amazingly, those rooftops are the stories with happy endings. I mean, they got out, right?

But where are they now? Do you think they have trouble sleeping at night?

The occasional rooftops still have painted messages: HELP US. I guess they had paint cans in their attic. And an ax, like meterologist Margaret Orr and Jefferson Parish President Aaron Broussard always told us we should have if we weren't going to evacuate.

Some people thought Orr and Broussard were crazy. Alarmists. Extremists. Well, maybe they were crazy. But they were right.

Perhaps 1 Dead in Attic should have heeded this advice. But judging from the ages on the state's official victims list, he or she was probably up in years. Stubborn. Unafraid. And now a statistic.

I wonder who eventually came and took 1 Dead in Attic away. Who knows? Hell, with the way things run around here—I wonder if *anyone* has come to take 1 Dead in Attic away.

And who claimed him or her? Who grieved over 1 Dead in Attic, and who buried 1 Dead in Attic?

Was there anyone with him or her at the end, and what was the last thing they said to each other? How did 1 Dead in Attic spend the last weekend in August of the year 2005?

What were their plans? Maybe dinner at Mandich on St. Claude? Maybe a Labor Day family reunion in City Park—one of those raucous picnics where everybody wears matching T-shirts to mark the occasion and they rent a DJ and a Space Walk and a couple of guys actually get there the night before to secure a good, shady spot?

I wonder if I ever met 1 Dead in Attic. Maybe in the course of my job or maybe at a Saints game or maybe we once stood next to each other at a Mardi Gras parade or maybe we once flipped each other off in a traffic jam.

1 Dead in Attic could have been my mail carrier, a waitress at my favorite restaurant, or the guy who burglarized my house a couple years ago. Who knows?

My wife, she's right. I've got to quit just randomly driving around. This can't be helping anything.

But I can't stop. I return to the Valley Down Below over and over, looking for signs of progress in all that muck, some sign that things are getting better, that things are improving, that we don't all have to live in a state of abeyance forever, but—you know what?

I just don't see them there.

I mean, in the 8th Ward, tucked down there behind St. Roch Cemetery, life looks pretty much like it did when the floodwater first receded ten weeks ago, with lots of cars pointing this way and that, kids' yard toys caked in mire, portraits of despair, desolation, and loss. And hatchet holes in rooftops.

But there's something I've discovered about the 8th Ward in this strange exercise of mine: apparently, a lot of Mardi Gras Indians are from there. Or were from there; I'm not sure what the proper terminology is.

On several desolate streets I drive down, I see where some folks have returned to a few of the homes and they haven't bothered to put their furniture and appliances out on the curb—what's the point, really?—but they have retrieved their tattered and muddy Indian suits and sequins and feathers and they have nailed them to the fronts of their houses.

The colors of these displays are startling because everything else in the 8th is gray. The streets, the walls, the cars, even the trees. Just gray.

So the oranges and blues and greens of the Indian costumes are something beautiful to behold, like the first flowers to bloom after an atomic explosion. I don't know what the significance of these displays is, but they hold a mystical fascination for me.

They haunt me, almost as much as the spray paint on the front of a house that says 1 DEAD IN ATTIC. They look like ghosts hanging there. They are reminders of something. Something very New Orleans.

Do these memorials mean these guys—the Indians—are coming back? I mean, they have to, don't they? Where else could they do what they do?

And—maybe this is a strange time to ask—who are these guys, anyway? Why do they do what they do with all those feathers and beads that take so much time and money to make? What's with all the Big Chief and Spy Boy role-playing?

As many times as I have reveled in their rhythmic, poetic, and sometimes borderline absurd revelry in the streets of our city, I now realize that if you asked me to explain the origins and meaning of the Mardi Gras Indians—I couldn't do it.

I have no clue. And that makes me wish I'd been paying more

attention for the past twenty years. I could have learned something.

I could have learned something about a people whose history is now but a sepia mist over back-of-town streets and neighborhoods that nobody's ever heard of and where nobody lives and nothing ever happens anymore; a freeze-frame still life in the air, a story of what we once were.

Despair
12/6/05

She had a nice house in Old Metairie, a nice car, a great job, a good man who loved her, and a wedding date in October.

A good life.

He was from Atlanta and had moved here to be with her because she is a New Orleans girl and New Orleans girls never live anywhere else and even if they do, they always come back.

That's just the way it is.

For the hurricane, they fled to Atlanta. His city. His people.

Meantime, her house was destroyed, her car was destroyed, and within days she was laid off from her job. And, of course, the wedding here in New Orleans was canceled.

When all settled down, he wanted to stay in Atlanta. But she is a New Orleans girl, and you know the rest. Equanimity courses through our blood as much as platelets and nitrogen—it is part of our DNA—so she was determined to return, rebuild, recover.

So they moved back here.

A few weeks ago, they moved into my neighborhood. She arrived first. That afternoon, she came over and joined the group that sits on my stoop every night solving the world's problems.

I introduced her to the local gang and welcomed her back to the neighborhood; she had been a neighbor many years ago.

Like many post-Katrina First Timers, she was a wreck on that first night. Didn't say much. Just sat there. Not the girl I used to know. But then, who is?

To add to her troubles that first night, her fiancé, who was following her to New Orleans that morning in a rented truck, had gotten a flat tire outside Mobile and was stranded on the side of the road.

She drove on because she had the pets in her car. He called the rental company for help; it wasn't the kind of vehicle with a tire that just any John Doe can change.

He called the trucking company all day. They kept telling him that they would be there within an hour and that's what he told her so she waited. We all waited.

By 8 P.M., he got fed up with the trucking company and called them and told them he had started the engine and was going to drive to New Orleans on the exposed tire rim. And that's what he did, calling the trucking company every few minutes to give a new location.

When she related this news to us, we all knew right then that we would like this guy.

Naturally, the trucking company showed up within minutes and changed the tire. He arrived late that night. He met all the neighbors and they all knew the story of his driving on the rim and they all thought it was hilarious.

And so their new life on my block began. They were one of us now, the survivors, the determined, the hopeful, the building blocks of the New City. Members of the tribe.

They settled in. I used to see them walking in the park and reading the paper on their front porch and occasionally they sat on my stoop, and life went on.

But I guess things were not going so well. She was always pretty grim—not the girl I used to know—but he seemed jolly enough and we would talk in the "Hey, how ya doin'?" kind of way.

Turns out, he couldn't stand it here. And truthfully, if you weren't from here, didn't have a history here, didn't have roux in your blood and a stake in it all: Would you want to be here?

I wouldn't.

But she is a New Orleans girl. To hell with no house, no car, no job, no prospects. This is where she belongs. And her mama lives here. End of discussion.

He moved back to Atlanta. She stayed. He came back. Try again. Work it out. Whatever it takes.

A few nights ago, they drank wine and, in some sort of stupid Romeo and Juliet moment, decided that they would kill themselves because all hope was lost and living here amid the garbage and the rot and the politics and the profound sense of failure was sucking the marrow out of their bones.

Not even love could overcome. Here, in the smoking ruins of Pompeii, sometimes it's hard to see the light.

She told friends later that she didn't really think they would do it. Said they got caught in the moment and let the bad stuff crawl all over their minds. The darkness can be so damn dark, and they weren't thinking straight. But she didn't think they were really going to do it.

But he did. Right then, right there.

So he's dead, and a family in Atlanta has lost a son, a brother, a friend. Another notch in Katrina's belt.

My stoop is empty these nights. None of us really knows what to say anymore.

This is the next cycle. Suicide. All the doctors, psychologists, and mental health experts tell us the same thing: this is what happens next in a phenomenon like this. But has there ever been a phenomenon like this?

Where are we now in our descent through Dante's nine circles of hell?

God help us.

The most open, joyous, freewheeling, celebratory city in the country is broken, hurting, down on its knees. Failing. Begging for help.

Somebody turn this movie off; I don't want to watch it anymore. I want a slow news day. I want a no news day.

A friend of mine who used to live here said on the phone from Philadelphia the other day, "I don't know how you guys can even get out of bed in the morning."

Well, obviously, some of us don't.

But we have to try. We have to fight this thing until there is no fight left. This cannot be the way we go out, by our own hands.

My neighbor is in a hospital in another part of the state now, learning how to deal. She talked to friends over the weekend and said she is not going to run away from this. She is a New Orleans girl, and this is where she is going to stay and try again. And again. And again.

She told her friends this weekend that she still has hope.

I don't know what flavor of hope she's got or how she got it, but if she's got a taste of it in her mouth, the rest of us can take a little spoonful and try to make it through another day, another week, another lifetime.

It's the least we can do.

The Ties
That Bind

My Introduction
to New Orleans
11/8/05

I was sitting in Donna's on Rampart Street last Saturday night, shaking my legs to a righteous swing session with the New Orleans Jazz Vipers, when a stunning realization hit me in the face: it was a hurricane, or something very close to it, that had brought me to this city in the first place.

It was November 1980. I was in school in Wisconsin, floundering both personally and academically. I had a friend in the same situation. We decided to blow off our classes and head out of town the week of Thanksgiving, pointing south with a tent and two sleeping bags in an attempt to decide whether we wanted to stay in college or find another direction in life.

I had told my parents in Maryland that I had a load of schoolwork and would not be home for the holiday. And off we went, destination South Padre Island in Texas, where I had gone for spring break the year before and had a gas.

But South Padre was miserable. It was deserted. Oil from a runaway well in Mexico was fouling the beach. And worst of all, the wind was relentless and borderline scary. It blew our tent all over the beach, and when we'd party a little and try to play Frisbee, the disc would get caught in the wind and take off three hundred yards down the beach.

A state trooper told us there was a mighty storm brewing out in the Gulf of Mexico; that the situation was certainly not going to improve and, in fact, might get a lot worse.

He suggested we leave.

So we packed up and decided to head for the Florida panhandle. Nice beaches, we'd heard. And so we hit the road again, passing through south Louisiana in the middle of the night.

Somewhere out in Acadiana, we stopped at an all-night gas station, and the girl at the cash register was wearing a baseball cap that said, "I'm a real Coonass, me."

Okay, I'm thinking. I'll take the bait. "What's a Coonass?" I asked her.

"Me," she replied.

I turned to my friend, also named Chris, and said, "Let's get the hell out of this state." Two hours later we were passing the interstate exits to New Orleans.

What did I know about New Orleans at the age of twenty? At this point in my life, I was already a Meters, Wild Tchoupitoulas, and Neville Brothers fanatic, having been turned onto them by my older brother, who had incorporated annual trips to Mardi Gras into his life's journey.

My sum total knowledge of the place was that it was probably a great place for a couple of lost college boys to do some serious partying.

We considered this option, but between us, Chris and I had less than $100 and we hoped to road-trip for at least a week or so, and then we'd need gas money back home—1,000 miles to Madison.

So we bypassed New Orleans, figuring to sleep on the beach in Florida and eat campfire beans, which is what we did. For one night. Then whatever storm had been brewing in the gulf descended upon us. The same lashing wind sent sand stinging into our legs.

Someone told us the storm had kicked east. It was going to get nasty. For two down-and-out, borderline depressed guys, this trip was simply not working out. We've got to get out of here, we said. New Orleans, we agreed, money or not.

The first New Orleans bar I ever walked into—a rite of passage as meaningful as your first car or your first kiss—was Tujague's on Decatur Street. I'll never forget the impression that the tiles and the sexy lighting and the lazy ceiling fans and slow-moving clientele had on me: What year is it? I thought. This place is gone, man, long ago gone.

We ate dinner at what I believe was Café Sbisa, but I'm not positive, all these years later. All I know is, we could afford only a couple of appetizers and we were surrounded by a busy and talkative staff of tall, thin gay men and this was all very exotic to us.

Next, naturally, we were on Bourbon Street. We put $40 in the glove compartment of our car for gas back to Wisconsin (forty bucks to Wisconsin, imagine that), and we decided we would hang out until we ran out of money.

That took about six hours.

Bourbon Street was jumping. The street was packed. The night before, Sugar Ray Leonard and Roberto Duran had sparred in the Superdome in one of boxing's truly legendary fights. It was the night Duran exclaimed, *"No mas!"*

We didn't know or care much about that. We just knew that we had never seen anything like this place before.

At the corner of Bourbon and St. Peter, there was a slow jazz band playing and a young black man singing "The Christmas Song." You know: "Chestnuts roasting on an open fire . . ."

The man was beautiful. I had never seen skin quite his color, and I don't think I had ever seen a black man with green eyes before.

And his voice. Wow. It wasn't Aaron Neville or Johnny Adams or even in their league, obviously, but to me it was angelic and new and soul-settling. I just stood there with my mouth open, filling my open mouth with much beer, but also just in plain awe.

He didn't use a microphone, and everybody in the place was quiet, just hanging on to the moment. I doubt that Bourbon Street has many musical "moments" anymore, having descended over the past few decades into a cacophonous sprawl, but to my young and nearly virgin ears, I had found something.

Something beautiful. Something that would stay with me, it turns out.

We listened to a few more songs and then left. I wanted to stay, but we agreed that this was no place to meet girls—too mellow and refined—and we wanted to meet girls, and so we wandered.

The story, at this point, becomes dramatically less poignant and sentimental, so I'll run through the details quickly: we were thrown out of three bars on Bourbon Street and were entering a fourth when a police officer took hold of my collar and said to beat it.

We were the exact same two guys I now witness from time to time lousing up our streets downtown. I see their immature, careless behavior and think: Idiots. They don't get this town and they never will.

But now I know there is hope for fools like me.

We ended up in Luther Kent's old bar over on Toulouse Street and the band was big and brassy and loud and we met these beautiful Scandinavian girls and the night was so far beyond perfect that I thought I was in Heaven.

I drove from New Orleans all the way to Wisconsin on Thanksgiving Day, pausing twice to stop at gas stations and once to eat Thanksgiving dinner at a Denny's in Illinois.

The following Monday, I returned to classes. Chris did not. I started listening to the Neville Brothers more and more. *The Neville Brothers*, their 1978 debut record, became my "date" music. I'd play "Washable Ink" and "Vieux Carré Rouge" and "Audience for My Pain" and I thought I was one very cool brother.

For my male friends, I'd play a cassette of the Wild Tchoupitoulas record with "Brother John," "Hey Pocky A-Way" and "Meet de Boys on the Battlefront" and I'd watch them try to figure out what the hell that was all about.

Not that I knew myself. I just knew I dug it. In between all the Springsteen and John Prine and Little Feat that consumed my musical interests back then, there was this deeper appreciation for sublime funk.

I graduated from college with a journalism degree, moved

back to Maryland, and was working there when a friend who had wound up at *The Times-Picayune* called me in the spring of 1984 to say there was a job opening here.

"You'd love this city," she told me.

I thought about that music. That six hours of immortality I had once lived there. I thought about that guy singing "The Christmas Song" and thought how sexy it all was in New Orleans. "Yes, I'd love that city," I agreed.

And Jesus, what a ride it has been.

I had not thought about that road trip to New Orleans in years, and when I was sitting at Donna's the other night, they were singing these great swing tunes without microphones and it was smoky and intimate and it felt like 1952 and it also felt like that moment I had in 1980. And then it hit me: I first came to this city because I was fleeing a storm.

I have spent hours online since I left Donna's the other night, Googling weather sites and other sources of meteorological data, trying to find out what was in the Gulf of Mexico that last week of November 1980.

I found that a moderate hurricane—Jeanne—was in the gulf about ten days earlier and Karl was off the southeastern United States that week. Neither amounted to much. But I can't find any reference to a severe storm rolling from Texas across the gulf to the Florida panhandle in those exact days.

Maybe it was just a tropical depression of some kind, or just the turbulence between Jeanne and Karl, but it was wild and windy when I evacuated into—not out of—New Orleans for shelter and safety and that's how I discovered the pulse of this magical place.

It's far past irony to reconsider this event. It's almost absurd, now, to realize how I got here. And it's also the best thing that ever happened to me, to have seen, known, loved, and lived this place called New Orleans.

The Funky Butt
12/9/05

When I moved to New Orleans twenty-one years ago, I was — to use a contemporary phrase — all in. I loved it from the minute I smelled the burning sugar cane from the Celotex factory across the river, a sweet stink I have always found oddly sexy.

But there was always a caveat to my love affair with New Orleans. I stood firm, fast, and unbending on one point: I was not going to raise my children here. No how, no way.

My reasons were obvious: school system, crime, litter, racism, politics.

I thought this place was great for getting my ya-yas out in my twenties and thirties, but I was off to Wisconsin when baby-making time came around. And I was going to make sure I found a wife who believed the same.

And I did. Sort of. We were vague about our discussions but talked often about where we might go — Wisconsin included — when the time was right. We both agreed: This is no place for kids.

But Sonny Landreth changed all that. Yes, that nebbish-looking, Ubangi-stomping guitar god from the southwest Louisiana musical stew made me rethink it all.

True story: It was JazzFest, 1999. My first child, Katherine, was five weeks old. Against the advice of our friends who had children, we took her to the Fair Grounds for an afternoon.

This was less for her, of course, than for us. She was too young for us to leave her with a babysitter—that new-parent protective coating being tough as tungsten—so if Kelly and I wanted to go, then Kate was coming, too.

It was hot. Scary hot, actually, and really humid, and that new-parent oh-my-God-we're-harming-our-new-baby thing kicked in. Total buzz killer.

But some nearby sage, and I wish I could remember who it was all these years later, comforted me with these words: five weeks ago your daughter was submerged in 98 degrees and 100 percent humidity. And she did just fine.

Interesting point. I'm sure the American Medical Association would find many flaws with this logic, but it helped for the moment. And we soldiered on.

We were wending our way through the crowd early on, unable to find a good spot to plant and actually listen to some music. Just one or two bands, we thought, then a plate of some wet, brown food and then we'll head home.

So we were up at the big stage—Acura, or whatever it was called then—and the crowd was too thick and we were trying to get through it and away from it when Sonny Landreth came on.

Have you ever heard this guy? He's making the whole thing up: the riffs, the chords, the notes. I'm no musical scholar, but I think he invented some things. I don't know if there is a specific genre to tag on his music, but it is primeval rock 'n' roll of the first element, a lowdown, fuzz-busting romp in the swamp. And we stopped to dig it.

And I looked down, and there, in the stroller, this beautiful child who had basically remained still and expressionless for the duration of her life—as newborns are wont to do—well, she started to move. To wiggle. And I swear to God, she smiled. For the first time.

I was awash. A Eureka moment: What a *great* place to raise kids. All this funk, the eccentricity, this otherness. Kind of like college, I thought: so much to learn outside the classroom.

It was a great afternoon. In a very small way, I was changed. As time went on, Kelly and I talked less and less about moving away and we had two more kids and we haven't discussed it in years and that's that.

I'm not making this up, nor is this some romantic, Katrina-induced revisionism; in fact, I told this exact story during a radio interview on WWNO last spring.

Just so you know. The record shows.

Today, my kids, they dance. They dig music, and that is the best gift I could ever give them, the best medicine they'll ever know.

At a school picnic in Maryland this fall, where they live in exile, a deejay was playing some contemporary dance club number of indeterminate provenance, and my two sons, Jack and James, started doing the funky butt.

No one else was moving—kids or adults. Some of them stared at my kids while they bounced their rumps up and down. I couldn't have been prouder.

When we go to Audubon Park on some Sunday afternoons, there'll be some massive and rollicking family cookout going on nearby and Katherine will start to shake her rear in a way I've seen only on music videos and she says to me, "Look, Daddy, I'm dancing like the brown people."

Ain't that something.

So what's the point? The point is, Sonny Landreth is playing tonight at Southport Hall. New Orleans veterans Paula and the Pontiacs are opening the show.

If you need to be reminded why we live here—and sometimes we all do—may I suggest this as a suitable alternative to whiskey, pills, shooting your refrigerator, and running naked through the streets.

The Hurricane Kids
9/20/05

I am writing this from the house where I grew up. It's a thousand miles from New Orleans.

Could be a million, really.

I have come to visit my wife and children, who have settled here among my family and old friends in a place we know and trust.

My gang, they live what looks like a normal life here now. School. Shopping. Playdates and birthday parties. Next week, my wife says she's going to start going to the gym.

A normal life. Without me.

Life goes on, I guess. But it's hard to bond the disconnect between what life was like before August 29 and what it's like now.

Talk about loose ends.

Don't get me wrong: Chevy Chase is an amazing place. It was a homey, professional-class neighborhood when my parents moved here in 1963 and is now a profoundly wealthy suburb of Washington, D.C., where famous people live.

It took a hurricane to make it happen, but now my family lives in the same zip code as George Will.

That's almost funny.

It's impossible not to like it here. It's so clean and everyone is so educated and polite and everyone cleans up after their dogs and we pass three crossing guards on our walk to school.

Although the streets are familiar to me—I've come back many times over the decades—I can't help but feel lost here. As if I were moving underwater.

After living in the specter of curfews and military troops and arson and desperate squalor, maybe for the first time in my life I get a hint of what posttraumatic stress really is. Low-grade, to be sure, but you feel it.

I don't recognize any of the kids and I don't know who the parents around me are and I suppose this happens to everyone who relocates to another city, but I don't think "relocate" is really the word for what we did.

What happened was, our lives and social structures and friendships and classmates and easy routines were blown across the globe on one fateful morning and now everything is different.

Just like that.

My daughter, she runs into the gym for her homeroom exercises and she starts playing one of those crazy hand-clapping games with a little girl I've never seen before, and who is that girl? What are they saying to each other?

I used to know the language and rhythm of her school in New Orleans, but here I stumble.

At the entrance to the school, there is a folding table set up where parents can contribute to a fund to buy backpacks and school supplies for the victims of Hurricane Katrina.

Victims. That's the mantle we wear now. And that sucks. In our lives—in all of our lives—the people we want to be are the rescuers in the boat, not the people plucked from the water, but that's what so many of us have become.

At my son's school, I was introduced to the teachers and administrators the other morning. "This is Jack Rose's father," they would say, and you could see it in their eyes right away: Oh, the Hurricane Boy.

Don't get me wrong, they're unbelievably generous and kind to us. In private, I cry when I think about what everyone here is willing to do, how much strangers here—everyone across this country, it seems—wants to help, wants to make us feel welcome.

But still, my son is the Hurricane Boy, and that's not going to change overnight. In my hometown, we are the Hurricane Family. Evacuees, refugees, whatever.

When I am introduced as someone from New Orleans, people sometimes say, "I'm so sorry."

New Orleans. I'm so sorry.

That's not the way it ever was before, not the way it's supposed to be. When people find out you're from New Orleans, they're supposed to tell you about how they got really drunk there once or fell in love there or first heard the music there that changed their lives.

At worst, people would say: I've always wanted to go there.

But now, it's just "I'm sorry."

Man, that kills me. That just kills me.

And by the time this runs in the newspaper, I'll be on my way back to the city, back to Sorry Town. And I'll leave my hurricane family behind here in what you could only call Pleasantville, and somehow I'll find the means to reconcile the two lives, the new and the old, the temporary and the permanent, a thousand miles apart.

It might as well be a million.

Not the biggest tale of hardship you're going to hear from this storm. Far from it. Just one man's journey. One guy wondering what the light at the end of the tunnel looks like.

Wondering where this all will take us. Wondering if any kids will come by our house on Halloween this year. Wondering who will set up their ladders on the corner where we always watch our Mardi Gras parades. Wondering who will be sitting under our shade tree at JazzFest.

It's not premature to think about these things. They are the familiar—and very special—touchstones of our lives.

They are the city where I live. The city that exists, at this moment, as a fond memory.

Traveling Man
10/10/05

I'm somewhat consumed by the topic of travel because I've done so much of it lately, hopping from one bankrupt airline to the next in an effort to see my relocated family in Maryland as much as possible.

If you're from New Orleans, the likelihood of running into someone you know at even the most random of American airports has dramatically increased since the storm. So many of us seem to be on the move, coming home, leaving home, visiting family, looking for a lost dog, looking for a job . . . but where is everyone going?

While changing planes in Memphis recently, I eavesdropped on a guy who was boarding my New Orleans–bound plane. Since he talked so loudly on his cell phone, I considered it to be fair game for columnizing.

Anyway, I don't want to get too far into this particular point, but let's just say this guy was not your run-of-the-mill stud muffin; not a guy you're going to see on the cast of *The Bachelor*, for instance.

In fact, he was round. And there's nothing all that wrong with being round; it's a personal choice, and I'm not going to judge here. And he was also considerably older than me, so we're talking borderline AARP zone here.

And what he was saying into the phone was that he could make $20 an hour in New Orleans hauling trees and debris, and then "All I have to do is pass the physical."

Mind you, the point of this is not to make fun of this guy. The point is: if you have two arms and two legs—or let's just say you've got three out of four—it appears that there's work for you in New Orleans if you want it.

As long as you can pass the physical.

I am so sick of airports. At Reagan National in Washington, I plugged my computer into the wall to power it up so I could write on the flight and it was still in my suitcase and I walked away for a second to chat with a friend. By the time I returned—and we're talking four minutes here—a gate attendant had been notified by an edgy passenger about this and they were pondering the situation and I was no doubt about to be responsible for shutting down all domestic air travel for the day until I sheepishly claimed possession of this menacing tableau.

I do admit—now, looking back on it—that the power cord running into the suitcase might have looked a little suspicious. I think I'll power the thing up at home before I leave next time. Or maybe just sleep on the plane.

My first Katrina-induced travel was, of course, the evacuation. I marvel to this day how my magnificently chaotic family of five managed to straighten up our house, pack our bags, secure our home and belongings, and be on the road on three hours' notice—and have the clothes that we threw together in such a hurry sustain us for more than two weeks.

I suppose a Category 5 hurricane rearing up your backside is a compelling incentive for effective time management.

In our mundane pre-K life, it would usually take us four or five agonizing days to (over)pack for a simple long weekend at the beach, and on the first night, someone (me) was always bound to complain that they (I) forgot some key element of wardrobe so essential to my relaxation that in its absence the vacation was now ruined.

You think leisure traveling with me is a pain? If you really want some jollies, you should try hurricane evacuating with me to some crack hotel in Vicksburg—the kind of place where the tub in the bathroom has a series of yellow-brown cigarette burns along the edge. Those are family memories for a lifetime; like telling your kids they can't take off their shoes even when they're inside.

"No, James! Put down that dirty needle!"

(If you only knew how little I was exaggerating here.)

And who smokes in the tub anyway? I guess people who stay in crack hotels, I don't know.

But now my children are safe and sound in the very leafy and upscale Chevy Chase, Maryland. When I was visiting last weekend, there was an aluminum foil display in the newly converted playroom in my parents' house and I asked my wife what it was and she informed me that it was my daughter's science project for her Brownie troop.

"What are they doing?" I asked.

"They're growing mold," my wife said. Growing mold. If my New Orleans daughter doesn't get the blue ribbon for that project—the state prize, in fact—then there is no justice in this world.

Have Barbie, Will Travel
11/1/05

Traveling back and forth to Maryland to visit my family in exile
has turned into a ritualistic exercise in tragicomedy.

On the lighter side: before each journey, I check with my kids
by phone to see what they need from our house in New Orleans.

Of course, they need everything, they tell me. Every toy, every
article of clothing, every piece of furniture, everything that hangs
on the walls, every piece of building material down to the studs.

"Itemize," I urge them.

"Barbies," they tell me.

"I can do that," I tell them.

And so my chore began one afternoon, as I crouched and
crawled into their secret places in our house—small, dark spaces
I have never been in, places that are not hospitable to people
larger than, say, a dorm refrigerator.

In the process, I discovered that there has been a population
of approximately fifty Barbies living under my roof. I did not
know this.

An absurd number, I was thinking, but then I remembered
that I used to collect empty egg cartons when I was a kid and I
probably had a couple hundred—a closet full of them—before
my mother brought the hammer down on that curious little
hobby of mine.

Truth is, I don't recall even the barest notion of why I collected egg cartons nor what I did with them. I just did. So who am I to tell my kids they have too many Barbies?

Let them be, I say. I mean, I turned out okay, right?

Don't answer that.

The other thing about our Barbies is that they are all naked. They lie in heaps and piles of tangled, plastic, not-quite-anatomically-correct nakedness—a truly discomfiting sight to a father who hopes to shield his children from any and all dissolute imagery, although I suspect a contemporary child would need to be at least thirteen before these tableaux would access the lurid pockets of the imagination.

My kids, they dress and undress their Barbies incessantly, obsessively, compulsively, but—at the end of the day—they are all naked. (The Barbies, not the kids.) They are bare canvases, so to speak, upon which to begin the next morning's sartorial exercises.

I decided I could fit about fifteen or so Barbies into my carry-on bag and began to try to dress them from the mounds of discarded dresses, gowns, and fashionable minis that litter my floors.

I found this task about as easy and pleasant as hanging Sheetrock. Apparently you need fingers smaller than toothpicks to accomplish this. I gave up the task.

And that's how I ended up recently wandering around several major American airports with a small satchel stuffed full of naked Barbies. All mashed together in a fleshy heap.

No other luggage to speak of. Nothing checked in. No personal clothes or items; I am fully outfitted in Maryland.

Just a laptop computer, a couple of notebooks, and a suitcase full of naked Barbies.

If anybody was ever wearing a sign at airport security that screamed "Full body cavity search!" it was me.

Guns, knives, drugs, explosives, cigarette lighters—that's old hat. A travel bag stocked with Lesbian Orgy by Mattel is a whole 'nother circumstance.

Mercifully, I made it from Point A (New Orleans) to Point B

(Maryland) without incident. That's because none of the security screeners would make eye contact with me. Or maybe I was only imagining that.

Maybe the X-ray machines render the plastic components of Barbies almost invisible. Or maybe the imagery was so creepy that no one wanted to deal with this haggard man with a carry-on bag full of naked Barbies.

Pass by, horseman.

And that's my story. Not much there, really. But there comes a point at which I choose to purge myself of the images and the smell and the dust and the sepia horizons of New Orleans. Of all the doubt.

Sometimes I just want to ponder something else.

Sometimes I just want to travel halfway across the country just to see my kids smile and to crawl under the covers with them at night and listen to their syncopated chorus of snores and nose whistles, wince at their involuntary spasms and howls, and stare at the ceiling and wonder at the wonder of it all.

Prep Boys and Jesuits
11/13/05

If you've done any traveling in the post-Katrina era, you already know this: it follows you.

Not only is The Horror the only thing anyone around here ever talks about anymore, it's also the only thing everyone Out There wants to talk about when they meet you.

I went to my high school's homecoming in Maryland recently and discovered I was practically a celebrity alumnus by virtue of the fact that I live in New Orleans.

We aging, potbellied guys shoved our hands in our pockets and rocked on our heels, standing down by the end zone watching the game.

"How is it?" they all ask, and I know they're being kind and really are concerned, but just how the hell do you answer that question in time to get back to the crucial third-and-long situation on the football field?

I mean, really: What can you tell them? Where do you start? Levees? FEMA? Looting? Do you really want to get into it?

So you lie and make it easier for everyone. "We're getting there," you tell them.

My high school is Georgetown Prep. It used to be affiliated with Georgetown University—way back a century or two ago—

but is now a stand-alone institution in the suburbs of Washington, D.C.

It's a coat-and-tie place, all boys, an academic and athletic powerhouse on ninety rolling acres; one heck of a place to spend your formative years. Latin was required when I went there; I'm sure it still is.

It was like living inside that novel *A Separate Peace*, which was also required reading when I was there.

It's composed mostly of day students, but there are a couple of dormitories there for boarders, and when Katrina blew through New Orleans, the folks at Prep contacted Jesuit High School in New Orleans and offered to take in some kids for the semester. No charge.

That amounts to considerably more than a nice gesture: it costs $25,000 to go there (which is a few more bucks than it was when I was a lad, to be sure).

There actually weren't any vacancies at Prep, so the academic brain trust there came up with a plan: any undergraduate roommates who agreed to make room for a Jesuit student and make it three to a room would be offered the coveted privileges allowed only to seniors: televisions and refrigerators in their dorm rooms.

Fifteen Jesuit kids wound up at Prep this fall. Maryland is a whole different world for these kids, trying to break into an alien East Coast social scene in midstream. Who are these girls? What are these people talking about? Don't they have any Abita around here?

After the football game, I met Jude Fitzmorris, one of the Jesuit kids. He's Tom Fitzmorris's kid; you know, that "Mr. Food" guy on AM radio.

Jude said he really likes it there. He's fitting in. He plans to stay the full academic school year. Most of the other guys, he said, are homesick as all get-out and they want to come back here.

In fact, some already have.

There's just something about New Orleans, I guess, even when it's beaten down like a wet three-legged dog. With mange and fleas. That's blind in one eye. And won't hunt.

That's us. The three-legged dog. But a confoundingly lovable cur all the same.

At that homecoming game (we beat St. Alban's by three touchdowns, by the way), I ran into my friend Rory Coakley, who happened to be in New Orleans the weekend Katrina began her ramrod track up our wazoo.

He had been moving his son, an incoming freshman—and recent Prep grad—into the dorm at Loyola University. In fact, this September, I was scheduled to host a dinner for Rory, Jr., and seven other incoming Prep freshmen at Jacques-Imo's Cafe on Oak Street.

Another local Prep alum and I were going to give the boys a little shrimp and alligator sausage cheesecake just to let them know they're not in Maryland anymore, then do the old-fart routine of welcoming them to the city and rendering our deep fonts of local wisdom and advice.

Of course, that didn't happen.

That Friday, Saturday, and Sunday before the storm, Rory called me from his room at the downtown Hilton as things were getting scary around here. I kept telling him to get the heck out of Dodge, but he couldn't find a flight. Or a car. Or a train. Or a bus.

I offered him one of our cars—told him to take it all the way to the East Coast; I didn't care. "You really need to get the hell out of here," I told him.

In my signature fashion, however, my car had zero gas in it and at this point there were no gas stations left open around here. So Rory, his wife, his son, and two other Prep grads were on their own.

"Godspeed to you, brother," I told him as I split town with my own family. "See you on the other side."

Rory's a creative and intelligent guy—and fairly well off, it turns out. As I said, we had a pretty good education, so, in thinking-outside-of-the-box fashion, he walked out of the Hilton lobby and up to a cabdriver and offered him a thousand dollars for a ride to Mobile.

In perhaps another characteristic of a typical Prep alum, Rory was delighted to discover that the cabdriver had a six-pack of Heineken in the car, which he threw into the deal as lagniappe.

Rory decided to drink one beer every hour. The six-pack was finished before they even made the Mississippi state line. The trip took so long that the cabdriver said he was too tired to continue, so Rory finished the driving duties, some sixteen or seventeen hours later.

A few days later, Rory and I were on the phone—he safely back in Maryland, me in Baton Rouge—watching the grim TV images of the Convention Center.

"You know, that would have been you," I told him. "That's the best thousand dollars you ever spent."

Anyway. At the homecoming game, Rory told me he would be back in New Orleans in January. Turns out, Rory Jr. and some of the other Prep guys are reenrolling at Loyola.

I wanted to ask him: Are you out of your mind? I mean, I think they're plumb crazy to do such a thing when they can comfortably remain in the safe, familiar environs of Georgetown University, where all the other Prep Loyola guys ended up.

But I swear to God, I wanted to kiss Rory when he told me this. It just slays me that there are people Out There who are committing themselves to this city when they have no other need or obligation to, no other reason than that they think it's the right thing to do.

They believe in us.

And this is so important. If our universities don't survive this thing, we're in deep trouble. And I will testify to you that a half-dozen boys from Georgetown Prep are a good place to start.

And yeah, sure, they'll probably wind up being among those really annoying shirtless yahoos you see sitting on living room furniture on the littered front lawns of the frat houses on Broadway, but they're also going to be young men who saw what went down here ten weeks ago and understand what went down here and they and their parents are still willing to stick it out with us.

Without them, we're toast.

And for that I say: Fried green tomatoes and eggplant pirogues at Jacques-Imo's on me, boys! Just give me a call when you get here in January.

Here to your new home, this crazy little three-legged dog named New Orleans.

Good-bye
12/4/05

Each time I go to Maryland to visit my children in exile, my daughter, Katherine, asks me the same thing: "Daddy, is everything in New Orleans broken?"

My first impulse is to tell her, "Only our hearts, darling. In a million little pieces. But our spirits will endure."

But Katherine, being six, isn't much for purple melodrama or lofty sentiment. She just wants to know if her swing set is okay.

So I tell her that a lot of things are, in fact, broken but that most of her stuff—that's what counts to a child, right?—is fine. Except for the swing set, oddly enough. It's history. But that's a small price, I tell her.

I try to teach my kids that they are the lucky ones, the fortunate few, and they saw all that stuff on TV, so I think they get it.

I think.

They see the piles of donated clothes at their schools in Maryland and the table where students were raising money to buy backpacks for Katrina kids and so they know: there are folks out there a lot worse off than us.

On TV, they saw the images of people sitting in baskets dangling from ropes out of helicopters and they thought that looked pretty scary but pretty fun all the same and they wish they had done that.

"No, you don't," I tell them and leave it at that.

Katherine and my son Jack recently asked me for status reports about their favorite places. The zoo: good. The aquarium: not so good. Creole Creamery: good. This is important. After all, who would want to live in a town without ice cream?

I try to paint a somewhat accurate picture of what life looks like here, filtered through their lenses; I want them to understand, in some small way, what they will come home to one day soon.

They need to know what will be different in their upside-down world. The fewer surprises, my thinking goes, the smoother it will all go down.

They seem to grasp the situation best by an accounting of their friends. Where are their friends? they want to know. Who will be here when they come back to New Orleans?

I tell them that Walker and Olivia and Margot are like us: they're all here and safe and settled in their own homes.

I tell them that Casey, Helen, and the twins Sisson and Tappan all lost the first floors of their homes in the flood but that they are going to live upstairs in their houses and they will be in school with us in January.

They think this sounds cool, this living upstairs thing.

"Can we live upstairs?" Jack asks me.

Hmm. "We can pretend," I tell him. "How about we make believe we live upstairs?"

He thinks this sounds like a good game.

Then I tell them that Lexi and Mila have moved away and they won't be coming back. Same for Miles and Cecilia. Ditto Charlie. They're gone.

They don't like this news, but they process it and they have been aware for a while that lots of families are spread around the country as they are, living in new places and going to new schools. Hurricane Kids, just like them.

They don't like the idea that they never said good-bye to Lexi and Mila and Miles and Cecilia and Charlie. I tell them we'll find these kids and we will tell them good-bye. I promise them that we will find these kids. So they can say . . . good-bye.

Continuing on the list of friends, I tell them that Sean is up in the air but that he will probably be coming back.

"Why is Sean up in the air?" Jack asks me. He's four. I try to picture what he is picturing. Sean. Up in the air.

That sounds even cooler than living upstairs. I guess it sounds as though he's dangling under a helicopter. I don't know. Sometimes I wonder how we're able to communicate with our children at all.

Katherine asks me about the specific fates of two other friends, Juliet and Nadia. I tell her that, truth is, I have no idea what happened to Juliet and Nadia. Not a clue. Vanished. They're just gone, and we don't know where to or for how long and maybe we'll see them again and maybe we won't.

I don't know.

Kids don't work so well with uncertainties.

"Will you find Nadia for me?" Katherine asks.

I tell her yes, I will find Nadia. But I don't know where Nadia is. I can't even find my barber; how am I going to find some kid who has been cast to the fates?

Where did everybody go?

Man, it's a hell of a thing that went down here.

Juliet, Nadia, are you out there? Somewhere? Anywhere?

If you are, Katherine says hello.

And good-bye.

Groundhog Day
12/18/05

We have been waking up with Groundhog Day Syndrome for a long time now, dragging ourselves out of bed with a sense of dread that the clock has stopped, the calendar pages don't turn, and nothing is changing.

We're Bill Murray. We're Sisyphus pushing the boulder up the mountain. We're trapped in an Escher print, walking down steps that actually lead up, down straight paths that lead us full circle.

Okay, for the four of you still reading, I'll stop with the cultural metaphors. You get the point. I get the point. We all get the point.

The point is: it's fourteen days until January.

Wait until January, people in New Orleans say. You hear it all the time. Things will get better in January.

It's our mantra of hope, optimism, faith. Or maybe delusion.

Maybe because we've been Saints fans for so long that we are willing to buy futures when the market is flat. So eager to accept promises we don't really believe.

It's always been "wait until next year," and we buy our season tickets and jerseys with the name and number of our new star player—the guy who's going to take us all the way!—and, like Charlie Brown, we keep running to kick the football and Lucy pulls it away.

Again and again. Wait until next year.

But there is merit to the current theory of an impending turn of events for the positive, empirical evidence to shore it up. For New Orleans, that is; the Saints, I'm afraid, are a lost cause, and they don't make levees big enough to plug that breach.

But January holds the promise of a sound that has been missing from our city for too long: the music of children. Lots of children.

Sure, there has been a refreshing repopulation of the little critters in recent weeks as schools opened and families trickled home, but the playgrounds still look pretty desolate and there's hardly ever a line for sugar cones at the Creole Creamery.

But there are legions of rug rats coming home this week or next or next, when the school semesters elsewhere end and the holidays are over.

True, my son Jack's nursery school class will have only twelve of the original twenty kids who were enrolled last September, but I guess that's a decent rate of return. A start.

And I think it will grow. The kid quotient goes up by at least three today.

My family is coming home.

This is wonderful news from a personal standpoint, but I am also filled with anxiety about this, and immeasurable . . . I guess I can say it: doubt.

Is it safe? Will they pick up on the air of despondency that seems to have engulfed three quarters of the adult population here? Will they be upset that they don't have a blue roof like everyone else?

These are the questions that nag me.

But I think my friend the barber Aidan Gill summed it up best: "A time will come when someone asks you, 'What were you doing about it?' You can't tell them, 'I was just watching it. I was just an innocent bystander.' Let me tell you something: there are no innocent bystanders in this."

My own call to arms has been that either you're part of the solution or you're part of the problem and it's time we become part of the problem because the solution, whatever it's been up to now, ain't workin'.

So I'm Charlie Brown now. New Orleans is Lucy. And I'm gonna kick that ball a country mile.

Come January, everything will get better. If not, we wait for February 2.

That's Groundhog Day.

Coming Home
12/27/05

On August 27, my family left our home in New Orleans with a duffel bag full of beach clothes, three sleeping bags, three teddy bears, and a basketball.

I always travel with a basketball. It's my security blanket. I never knew how much I'd need one on this trip.

There was a hurricane coming to town, and, well . . . you know the rest of that story. I returned to New Orleans a week later. My family wound up in Maryland, in the town of Somerset, just on the D.C. border, in the house where I grew up.

There has always been much hand-wringing over what you were supposed to call people like us—refugees, evacuees, etc.—but the terminology I prefer is that my kids were "embedded" at their grandparents' house. They became minicelebrities in my hometown. Katrina Kids. A name recognized the world over.

When I went to visit, it seemed like everyone knew who we were. Several times, while trick-or-treating on Halloween, other parents stopped me and said, "We've heard about you." People gave us clothes and toys and tuition (thank you, Concord Hill School) and such an outpouring of generosity that it boggles the mind to realize just how kind strangers can be. My sister loaned us her car for four months, and if that's not love, I don't know what is.

My wife and kids used to spend weekends at my brother's house in Poolesville, Maryland—forty-five minutes away—and one morning, three bicycles appeared on the front lawn.

No note. No explanation. Just like that.

They'd heard about us.

We made the Somerset town newsletter but not the local daily, as some of our friends did in smaller towns across America. That's the price you pay when you become Katrina Kids in the *Washington Post* distribution area; you have to fight with Tom DeLay and Saddam Hussein for front-page space.

On the other hand, the crew at the local Starbucks wouldn't let my wife pay for coffee when they found out she was from New Orleans, so it was a two-way street, the good and the bad.

My wife and daughter became social mavens in town; the women of Somerset smothered them with attention and invitations. They thrived. It is a great place, that old town. But the gig is up.

We said good-bye to our extended family and new friends last week, and here's the thing about that—from the Can't Catch a Break files: what should have been the happiest day of the year for us—our homecoming—was actually Teardrop City, saying good-bye to my sister, my brother, their families, and, worst of all, my parents, who let us turn their house and their lives upside down and asked in return only that we not break the frail staircase banister or destroy my mother's favorite old sofa, and, naturally, we did both.

My parents are heroes. Among the tens of thousands of people who allowed their lives to be jolted by those of us who came seeking shelter from the storm. I felt as though we broke their hearts when we left.

But my kids got to know them, and if there's one thing I can thank Katrina for, it's that. And also, my kids got to see snow, make a snowman, throw a snowball, catch flakes on their tongues.

That was a nice finishing touch.

But I'm tired of spending all my life surrounded by good-byes. That's a lyric by Fred LeBlanc, the Cowboy Mouth drummer, but it captures my core right now. Every day, it seems, it's good-bye to somebody.

But bringing my family home also brought with it the very welcome sound of hello. It was a sound I needed to hear. Hello to all — well, some — of our old New Orleans friends and neighbors.

And it's funny: it wasn't until my wife and kids walked into our house that I realized I had been living with a bunker mentality for a long time.

For instance, I had cleaned out our refrigerator months before, but the shelves were still in the backyard. My back deck was still a repository for seven red gas cans, even though I hadn't run a generator since September.

My closet and drawers were almost exactly as they had been the day we evacuated; I have worn two sets of clothes since everything went down. Jeans, T-shirts. I look at the suits hanging in my closet and wonder what use I'll ever have for them again.

What did I used to do?

Some folks say it's insane to bring children into this environment, this beaten-down town, and certainly there is merit to that argument.

Is it depressing here? Yes. Is it dangerous? Maybe. The water, the air, the soil . . . I don't know.

And there's little doubt that the kids have picked up the vibe. My six-year-old daughter started writing a book this week — a writer in the family! — and she has a page about the hurricane in it and it says, "A lot of people died. Some of them were kids."

Mercy. God in Heaven, what lives are we handing to these children of the storm?

Then again, there is much about the aftermath that amuses them greatly. For example, where adults see rows and rows of spoiling refrigerators fouling the side of the road, children see mountains of empty appliance boxes to replace them.

It used to be that when a neighbor on the block bought a major appliance — a once-a-year event — we would commandeer the box and make four or five days of fun out of it. A fort. A playhouse. A cave.

With all these empty boxes around, I thought it would be

nearly criminal not to make some lemonade out of all these lemons bestowed upon us, so I borrowed a friend's truck and brought six refrigerator boxes home and built a Christmas village for the kids.

They disappear for hours. In all the muck, you gotta dig for the magic.

When we drove to City Park the other night to look at the holiday lights, we plowed through blighted streets, total darkness, total loss and devastation on the sides of the road.

"Ooh, scary!" was all my son could muster. They thought it was pretty cool, actually, and I'm not going to call them out on that and tell them that in fact it's not. In due time, they will find out.

They will learn what went down in this town.

They see the ubiquitous brown stain that marks where the floodwaters settled for three weeks, and they see not the criminal failure of the Army Corps of Engineers but . . . a bathtub ring around the city.

What other place has that?

They love this town, my kids. They had a blast in Maryland, but they all said they wanted to come home and they've not said otherwise since they got here.

They know that Al Copeland's house is all lit up for the holidays like some crazy Disney castle and they know we'll go check it out this week, and that alone, for them, is a reason to live here.

They'll go back to their schools in January, and we will move on.

It's a big deal, what's happened here and what lies ahead. Rebuilding this city is history in the making, and my family—as we're fond of singing around here—is going to be in that number.

This is not just Anywhere USA we're talking about. This is New Orleans. This is our home. Our future.

It's a hard-luck city right now, and you can look at it as a half-empty, half-full conundrum, although, in New Orleans, the truth is that the glass is shattered.

But we're going to help pick up the pieces. Starting today.

Life in the Refrigerator City

Civil Unrest
10/18/05

Refrigerators are poignant symbols of our city's destruction and our government's inertia; many are now painted with political slogans.

The refrigerators of New Orleans are also the weapons of choice in the rapid deterioration of civility Uptown. Weapons of our Mass Destruction—literally.

It's all a part of NIMBY syndrome—Not In My Backyard—the bane of political processes nationwide (think Wal-Mart, landfills, and halfway houses), but these are particularly wicked and stinky cases.

A small instance would be the case of the jerk who loaded his dead and smelly fridge into his pickup truck one night and drove around Uptown looking for a place to get rid of it, rather than putting it on his curbside like the rest of us and taking his chances on the latest gambling craze sweeping our town: FEMA Garbage Pickup Lotto.

And did he dump it in the river or on some abandoned lot on Tchoupitoulas? No, this pillar of society chose Audubon Park—at the corner of Laurel Street and West Drive—to dump his offensive icebox. Smooth move. What a prince.

There's one oasis for miles in this community that has been cleaned and groomed for repopulation (Thank you, Oklahoma

National Guard)—a place to bring kids and pets and grandmothers and see what little remains of nature in this godforsaken wasteland—and somebody dumps a fridge on the corner and drives off into the night.

This kind of crap makes me hubcap-stealing angry. But this was just a skirmish in what has become the Uptown Refrigerator Wars.

Refrigerator clusters have started appearing all over the area, as one guy dumps his fridge on a corner away from his house and then—like iron shavings drawn to a magnet—suddenly there are five appliances on the corner, then ten, then fifteen.

But it gets worse. It gets personal. The above crimes are random and anonymous. The two I shall now describe involve direct confrontations followed by covert actions and now, no doubt, smoldering resentments among neighbors.

Full disclosure: I was involved in one of these episodes. I'm sure this comes as a great shock to, say, my wife and close friends, to hear that I interjected myself into a petty and juvenile refrigerator dispute but, hey: like everyone else, I'm mad as hell, and I'm not gonna take it anymore.

To wit: On Friday night, the garbage crews rolled onto my street—huge dump trucks and backhoes and cranes and Bobcats. It was the closest to a parade that we've seen in a while, and we all poured out of our houses to cheer them on. Finally, our six-foot wall of debris, stretching from one end of the block to the other, was going to be hauled off, and we could begin to try to forget what has happened here.

But while the hard-hatted cleanup crews were doing their massive sweep-up, a guy from around the corner drove up in his pickup truck and dumped a fridge on the corner.

My neighbor Franke jumped off his stoop and ran over to explain that the refrigerators and other hazardous waste had already been cleaned from this block; that these guys on Friday night were just picking up trees, branches, household debris, and regular old garbage.

The guy insisted that the trucks would take his fridge, too, and then he drove off, even as we told him: Don't leave this here.

Well, it took an hour, but the federal contractors got my block clear. We could see our curbs and sidewalks for the first time since the hurricane. The place was swept spotless. It was a time for celebration.

Except for that damn smelly fridge they left on the corner, just like we said they would.

Man, that really chapped me. So, in the middle of the night, I borrowed a friend's dolly and I loaded up the fridge and I dragged it back to the offender's house and unloaded it at his front steps. Since they hadn't picked it up, I was sure he was going to want to do the neighborly thing and take it back.

Now, I ask you: Was I wrong to do this?

Don't answer that. First, let me tell you another story, as reported to me by a very reliable source who shall remain nameless for his own protection. (Me, I'm not circumspect enough to perform my urban civic warfare anonymously.)

Over in another part of Uptown, several neighbors were working together to roll their refrigerators out to the curb. Everyone explicitly agreed to tape them shut to lock in the stink and foulness and take the necessary precautions to prevent widespread dysentery.

Often, as you probably know, getting a full refrigerator out to the curb takes a couple of people, but one guy got restless and refused to wait and he wrestled out his appliance to his driveway alone. He had attempted to tape it shut but had done an obviously inferior job and he wouldn't wait for help.

Then he tied the dang thing to his car to drag it down to the curb. And it fell open. And your mama's seven-week-old casserole spilled out. And it stank. And he left it there, an open and stinking invitation to all manner of biblical-proportion infestations and plagues.

Naturally, everyone on the block got ticked off. And then one got even.

When a contractor drove by later that day, a guy on the block offered him $20 to use his Bobcat to grab ahold of the offending refrigerator, move it into the middle of the offender's driveway, and drop it—thereby blocking ingress and egress to said driveway.

The contractor accepted the offer and moved the fridge into blockade position. Now the neighbors all eye one another suspiciously and goodwill is withdrawn and there you have it. This is what it has come to.

Now, I know what a lot of you are thinking: There are people in this town who lost *everything*. Their loved ones, their homes, their jobs, their pets, their precious photos and memories.

And their refrigerators.

And all that you rich and idle Uptowners on dry land can find within your hearts to do is bicker over appliances?

You're thinking: You people didn't have a right to survive this storm.

Maybe you're right. Maybe we should go back to fighting one another over Wal-Mart and Whole Foods and college bars. But consider this:

Maybe this signals a return to normalcy. Maybe this is even a healthy sign of the human spirit.

Or maybe we're all just a bunch of petty ingrates.

Really, it's not for me to decide. I am merely the chronicler of events and, okay, a minor participant in the civic unrest.

I am willing to share the blame. But I also view this story as a cautionary tale, a call for civility, a cry of help to the community at large before we tear ourselves apart.

And while we're talking about civility, one more thing:

Keep your stinking fridge to yourself.

Refrigerator Town
10/30/05

In Refrigerator Town there was a Council Full of Clowns
And a tall and savvy king as bald as Cupid.
In Refrigerator Town, while all the poor folks drowned
FEMA and Mike Brown were stuck on stupid.
In Refrigerator Dome, which was temporary home
To the terrified and downtrodden masses,
In Refrigerator Dome, the people waited all alone
While the buses showed up slower than molasses.
In Refrigerator Village, some coppers loot and pillage
And we still don't know how many won't come back.
In Refrigerator Village, they'll have to pass a millage
Just to pay for all those stolen Cadillacs.
In Refrigerator Town, not a child can be found
And the classrooms are as empty as the Dome.
In Refrigerator Town, School Board antics still abound
And you wonder why you'd ever move back home.
In Refrigerator Void, all the houses were destroyed
And you get a sense of widespread fear and panic.
In Refrigerator Void, all the folks are unemployed
And everyone you meet is taking Xanax.
In Refrigerator City, Congress seems to take no pity
On the businesses that cease to operate.

In Refrigerator City, there's a VIP committee
To which nobody can possibly relate.
In Refrigerator Parish, the bickering is garish
And the politicians seem to have no clue.
In Refrigerator Parish, it really got nightmarish
When the sharks showed up on Cleary Avenue.
In Refrigerator 'burbs, the trash is piled up on the curbs
And the neighborhoods are ugly and they smell.
In Refrigerator 'burbs, folks are getting quite disturbed
That their quality of life has gone to hell.
In Refrigerator Land, we have no leg on which to stand
While the politicos can't seem to do a thing.
In Refrigerator Land, it seems the only helping hand
Is the signing bonus at the Burger King.
On Refrigerator Planet, if you can't bag or box or can it,
Just push it out your door onto the street.
On Refrigerator Planet, pick up the garbage, dammit!
'Cause the whole place smells like fetid, rotten meat.
In Refrigerator Wasteland, you have to dress up like a spaceman
Just to rescue your old family photographs.
In Refrigerator Wasteland, stretched from Chalmette clear to Raceland
We're in misery while Halliburton laughs.
From the Refrigerator Pulpits, the preachers said the culprits
For the storm were all the lesbians and queers.
But Refrigerator Church was left in quite a lurch
When it turned out to be the Corps of Engineers.
In Refrigerator Dome, the Saints no longer call it home
No more runs or kicks or punts or touchdown passes.
In Refrigerator Dome, no more famous cups of foam
And Tom Benson's heart's as cold as Minneapolis.
In Refrigerator Land, the levees all are made of sand
And there's no gas, no food, no water, and no sewage.
But in Refrigerator Land, we will make our final stand
Because anything beats rush hour in Baton Rouge.

Lurching Toward Babylon
11/11/05

People ask me: What do you cover now that the entertainment industry has fizzled away? After all, for the past ten years, that was my beat.

My answer: Basically, I spend my days like everyone else, lurching from one "episode" to the next, just trying to live, just trying to survive, just trying not to crack up and publicly embarrass myself, my family, and my newspaper.

It's hard, man. It's hard, just to live. I don't mean to be overly confessional here, but sometimes I feel I am no longer fit for public consumption, no longer fit for publication, and definitely no longer fit to operate heavy machinery.

I was at my local Circle K the other day, sitting in my car in a borderline catatonic state, when I witnessed a guy in a truck in the parking lot wadding up a ball of trash and throwing it out his window.

I have silently witnessed this sight a million times over the past twenty years. On Broad Street, on Magazine Street, in the French Quarter, everywhere. We all have. It's almost as if litter is a part of our heritage.

Well, I snapped. I got out of my car and approached the offending vehicle and I tapped on the guy's window.

During my walk to said vehicle, a very loud voice inside my

head said to me: Don't do this. You are not well. It's none of your business.

But there are lots of voices in my head these days. You can probably relate. So I wrote this cautionary device off as just so much cacophony and decided: It is your business. The guy rolled down his window, and I asked, "Are you from here?"

I expected him to say no, and I had this thing in my mind that I was going to tell him, this thing about the sanctity of my city, about the care he needs to take, about how delicate our balance is right now.

But he said yes. And I lost it. Completely. Stark raving mad, if you must know the truth. "You can't do this anymore," I said to him in a voice that wasn't particularly loud but in a tone I hardly recognized from myself and that was probably laced with just enough tonic to catch his attention.

We looked at each other. And then I said—or maybe I screamed—"You can't do this anymore!"

I'm not sure who was more frightened, he or I, but I kept going. I said, "You can't just throw stuff out of your car window anymore. I realize that there is garbage everywhere—all over our streets—but, still, you can't just throw stuff out your window like it doesn't matter. *It matters!*"

The guy was frozen in his seat. He was no doubt wishing he had gone to Winn-Dixie or the Stop-N-Go or anyplace else but this Circle K. But here we were. I laid it out on this poor sap. I said, "We've got to change. We can't go back to the way we were, and the way we were was people just throwing crap in the streets like it doesn't matter. We need to do better. We need to change.

"*It matters!*" I said again—as if he hadn't heard me the first time—and then I just stood there in a forwardly lurched position, and I can tell you: I'm tired of lurching. I want to stop lurching. But I can't stop lurching.

Needless to say, I freaked the guy out. His eyes got wide, and I think he wanted to answer me but no words came. He mumbled something like "All right," and then his arm got busy rolling his window up and he nodded to me in a fashion that said some-

thing between "Don't kill me" and "Seek professional help" and
he backed out of the parking lot.

Slowly.

And he was gone. And I was standing there.

Lurched.

He probably got on his cell phone to his wife and said: "We're
moving to Houston."

I don't know. I don't mean to push my existential dread on
complete strangers, but there I stood, now in an empty Circle K
parking lot, thinking: What the hell are you doing? I lurched
back to my car. I lurched home. And I'm sitting here at my
desk—lurched, I might add—wondering where all this comes
from.

There is no lesson here. No moral. Other than that we have to
erase all the bad things we used to do around here—big and
small—if we want to survive. We need to be civil. We need to be
clean. We need to change. We need to respect ourselves and our
city.

Otherwise, some disengaged crazy guy is going to accost you
in a parking lot someday and make you wish you'd never gotten
out of bed that morning. It will leave you in one serious lurch,
my friend.

The Cat Lady
9/29/05

Ellen Montgomery's house near Audubon Park was already almost invisible from the street before Hurricane Katrina shattered the massive cedar tree in her front yard and left a tangled, camouflaged mess that now obliterates the view of just about everything.

If anything, that helped her hide from the National Guard during the tense days—now ancient weeks ago—when word came that they were forcing those who had remained in New Orleans to leave.

"If I was out walking in the neighborhood and I heard the Hummers coming, I would duck down behind a porch or some broken shutters," she said. "I felt like a Confederate spy in enemy territory."

Montgomery was a holdout. A straggler. The resistance.

She stayed behind without power or running water or even a generator. The simple reason: "My babies," she says. Thirty-four cats. (It was thirty-three for several weeks, until one that had gone missing returned home last Saturday night, "to say hello," Montgomery says.)

She knows what you're thinking. It used to bug her but not anymore.

"Years ago, I said to my vet, 'But I don't *want* to be a cat lady!'"

Montgomery recalls. "And he says to me, 'But you *are* a cat lady.' So there you are."

And so, for thirty days, what has she done?

"Well," she pauses. "I sleep late. Let's see . . . and then I feed the cats. I read *The Journal of Beatrix Potter*. It's a lovely book. And then I have my cup of coffee. And that usually lasts a couple of hours. And then I paint and—I don't know. The days just fly by. I'm in another world here. I don't feel the heat. I don't feel anything. I am very able to exist on my own. I just paint, and that's what keeps me from going bonkers. That's my therapy."

Montgomery has been painting since 1977, when she read the book of Vincent van Gogh's correspondence, *Letters to Theo*.

"I read it and I said, 'I want to do that,' " she says. "So I got down and did that and have been doing it ever since."

Indeed. She sits on the floor in the front room of her house— it would be a stretch to call it a "studio"—and she fills canvas after canvas, board after board, paper after paper. If you stood still in front of her for long enough, she'd probably paint you.

Her home is filled with thousands of paintings she has made over the past three decades. Admittedly, she has sold few works, so mostly they line her walls, floor to ceiling in every room, and then they fill stacks and piles randomly assigned through her cluttered 1890s cottage.

And, having recently run out of canvases to work on, she is now working a medium that only a hurricane could provide: she has gathered scores of slate roofing tiles that were scattered off the roofs of her neighbors' homes into the street, and now she paints them.

"They're so beautiful," she says. "I couldn't bear the thought of the National Guardsmen or some contractors trampling over them, so I collected them. I won't have enough time in my life to paint them all."

Over the years, she has painted various abstracts and florals and faces and landscapes, but now her work is fairly dark and muddied and swirly, work clearly influenced by the monstrous forces that have visited her life this past month.

Funny thing is, in the beginning, she didn't really know what had happened.

Montgomery has been living the consummate, isolated cat lady existence for years, and she was only vaguely aware that a storm was even coming.

The shattered cedar tree and the loss of power, water, and phone—and the disappearance of all her neighbors—told her it was something big.

"I went to church that Sunday morning before the storm, and a sign on the door said, 'Services canceled,' so I bought a paper and that was the last news I heard," she says.

"There were four or five days where I had absolutely no idea what had happened. But I was safe, the cats were safe, so I thought: Why be scared? I firmly believe in God and prayer. I knew I would just ride it out. I am probably more prepared than anyone else in the world to spend time alone."

It wasn't until several days later, when a neighbor returning to retrieve some items loaned her a radio—and stocked her with food and water before leaving again—that the magnitude of the event settled upon her.

"I try to listen to the news a couple of hours a day, and it's unimaginable, really," she says. But she has seen no images of it all; has not seen that more than half the city was underwater and has not seen the human misery that filled the Superdome and Convention Center, sights that are now burned into the American consciousness.

"At first, actually, it was kind of nice around here," she says. "The birds came back, and the squirrels would come deliver me the news. It's all been so peaceful, really. But it's nice to have the thought of people coming back. I suppose there'll be lots of chain saws and hammers and all that, so I might miss the silence. But, the truth is, I'm just about out of candles."

Caving In
10/2/05

It's not hard to identify the point at which, during my second tour of press duty here, it was time to get out.

That would be when, in the course of accompanying a photographer to shoot pictures for a feature I was writing, I stood up, blacked out, pitched face forward into a tree, and lay in the grass drifting in and out of consciousness for the next couple of hours.

It was during those "in" points of my in-and-out consciousness, looking up into a profoundly beautiful blue New Orleans sky, that I thought: Maybe I need to eat more. Maybe I need a break. I wonder what my kids are doing today? I wonder if there are any job openings in the Midwest?

There I was, a body lying face up in the grass on the side of the road for several hours in a once-major metropolitan city, a sizeable gash across my forehead, one that—as I study it in a mirror—actually seems to be in the shape of the letter K, which seems a fitting lifetime reminder of what has happened here.

A little more authentic than a tattoo, no?

I was also thinking: Isn't anyone going to come get me? Several notions came to mind.

First of all, even before Katrina (pre-K, let's call it), a man passed out on the side of the road in New Orleans was not a uniquely alarming sight. But that's usually a vision reserved for the tourist areas, not the shady streets of Uptown, where my meltdown occurred.

Second—and I don't mean to be too macabre here—in the days since Katrina, a body lying anywhere on the street around here has not been a completely unusual circumstance.

You may ask: Why didn't the photographer get me out of there? But he was the only shooter we seemed to have in the city that day and the police chief was about to resign and he had to go get the picture and so I waved him off. "Go ahead," I said. "I'll be fine."

The story is important, I was thinking. Go get the story.

That was about 3:30 in the afternoon. I heard birds singing, and every now and then, I could hear the woman we had come to photograph—a Katrina holdout and survivor—cooing to her cats in the distance.

It was not altogether unpleasant, the parts where I was awake. I had some shade. But it occurred to me that this environment is no place for the overemotional and faint of heart.

If you cry when you watch *Terms of Endearment*, you don't need to be here. Problem is, I even cry at the end of *When Harry Met Sally*, so this whole experience is Stress City.

Though people are trickling back into town and businesses are starting to light up, it's still an impossible vista, this whole damn city, where Lakeview looks like a nuclear wasteland with automobile trunks, doors, and windows imploded from being underwater and so many things lying upside down in the street that shouldn't be upside down.

Including reporters.

There's a car down the street from my house that careened over a concrete retainer wall and through an iron fence and crashed into the front porch of the Cafe Luna coffee shop and I've actually gotten used to the sight, after all these weeks.

This little tableau is so far down on the list of priorities around here that it could be four more weeks until somebody thinks to drag that thing away.

Those are things you think about while lying on the side of

the road, stuck somewhere between Armageddon and the Dawn of a New Day.

Nobody drove by. Nobody walked his dog past me. No kid rode up on a bicycle and asked, "Are you okay, mister?"

When I noticed it was starting to get dark, I got up, a little more than wobbly, and wandered to my car and drove to the Sheraton Hotel downtown where I am staying; and in the morning I wrote the story about the cat lady we were photographing Uptown by the tree that now bears an imprint of my head.

Because the story is important. We have to get the stories. This is an assignment bigger than any of us. It's history in a hurry.

But if it's okay with you, I think I'm gonna take a few days off.

The Magnet Man
11/20/05

With a measure of modesty you don't often find among the creative class, Chris Cressionnie describes his vocation thus:

"I used to be an artist who waited tables. Truthfully, now I'm more of a waiter who happens to paint pictures. But since the hurricane, I really don't do a damn thing."

Cressionnie's employer, Gautreau's restaurant, has not reopened yet. And he hasn't found the muse or concentration to stand at a canvas and paint. Thus, after nature's furious upheaval, a man is reduced to his fundamental primeval nature: hunter and gatherer.

And that's how Cressionnie has created one of the most stirring and amusing post-Katrina visual displays: his 1994 Chevy Blazer is covered with, of all things, refrigerator magnets.

And not just any old souvenir magnets you pick up at a gift shop. In fact, these are your magnets. And my magnets. And everybody else's magnets.

For weeks, Cressionnie has been collecting these delicate little tokens, at once so frivolous and common, but that tell a story of our city. They say where we go to school, what teams we root for, where we order pizza, what gods we pray to, what veterinarians we take our pets to, when our next dentist appointment is, where we like to go on vacation, and—this part stays with you—who we love.

At risk to life and limb (sudden stops of the car) and at risk to his senses (he gets into some seriously stinky situations), Cressionnie drives our streets by day—in the dead hours between dropping off and picking up his son at school—and he gathers mementos off discarded refrigerators and, in the process, has created a rolling art installation that is a snapshot of our culture.

American flags. Jesus. Mother Teresa. Daffy Duck. Saints schedules dating back to 2001. Fruits. WWOZ. Tulane. Elysian Fields, spelled out in those classic street tile replicas. Hollywood. Country Day. California. St. Francisville.

I ♥ New Orleans. All those Harry Lee magnets that the sheriff throws off Mardi Gras floats every winter; each year a different design. Dozens of insurance agents. The same for veterinarians. A photo of two young lovers standing on the Great Wall of China.

Who are they?

On March 27, someone has a doctor's appointment at 9:15 A.M. on Napoleon Avenue. Will he or she remember? There is a white magnet with wedding bells on it that commemorates the marriage of Essence Allen and Wright Ellie Wright, November 11, 2003.

And there are the children: all these discarded pictures of someone's kids staring out at you from the side of Cressionnie's car. There's one that says: "Happy 1st Birthday Micah. March 12, 2003. Little Fingers, Little Toes. Today you're one. And everybody knows."

There is something maudlin—maybe even mildly predatory—about picking over the remains of our devastation. But there is also something noble about archiving the personal details of our citizenry, particularly when those details were otherwise bound for the dump.

"In many ways, this is kind of sad," Cressionnie said one day while combing the Mid-City and Pigeon Town neighborhoods. "They're like little trophies of people's lives. Keepsakes. But it also seems significant. In my art, I've always tried to make light of things; I've always been a bit of a thorn in the side."

Indeed. As he climbs through piles of waste and abandoned appliances, he receives many odd stares. "People kind of check you out when you stop in front of their house," he said. "You just give them a little wave, and everything's okay."

Not all are so friendly, though. Once, when a guy figured out what he was doing, he barked at Cressionnie, telling him to just come inside his destroyed house and take whatever he wanted. Just take it all, the man said.

That's why Cressionnie travels with his boxer, Mika. "Just in case anything happens," he said.

But nothing does. It all settles. And truth is, Mika seems pretty bored with the project after all these weeks. "She doesn't even try to get out of the car anymore," he said.

The job of an artist is never easy. Sometimes he has to wrestle with duct tape that has pinned down a particularly attractive magnet—maybe a religious icon or a good Disney character.

Then there are the maggots to deal with. Maggots on Magnets. Now, there's a great name for a punk band if I ever heard one.

To be sure, he tries the patience of anyone who happens to be driving behind him. "I slow down everywhere," he said. "It's become an addiction, almost. The hunt for the hunt's sake."

On Colapissa Street one day, Cressionnie asked a resident, Donald Murray, if it was all right to grab the magnets off his fridge by the sidewalk. Murray said sure and called over to some friends to witness the event in a sort of check-this-dude-out kind of way.

"That's nice," said Murray, an African American, hands on hips, inspecting the car. "Real nice. But I'm going to tell you this to your face: Only a white guy would think of something like this."

They all laughed. A lot and loud. Murray and his friends stared in silence and wonder again. Then Murray said, "You're going to need a bigger truck."

The Last Ride
11/27/05

In the trail of tears left by Katrina and Rita, blanketing an entire region of American geography, culture, history, and memories, it will be years, maybe decades, before we've compiled the compendium of what we've lost.

There are a million small stories to be told after the hurricanes: stories about corner stores, neighborhood bars, barbershops, local bands, local characters, influential teachers and football coaches, roadside attractions, and local institutions.

So much of this stuff, gone now, ingloriously surrendered or disappeared in the wake of the storms.

On August 29, many of these stories ran their final chapter with no two weeks' notice given. No going-out-of-business sale, farewell performance, or going-away party. Not even good-bye and thanks for the memories.

The Circle G Riding Stable in Picayune, Mississippi, is one of these stories.

If you are from southeastern Louisiana or Mississippi and ever rented a horse for a day ride in the country, you probably found yourself at one time or another at the Circle G.

For thirty-five years, it was a destination for summer campers and church groups, young lovers, city slickers, family picnics, office parties, conventioneers, and plain old looking-for-something-to-do weekend adventurers.

And reporters; the Circle G amassed an impressive portfolio of regional press clippings over the decades, including at least a half-dozen features and profiles in this newspaper alone.

That's because at Circle G you generally got more than just a horse ride for your money. With it you got an education in country living and plain speaking from the proprietor, a master raconteur named David Gluth, a former shirt-and-tie New Orleans businessman who moved to Picayune in 1969—at age twenty-seven—and transformed himself into a rural wag with a large and loyal New Orleans clientele.

He is also my father-in-law.

Picayune is where my family first evacuated for Katrina, figuring on getting out of New Orleans for a few days to avoid the predictable street flooding and power outages.

As the storm grew bigger and turned its eye toward the Mississippi coast, the tall, tall pines of Picayune—and its relative isolation fifteen miles inland—made me think it was no place for my wife and three city kids to ride out a major storm. I was right. On the western edge of the eye, Picayune got hammered.

"I had never really been concerned about hurricanes before," David told me later. "I had weathered them my whole life. But the morning it came in, I was out on our deck and I was watching as sixty-foot trees came out of the ground and just flew across the property.

"Huge oaks and tremendous pines—ten feet around—were just falling all over us. There were tornadoes everywhere and that freight train sound. I started to worry that the roof might blow off, the windows would blow in, and the house would collapse. And for the first time in my life, I felt fear."

When it was over, the arboreal devastation was nearly complete. Katrina simply cleared the place out, a once tree-canopied paradise laid open to bare sunlight. Miraculously, the house—and the horses, thirty of them—survived.

"Animals know how to take care of themselves," David said. "They've been dealing with storms for thousands of years; that's how they have survived. In a storm like this, horses just put their butts to the wind, their heads down, and their ears forward—and they say their horse prayers." Nevertheless, by that Monday afternoon, it was clear that the Circle G had hosted its last rider.

The deep, slow-rolling, fourteen-mile path through the woods was a litter of fallen trees. All access to Catahoula Creek, where riders stop for picnics on a long sandy white beach, was blocked; the trail, carved out by more than thirty-five years of riding, was, in a word, obliterated.

In a matter of hours, a beloved local business was wiped off the books.

Aside from the massive cost and time to rebuild and clear the trails—and fix the barn—there were other concerns.

"I realized that the majority of my customer base was probably gone and those who remained would be involved for a long time in other pursuits that don't include horseback riding," David said.

So he folded his hand. Over the past few weeks, David has torn down the barn and sold the horses, kissing each one goodbye before they were led away. "I've cried more than a few times," he said.

"We get calls every day now from our old customers," he said. "Some are ready to come back, and they get very upset when we tell them what has happened. They say, 'No! I rode there when I was a kid and now I ride there with my granddaughter. It's our tradition. You can't do this!' "

Some folks even offer to bring their own chain saws to help clear the place out, but they don't realize the enormity and futility of the task at hand. The Circle G—it's toast. Another notch in Katrina's belt.

"I'm too old to start over," David said. "This has been my life for thirty-five years, but I'm ready for page two of my life—or page three or four or whatever page I'm on now."

But it was a good run. Over three and a half decades, David was joined in the business by his parents, his son, David, Jr., and his family, and eventually his fourth wife, Augusta.

Quite the family affair they built, from taking phone reservations in the morning to laying out the hay in the evening and everything in between; a small, self-contained private paradise in the woods.

"When I was a little boy, six or seven or eight years old, I always wanted to be a horse farmer," David remembers. "I wanted to move to Montana or Wyoming and own a ranch. Well, I never made it to Wyoming, but I got to make tens of thousands of people happy, and I guess that's the best thing.

"I never had to work for a boss, and I wish I had saved more money, but I guess you could say I was a little kid whose dream came true."

Lights in the City
12/11/05

At this time of year, many of us are asked to ponder the true meaning of Christmas as some way of recalibrating our actions, lifestyles, and character.

Tooling around the Fontainebleau neighborhood the other day, I came across a wasted yard in front of a wasted house in the middle of a wasted neighborhood with trash, debris, and the specter of loss everywhere, and there, on the corner of this pathetic lot, was a wasted little brown tree wrapped in a single strand of white Christmas lights.

One might ask: What is the point? What are they trying to prove? Are we even on Santa's itinerary this year? Or will he write off New Orleans, grab a quick bite at Ruth's Chris in Baton Rouge, and continue on to cities that have Fortune 500–based companies, there to stuff their CEOs' stockings full of FEMA contracts?

Besides, all our chimneys either fell down or are covered with blue tarps. What's a jolly old elf to do?

Whether this small effort—this one pathetic little Charlie Brown Christmas tree in a town full of Charlie Brown Christmas trees—represents hope, delusion, or faith, I am not sure. I suppose time, God, and the Corps of Engineers will be the ultimate judges of that, and not necessarily in that order.

But tradition marches on, and so it must be. Out in a Kenner neighborhood where I often take my kids to look at the spectacular holiday light displays put on by the rich folks, many of the houses are gutted. But the FEMA trailers parked in the front yards are decorated with twinkling white lights instead.

It is both the saddest and most beautiful thing you ever saw.

And in places with no trailers, some folks have just decorated their curbside refrigerators and left it at that. Merry stinking Christmas to you, Uncle Sam.

Never mind that Entergy is going to bill you $800 for the use of a single strand of lights this month ($1,400 if you blink those suckers), the weird and oddly celebratory manifestations of the holidays around here are just another sign that *you can't stop us.*

Sure, you can slow us down, pare our ranks, tear at our foundations until we cry for mercy. But *you can't stop us.*

Perhaps no civic organization has shown its resilience in the face of all odds more than the Drunken Santas, a tight-knit group of New Orleanians who, after a round of drinking games at Madigan's bar one night in 1998, decided to take an activist role in the holidays rather than sit around getting soused by themselves.

So they decided to get soused with others. Spreading the cheer is their aim. So they dress up in Santa costumes (or skimpier facsimiles thereof for the female members of this organization, the Ho-Ho-Hos) and they charter a fleet of limos and they pub-crawl.

These guys are right up there with the Salvation Army and Rex when it comes to giving back to the community this time of year. As Ho-Ho-Ho Natasha Daniel put it, "We have a good time. We push people into garbage piles. Make them take shots with us. You know: all the reindeer games."

Now, I realize that at this point in the story the eyes of the righteous are rolling. Wait until they hear about this in Congress, I hear you saying. Now they're *never* going to give us that $2 billion we need to rebuild New Orleans.

Well, frankly, Congress can go Scrooge itself. And so can the eye rollers, holy rollers, and professional bowlers. (Sorry, I need a third entity to make the rhythm work in that last phrase and I couldn't come up with a damn thing.)

They'll never understand the hardships the Drunken Santas have been forced to endure: from ninety-two participants and twelve limos last year, their ranks were devastated by Katrina to the tune of just twenty-two riders this year—only three of them Ho-Ho-Hos, perhaps the worst part of this whole tragedy.

One fellow named Jonathan drove in from Baton Rouge for the event Thursday night only to find that the tree that had fallen through his roof had caused significant water damage to his auxiliary closet (or whatever you call the closet where you keep things like Santa suits) and destroyed his costume.

He was forced to participate in street clothes. When will the horror stop! How much more can we take!

Anyway. Shrunken Santas might have been a more appropriate name for the group this year. But they endured. "We love this city and we love this tradition and we want normalcy and we're not going to be stopped," said Drunken Santa Matthew Dwyer as the group filtered out of the Monkey Hill Bar toward their limos and into a night of destinations unknown.

The Drunken Santas did what they did for no other reason than it was something to break pattern in this wretched little city and—as distasteful as this behavior may strike some—truthfully: it's nobody else's concern. They rented limos to take everybody home, so no one crashed into your house, so let it be.

Actually, if they had crashed into your house, that might have helped out with the lousy insurance check you're going to get, but that's a cause I'm somewhat hesitant to get behind: *More drunk drivers!*

Now, the more astute of you readers out there may have sensed a metaphorical undercurrent here in this sordid tale of debauchery and weirdness.

Yes, I'm talking about Mardi Gras. And why we can't even think about canceling it. I was going to go into that in far greater detail in this story but I'm out of room here and sometimes even I get tired of reading me so I'll pick up that thought in my next column and I'll let you go after one more thing:

Christmas is a mangled institution and taken all out of context by crass commercialism, awkward passes at co-workers at the office party, and a cacophony of maudlin Christmas carols by Dolly Parton.

But does anyone say: *That sends the wrong message! Cancel it!*

Do what you do. This Christmas, Hanukkah, Kwanzaa, New Year's Eve, Twelfth Night, Valentine's Day, Mardi Gras, St. Paddy's Day, and every day henceforth. Just do what you do. Live out your life and your traditions on your own terms.

If it offends others, so be it. That's their problem.

Personally, I think blinking white lights on those stark white FEMA trailers is all wrong, totally missing the point, but I'm not going to knock on your door and tell you that you've got your priorities messed up and you're sending the wrong message and that the Senate Finance Committee is going to kill the appropriations bill that could save us all because of your stupid trailer.

No, instead, when I drive by your house with my kids next week, I'm sure we'll all agree in the privacy of our car that a subtle combination of red and green—nonblinking, I might add—would have looked much better.

Now, about that inflatable snow globe . . .

Let the Good Times Roll
12/13/05

Mardi Gras. It's not on the table. It's not a point of negotiation or a bargaining chip.

We're going to have it, and that's that. End of discussion.

Folks in faraway places are going to feel the misery of missing it, and that is a terrible thing. In the past, I have missed the season a couple of times because of story assignments elsewhere, and it sucked to be away from the center of the universe and not be a part of this city's fundamental, quintessential, and indelible cultural landmark.

But we can't turn off the lights and keep the costumes in storage and ladders in the shed for another year just because we are beaten and broken and so many of us are not here.

In fact, we have to do this because we are beaten and broken and so many of us are not here.

Katrina has proved, more than ever, that we are resilient. We are tougher than dirt. Certainly tougher than the dirt beneath our levees.

The social and celebratory nature of this event defines this city, and this is no time to lose definition. The edges are too blurry already.

Some folks say it sends the wrong message, but here's the thing about that: New Orleans is in a very complicated situation as far as "sending a message" goes these days. It's a tricky two-way street.

On the one hand, it is vital to our very survival that the world outside here understand just how profoundly and completely destroyed this city is right now, with desolate power grids and hundreds of thousands of residents living elsewhere and in limbo.

Jobs, businesses, and the public spirit are all about as safely shored as the 17th Street Canal floodwall. We're leaking. And we could very well breach in the coming year or two.

We very well could.

On the other hand, we need to send a message that we are still New Orleans. We are the soul of America. We embody the triumph of the human spirit. Hell, we *are* Mardi Gras.

And Zulu can say they're only playing if they get it their way and Rex can say nothing at all and the mayor—our fallen and befuddled rock star—can say that he wants it one day and he doesn't want it the next day, but the truth is: It's not up to any of them. It's up to me now. And we're having it.

And here's a simple, not-so-eloquent reason why: If we don't have Mardi Gras, the terrorists win. The last thing we need right now is to divide ourselves over our most cherished event.

If the national news wants to show people puking on Bourbon Street as a metaphor for some sort of displaced priorities in this town, so be it. The only puking I've seen at Mardi Gras in the past ten years is little babies throwing up on their mothers' shoulders after a bottle.

To encapsulate the notion of Mardi Gras as nothing more than a big drunk is to take the simple and stupid way out, and I, for one, am getting tired of staying stuck on simple and stupid.

Mardi Gras is not a parade. Mardi Gras is not girls flashing on French Quarter balconies. Mardi Gras is not an alcoholic binge.

Mardi Gras is bars and restaurants changing out all the CDs in their jukeboxes to Professor Longhair and the Neville Brothers, and it is annual front-porch crawfish boils hours before the parades so your stomach and attitude reach a state of grace, and it is returning to the same street corner, year after year, and standing next to the same people, year after year—people whose names you may or may not even know but you've watched their kids grow up in this public tableau and when they're not there, you wonder: Where are those guys this year?

It is dressing your dog in a stupid costume and cheering when the marching bands go crazy and clapping and saluting the military bands when they crisply snap to.

Now that part, more than ever.

It's mad piano professors converging on our city from all over the world and banging the 88s until dawn and laughing at the hairy-shouldered men in dresses too tight and stalking the Indians under the Claiborne overpass and thrilling the years you find them and lamenting the years you don't and promising yourself you will next year.

It's wearing frightful color combinations in public and rolling your eyes at the guy in your office who—like clockwork, year after year—denies that he got the baby in the king cake and now someone else has to pony up the ten bucks for the next one.

Mardi Gras is the love of life. It is the harmonic convergence of our food, our music, our creativity, our eccentricity, our neighborhoods, and our joy of living. All at once.

And it doesn't really matter if there are superparades or even any parades at all this year. Because some group of horn players will grab their instruments and they will march down the Avenue because that's what they do, and I, for one, will follow.

If there are no parades, I'm hitching a boom box to a wagon, putting James Booker on the CD player, and pulling my kids down the Avenue and you're welcome to come along with me and where more than two tribes gather, there is a parade.

We are the parade. We are Mardi Gras. We're Whoville, man— you can take away the beads and the floats and all that crazy stuff, but we're still coming out into the street. Cops or no cops. Postparade garbage pickup or no garbage pickup—as if anyone could tell the friggin' difference!

If you are stuck somewhere else, in some other town, bring it to them. If you've got a job somewhere else now, take off that Tuesday and get all the New Orleanians you know and gather in a park somewhere and cook up a mass of food and put some music on a box and raise a little hell.

And raise a glass to us, brothers and sisters, because we're in here fighting this fight and we'll raise a glass to you because you cannot be here with us and we know you want to. Let the whole damn country hear Al Johnson yelling "It's Carnival time" and let them know we're not dead and if we are dying, we're going to pretend we're not.

Fly the flag. Be in that number. This is our battle to win or lose. Hopefully, of one mind and one message. That we are still here. And that we are still New Orleans.

Our Katrina Christmas
12/25/05

To call this a Christmas like no other would be stating the obvious, I suppose. What an upside-down world we've found ourselves in here at the bottom of America.

In the big picture, maybe that helps one focus on the True Meaning of Christmas. Which is shopping, of course, but here's the thing: my local Pier One didn't sell wrapping paper this year and the Elmwood Wal-Mart didn't have strings of Christmas lights and—as I write this story—my family has been unable to find a lot around here that still has Christmas trees in stock.

Just how were we to engage in the most holy and traditional of holiday sounds—the cash register printing out debit card receipts—without purchasing all the physical trappings that mark the birth of Jesus?

Without that, all we've got is José Feliciano singing "Feliz Navidad" on the radio.

Man, that song drives me crazy . . . er, loco.

As unfathomable as it seems, my kids might not have a tree to congregate around this morning—although, as my deadline looms, my wife tells me she's making one last, desperate sweep through Metairie to find one, which worries me because I don't know if she'll make it back home before, say, Tuesday.

What about my dinner?

Which brings up this point: How is it that we lost 80 percent of our residents around here but traffic got worse? Can somebody explain that? How is it that bars close earlier but people drink more? Ah, don't get me started.

Under the circumstances, it's pretty hard to get worked up about it. It's pretty hard to get worked up about any of life's little inconveniences these days; odd, since there are more inconveniences than ever before and some of them aren't so little.

We have a house. I have a job. We're way ahead of the game. We're like royalty in one of those old Monty Python movies: we have clean clothes.

But my daughter fell to pieces about the tree thing. I thought it was the sentimentalist in her, driven to despair because a part of our revered process might be missing this year, part of our seasonal custom gone to seed.

In fact, it was because she told me that Santa wouldn't have anywhere to put her presents. Good to know that she's got her priorities together.

So I told her Santa is not about trees, he's about kids, and we've been through this before anyway, when she discovered a few years ago that we don't have a chimney, either. Man, those old storybook legends make it a hard go-round for parents in the twenty-first century.

I mean, if Santa rode a Humvee pulled by, say, a bunch of potbellied pigs, this whole Christmas thing would be an easier sell. (Funny, though, my kids never cry out for Old World porridge; they're cafeteria traditionalists, picking those they like and dispensing with the rest.)

Anyway, I wound up pulling that old parenting trick of instilling sadness and guilt in children to make them come around to your point of view.

"You know, some of our friends don't even have houses to put trees in this year," I told them, and, unlike when my parents used to invoke starving children in Africa as a reason to finish my dinner—an oblique reference at best to a six-year-old—the fact is, they understand what it's like to be homeless.

For the past four months, they have been living a thousand miles away with hand-me-down clothes and borrowed toys.

But now they are home. And I wanted to wait until they were here so we could get the tree together, but maybe I waited too long and so it goes.

A Christmas like no other.

I suppose one positive aspect of the circumstances is that my family didn't receive any holiday photo cards with pictures of our friends' pets wearing Santa hats this year.

And we received no tiresome family newsletters from faraway friends whose children are way above average, sweeping everything from the gold medal in the 400-meter backstroke to the blue ribbon for animal husbandry at the Iowa 4-H fair this summer.

But this is small recompense. Truth is, we didn't get any Christmas cards at all this year. That has never happened. I suppose they'll show up in June. With our Christmas catalogs, no doubt. And my *Newsweek*s from October.

Funny how you recalibrate your priorities in life: No mail, no problem. Whatever.

That's Christmas in New Orleans this year. Shape-shifting. Adapting. Getting along and getting by. Pondering the heretofore unknown dilemma: what to get for that special someone on your list who has . . . nothing.

Today it will be my family and my in-laws from Baton Rouge and Mississippi coming to join us in our winter homecoming, to celebrate over a warm meal and probably a few tears and a lot of laughter.

Kind of a simple formula, really. A chance to eat, breathe, forget, and remember. One more day to just be alive and be thankful for that and to carry on and up.

And José Feliciano on the radio. Singing that dang song.

Tears, Fears, and a New Year
1/1/06

When I look back on the year 2005, nothing comes to mind more than the opening line of Dickens's *A Tale of Two Cities:* "It was the best of times, it was the worst of times."

Except for that "best of times" part, it describes New Orleans perfectly.

How did we get here? What happened to my tough-lovin', hard-luck, good-timin' town?

Mercy.

I have cowered in fear this year from the real and the imagined. The fear of injury, the fear of disease, the fear of death, the fear of abandonment, isolation, and insanity.

I have had seared into my olfactory lockbox the smell of gasoline and dead people. And your leftovers.

I have feared the phantom notions of sharks swimming in our streets and bands of armed men coming for me in the night to steal my generator and water and then maybe rape me or cut my throat just for the hell of it.

I have wept for hours on end, days on end.

The crying jags. I guess they're therapeutic, but give me a break.

The first time I went to the Winn-Dixie after it reopened, I had all my purchases on the conveyor belt, plus a bottle of mouthwash.

During the Days of Horror following the decimation of this city, I had gone into the foul and darkened store and lifted a bottle.

I was operating under the "take only what you need" clause that the strays who remained behind in this godforsaken place invoked in the early days.

My thinking was that it was in everyone's best interest if I had a bottle of mouthwash.

When the cashier rang up my groceries all those weeks later, I tried, as subtly as possible, to hand her the bottle and ask her if she could see that it was put back on the shelf. She was confused by my action and offered to void the purchase if I didn't want the bottle.

I told her it's not that I didn't want it but that I wished to pay for it and could she please see that it was put back on the shelf. More confusion ensued and the line behind me got longer and it felt very hot and crowded all of a sudden and I tried to tell her: "Look, when the store was closed . . . you know . . . after the thing . . . I took . . ."

The words wouldn't come. Only the tears.

The people in line behind me stood stoic and patient, public meltdowns being as common as discarded kitchen appliances in this town.

What's that over there? Oh, it's just some dude crying his ass off. Nothing new here. Show's over, people, move along.

The cashier, an older woman, finally grasped my pathetic gesture, my lowly attempt to make amends, my fulfillment of a promise I made to myself to repay anyone I had stolen from.

"I get it, baby," she said, and she gently took the bottle from my hands and I gathered my groceries and walked sobbing from the store.

She was kind to me. I will probably never see her again, but I will never forget her. That bottle. That store. All the fury that prevailed. The fear.

A friend of mine, a photojournalist, recently went to a funeral to take pictures. There had been an elderly couple trapped in a house. He had a heart attack and slipped into the water. She held on to a gutter for two days before being rescued.

It was seven weeks before the man's body was found in the house, then another six weeks before the remains were released from the St. Gabriel morgue for burial.

"Tell me a story I haven't heard," I told my friend. Go ahead. Shock me.

When my father and I were trading dark humor one night and he was offering advice on how to begin my year in review, he cracked himself up, proposing, "It was a dark and stormy night." That's close, but not quite it. "It was a dark and stormy morn- ing" would be closer to the truth.

What a morning it was.

I was in Vicksburg. I had just left the miserable hotel crack house to which my family had evacuated—it must have been the last vacant room in the South—and was looking for breakfast for my kids.

But the streets and businesses were abandoned and a slight but stinging rain was falling, the wind surging and warm, and while my kids played on a little riverfront playground, I got through on my cell phone to the *Times-Picayune* newsroom, where scores of *TP* families had taken refuge, and I remember saying to the clerk who answered the phone, "Man, that was a close one, huh? Looks like we dodged another bullet."

I suppose around a million people were saying exactly the same thing at exactly the same time. What I would have given to be right. Just that one time.

I was trying to get through to my editor to ask, "What's the plan?"

By late afternoon, that's what everyone in the gulf region was asking.

Of course, it turns out there wasn't a plan. Anywhere. Who could have known?

The newspaper was just like everyone else at that point: as a legion of employees and their families piled into delivery trucks and fled the newspaper building as the waters rose around them, we shifted into the same operational mode as everyone else:

Survive. Wing it. Do good work. Save someone or something. And call your mother and tell her you're all right.

Unless, of course, your mother was in Lakeview or the Lower 9th or Chalmette or . . . well, I've had enough of those horror stories for now. I don't even want to visit that place today.

This was the year that defined our city, our lives, our destiny. Nothing comparable has ever happened in modern times in America, and there is no blueprint for how to do this.

We just wing it. Do good work. Save someone or something.

You'd have to be crazy to want to live here. You'd have to be plumb out of reasonable options elsewhere.

Then again, I have discovered that the only thing worse than being in New Orleans these days is not being in New Orleans.

It's a siren calling us home. It cannot be explained.

"They don't get us" is the common refrain you hear from frustrated residents who think the government and the nation have turned a blind eye to us in our time of need. Then again, if they did get us, if we were easily boxed and labeled, I suppose we'd be just Anyplace, USA.

And that won't do.

We have a job to do here, and that is to entertain the masses, and I don't mean the tourists. They're part of it, of course, but what we do best down here—have done for decades—is create a lifestyle that others out there in the Great Elsewhere envy and emulate.

Our music, our food, yada yada yada. It's a tale so often told that it borders on platitude, but it is also the searing truth: We are the music. We are the food. We are the dance. We are the tolerance. We are the spirit.

And one day, they'll get it.

As a woman named Judy Deck e-mailed me in a moment of inspiration: "If there was no New Orleans, America would just be a bunch of free people dying of boredom."

Yeah, you write.

That, people, is the final word on 2005.

Misadventures in the Chocolate City

Chocolate City
1/18/06

I wake up in the Chocolate City mad as hell.

It's like this: I'm supposed to be on vacation this week, cooling my heels, and then our mayor, Willy Wonka, loses his grip in public again and that's hardly headline news in and of itself, but this time he really lets one go.

I mean, he really gasses the place up, if you know what I mean. Now, how am I supposed to sit this one out?

First thing I do, I follow the mayor's lead and call Martin Luther King, Jr. Of course, it takes a while to get through because he died in 1968 so he still has one of those avocado green rotary dial phones on his kitchen counter and no call-waiting.

As you might imagine, his line was pretty tied up Tuesday morning.

"King!" I holler when I finally reach him. "What in blazes are you thinking? You're writing speeches for Wonka, and the best you can come up with is 'Chocolate City'? Meet me at CC's Coffee House, bruh. Pronto. We gotta talk."

"I'm tired," he complains. "I had a big day yesterday."

"We all had a big day yesterday, King," I tell him. "Eleven o'clock. Be there."

Then I call God.

Of course, my call is answered on the first ring, but it's some lackey working out of a phone bank in Singapore. We tangle a bit; she's giving me the runaround about him being busy and can she help me, and I'm wondering: What's with authority figures these days?

"Just who does he think he is, he can't take my call?" I say. "What, he's Dan Packer now? *Put him on!*"

I finally get him, and I calm down a bit because he's got that comforting voice, kind of like Barry White, but I'm still all dandered up and I tell him, "Eleven o'clock, CC's. We gotta talk."

He starts to make excuses, tells me he's got lunch at Ruth's Chris with Pat Robertson, but I'm all over him like white on rice.

Unless it's brown rice, of course.

I suppose it could be brown.

Anyway, I wear him down and he finally admits that he thinks Robertson is a lunatic blowhard who's always asking God to take out some foreign leader or burn down a place like Oklahoma because there are sodomites reportedly living there, so he says to me, "All right. Chill, amigo. I'll be there."

So me, King, and God all meet up and I'm ready to tear into these guys about the advice they're giving Mayor Wonka, who's gone all Shirley MacLaine on us and has had almost five months to compose himself since his multiple meltdown and the best thing he could come up with was this?

We're standing in line to order, and I let loose: "All right, you knuckleheads, which one of you wrote the 'Chocolate City' thing?"

They are aghast at my strong language, "knucklehead" being the harshest term our mayor can come up with to describe the dirtbag, scumbag, dope fiend gang-bangers who have run roughshod over this town for the past decade, making us the Killing Fields of America.

Knuckleheads. Yeah, that's great, like they're the Three Stooges now. "Hey, I'm gonna cap yo ass with my nine. Nyuk, nyuk, nyuk."

Anyway, King waves me off. "Can we order before we get into this?" he asks.

The barista, one of those bright and perky *Uptown* people —
and I think you know what kind I mean — says, "Hey, guys, what
can I getcha?" and sure, she acts all Ladies' Auxiliary toward us,
but we all know — me, King, and God — that all this white girl
really wants is to grab up as much property as possible in the
Lower 9th and build a couples resort and day spa.

Me, King, and God — we're not stupid.

King orders first. "Coffee," he says. "Black."

Well, do I need to tell you: the whole shop is paralyzed into
the most uncomfortable silence you ever heard.

"Jesus!" I mutter under my breath, and God pokes me in the
eye. "Watch it, knucklehead," he says.

The barista, she goes, "Nyuk, nyuk, nyuk," and I'm beginning
to think I shouldn't have gotten out of bed; I should have just
stuck to my original plan to meet Kafka for racquetball at noon.

Coffee. Black. This King guy, he just doesn't get it. Then it
turns out he's just joshing around. Suddenly he breaks the uncomfortable silence and screams, *"I'll have a cream!"*

And he starts wagging his finger all around like he's back at
the Lincoln Memorial, and he starts yelling, "And my children
will one day live in a nation where they will not be judged by the
color of their coffee, but by the content of their character."

God, he cracks up at this. He starts nudging his elbow into my
side, and he's practically got tears in his eyes.

"What are you, Chris Rock?" he says. "That's hilarious, King.
You are one loco dude!"

They do that knuckle-knock thing, and God orders. Café au
lait — who would have guessed?

So we sit and I ask them, "Guys, what's the deal? Wonka says
he consulted with both of you before that blasted speech yesterday. Tell me you're not behind this Chocolate City thing. It's tear-
ing us apart!"

King falls silent; he's eyeballing all the Uptowners like they're
going to steal his hubcaps.

God pipes up, "Listen, hombre. Me and King, we had nothing
to do with that speech. We told Wonka to go with a unity theme,
black and white together as one. We did have this thing about

Oreos in it, but we scratched that long before the final draft.

"Your boy Wonka, that was all off the cuff, man. Extemporizing, you dig? He was off the script on that one. Completely off the reservation."

This gets King's attention. There's another uncomfortable pause as the whole place goes mute again.

"Sorry, cats," God says. "Poor choice of words. My bad. But listen: You people have got your race thing so screwed up down here that even I'm having trouble concentrating. You've got to get your house in order, folks. Your boy Wonka is walking around tossing matches on kindling. If you don't watch out, the whole place is gonna blow.

"And that will put us all out of work," he says, and he pushes his chair back and stands up.

"Gotta vamoose, bruh!" he says. "Been real, but there's mucho work to be done in the Chocolate City. *Hasta la vista.*"

Silence again.

"All right, I'll take the bait," I tell him. "What's with all the gringo lingo?"

He looks at me like I'm crazy. He reaches into his wallet, grabs a card, and hands me one before he rolls out the door.

The card, it says, "God & Sons Roofing. Reasonable Rates. Fully Insured. Habla Español."

I look at King. I stutter, "Did you know . . . ?" But he's just shaking his head at me.

"Go figure," he says. "But it makes sense, when you think about it. His son's name is Jesus. The stepfather was a carpenter. All of them living in a Kenner hotel without electricity and running water like it's no big deal. It just goes to show, you never can tell. I guess you really need to be careful about what kind of assumptions you make about people."

We both take a sip and pause for a moment, and he adds, "And God, for that matter."

I nod at him over my tall glass of milk. "Now you're talking, King," I tell him. "Now you're talking."

Tutti-Frutti
1/22/06

When the mayor broke onto the political scene with a Starburst four years ago, he was our Mr. Goodbar, the Sugar Daddy we needed to lead us out of our intractable cycle of political Trix and Twizzlers.

Well, some folks suggest his Lucky Charms wore off this week with that Milk Dud of a speech, in which he handled Dr. King's legacy with Butterfingers and sent a fudge ripple over America's airwaves and Snickers through the halls of Congress.

He looked a little Zagnuts on TV, telling all those Whoppers and getting himself in Mounds of Dubble Bubble trouble. Sociable Crackers around here got Good & Plenty mad about that, wondering how we let this Cadbury the collective goodwill of the citizenry.

Oh, Henry!

Forthwith, his detractors would have you believe his Very Berry ill-timed comments threaten the city's Rocky Road to recovery and may even leave him wondering where the next Payday might come from after the elections.

To be Frankenberry with you, I disagree. With his admitted lack of political Skittles and his Neapolitan savvy, the chocolate chip on his shoulder, and that Jujube in his swagger—to say nothing of his knack for the perfectly timed Quisp—I find him a breath of fresh air.

A real Altoid of a guy. Therefore, I don't think we should pecan him anymore.

After all, rather then curry favor with political Jawbreakers, corporate Cocoa Puffs, and sycophantic Goobers like our former city leaders, our mayor made City Hall a haven for Smarties and Nerds, bringing the city's standards and technology up to the twenty-first century.

Okay, maybe his advisory team is not so Cracker Jack, a little top-heavy with dilettantes and Raisinets. And you have to wonder: What got into the guy? Was he dipping in the Laffy Taffy again? What made him Krackle up like that and go all Chips Ahoy on us?

It seems like he might have hit the Frosted Flakes a little too hard on his recent vacation in Jamoca; you'd swear he was eating Sno-Caps, all in a Häagen-Dazs like that old dude from the Grateful Dead.

Whatchamacallit?

Cherry Garcia. Yeah, that's the guy.

And now what a Chunky Monkey this city has on its back. We need our Big Shot mayor, Count Chocula his bad self, to lead us out of the Sierra Mist to Fruitopia, where levees are fifty feet tall and not made of Mallomar—and where we all worship at the same Oreo altar. Otherwise, you can just Kiss all our MoonPies good-bye.

So just say your Breyer's and hope everything turns out for the best, and let's have a little faith in our mayor, our leader.

Our Nutty Buddy.

He Had a Dream
5/26/06

Did you know there was a plan? A secret plan?

There was talk, of course, in the months before the mayoral election that white folks were intent on taking over this place and remaking it in our own image and we pooh-poohed that notion, of course, because it was politically expedient to do so, but it was, in fact, true.

There was a grand design for the New Vanilla City.

The first thing we were going to do was default on our contract with the Hornets and bring in NASCAR. Nothing gets white folks excited like really fast cars making a left turn for three hundred miles.

That, sports fans, is entertainment.

Second, we were going to get rid of this city's bizarre infatuation with chicory coffee. Man, that stuff is as bitter as birch bark. The new official drink of New Orleans: double chai latte. With skim milk.

Yes indeed, we were going to put some soul into this city at last.

Sunday afternoon second lines were to be replaced by line dancing. Instead of strange incense, oils, and rasta caps, the sidewalk vendors on Canal Street would sell exotic Dutch cheeses and bootleg Jimmy Buffett CDs.

We were going to put some culture into this place. Finally.

What a funky city it could have been, had the voting gone the other way—a city where gospel brunches were replaced by Gregorian chant breakfasts and the big clarinet on the side of the downtown Holiday Inn would be replaced with a really big banjo.

The menus at Dookie Chase's and Willie Mae's in the Treme would be reworked to add a little excitement to the dull palettes around here. No more of that turkey-neck whatever and all that okra stuff.

Instead, bagels and lox on every plate! And potato soup. Finally, a little flavor around here. A little excitement! Imagine a city restaurant critics would flock to for new and daring ideas.

New management at WWOZ would dispense with all that crazy jazz and R&B and would instead offer twenty-four-hour programming of *A Prairie Home Companion* with occasional weekend specials featuring all ABBA, all the time.

God, I love ABBA.

Oh, to think of the possibilities that slipped away in the voting booth last Saturday! What were you people thinking?

Imagine a JazzFest where the Polka Tent replaces that unfathomably dull Gospel Tent and instead of Congo Square we get— are you ready for this?—Scandinavian Square!

Something in a tasteful woodwind quartet, I'm thinking. Some barbershop quartet. Some college chorales. Something— anything!—to bring a little life to that same ol', same ol' JazzFest dullsville lineup.

One thing we would have kept is Lionel Richie as the closing act on the Second Sunday. I thought that worked out pretty good.

Yeah, we were gonna keep Lionel. Have you ever listened— and I mean *really* listened?—to the lyrics of "Sail On"?

Unbelievable. And tell me the truth: Does anyone even know what "Hey Pocky Way" means? The Neville Brothers are so yesterday.

This town, people—this town was gonna change. We were finally going to have something special here, something that people from around the world would want to come see and experience.

In the Quarter, we were going to get rid of all those noisy street-corner brass bands and break-dancers and the tap-dancing kids and replace them with: more mimes. Mimes, man. They crack me up.

How do they stand still for so long?

Shoeshine hustlers would change their con. No more crazy vernacular. The pitch would now be "Would you care to make a wager on the location of the procurement of your footwear?"

Other phrases around here would be reworked for clarity and precision. "May I inquire as to the health of your mother and her extended family?"

And no more "Yeah, you right." Instead: "That is correct, sir!"

And "Who is that to intimate they are going to defeat our football team? Who is that? Who is that?"

We've got streets here named after African-American icons like Martin Luther King, Oretha Castle Haley, and Rosa Parks, but nothing for the truly great Caucasians this city has produced.

I mean, how come there's no Richard Simmons Street? Kitty Carlisle Avenue? I'm telling you, it's simply not fair.

Did you know that the Backstreet Cultural Museum doesn't even have an exhibit on lacrosse? What's up with that?

There was a new world order in store. Polo! *Will & Grace* film festivals! Brooks & Dunn! Zulu outfitted by Perlis! Oh, glory lost!

We could have been the most interesting city in America.

But no. Not now. The dream is dashed. Crazy voters.

I am despondent. I need a mojito.

Tennis, anyone?

He's Picking the Pairs for Nola's Ark

6/13/06

The Big One's coming and it's going to wash us all away and I don't know what you're doing to prepare for it, people, but I've got my own plan: I'm building an ark.

The way I see it, some pissant Category 2 storm is going to drown this whole place this summer and New Orleans as we know it will cease to exist.

So I'm going to load up an ark and sail to an alien, distant shore with a pair of everything that makes New Orleans what it is—so unique, charming, and eccentric—and we're going to start all over again, two by two.

We'll go wherever the fates and currents take us—the Caribbean, the Indian Ocean, Toledo Bend Reservoir; I don't know. I just know we're going to load the ark and sail away, and—when the deluge is over—we're going to start from scratch, just like that Noah guy did.

Just call us Nola's Ark.

We're going to need a king and queen wherever we go, so I'm bringing Ella Brennan and Norman Francis. I'm bringing Leah Chase and Paul Prudhomme to run the ship's galley.

Al Copeland and Chris Owens will board the ship together in the hope that their union will produce a legion of offspring who inhabit their quintessentially New Orleans spirit—that certain *je ne croissant pas.*

We're going to bring Bob Breck and Margaret Orr for our Accu-Weather needs, because Lord knows we need AccuWeather. Our new false idol in this strange new land will be a Super Doppler.

I'm going to pair up Becky Allen and Ricky Graham to promulgate a new generation of New Orleans theater. We'll bring John Scott and Mignon Faget because we need pretty things—very thoughtful pretty things.

Dr. John and Irma Thomas will board this ship to create a new legacy of New Orleans musicians and we're bringing along Theresa Andersson also but she can't bring anyone with her because, well . . . because I said so.

I'm going to bring Blaine Kern and Quint Davis to rebuild the city's two most cherished public celebrations. And because I can't think of any suitable female companions for this pair, I guess we're going to allow gay marriage in this new New Orleans so their progeny will bring us JazzFest and Mardi Gras in perpetuity.

I guess that means David Vitter's not coming with us. And that's just as well. There will be tolerance and science where we're going. I realize those are outrageous notions, but keep in mind, this is just a fantasy.

We'll bring the Neville Brothers if they will join us.

But in this strange, new land where we are going there will be no Corps of Engineers, insurance adjusters, meter maids, assessors, or people who park their SUVs in two spaces at the Ochsner parking garage.

It will be paradise.

We're going to bring Bill Jefferson and Cleo Fields because we're going to need a lot of disposable cash on hand and—as far as I can tell—they've got more disposable cash on hand than anyone else around here.

I'm going to load up seedlings of celery, onions, and bell peppers to plant in this new Utopia. I'm going to bring two old guys who look like serial killers dressed in soda fountain vests to sell

Lucky Dogs and I guess we'll need to bring some cows and pigs to make those hot dogs.

Lucky Dogs are made of cows and pigs, aren't they?

Whatever. I'm going to load up two mosquitoes, two mimes, two indifferent waiters from Napoleon House, two strippers, and two United Cab drivers. It will be New Orleans again!

Two by two, New Orleans will survive. Deuce and Reggie. Garland and Angela. Frankie and Johnny. Crawfish and Monica.

We're going to need a pharmacist, I guess. Definitely need a pharmacist. And that guy who runs Creole Creamery because we're going to need ice cream.

Before we leave, we'll swing by Lee Circle and pick up two guys hanging out by the Shell station in case we need any roofing work done on our voyage.

I thought about bringing Frank Davis and Jackie Clarkson, but I'm afraid they'd just chat and natter on the whole darn voyage and we wouldn't get any peace at all. Besides, I want fish and music in the streets where we're going, and with them around I don't think either would last very long.

I'll bring Ron Forman, but he's not allowed to run for office; we just need someone to keep the animals in line. We're going to bring lots of animals but no animal rescue people because they'll end up spray-painting the whole damn ark.

And no blue dogs.

That blue dog drives me bonkers.

Where we're going will have neatly trimmed grass in public places and no dog poop on the sidewalk and nice playgrounds and regular garbage pickup and everyone's weight will be proportional to their height.

Then again, that doesn't sound much like New Orleans, so scratch that.

So I guess we're ready to go. Onward to Utopia. Oh, wait . . . I see through my field glasses that there's one more pair standing in the rain waiting to board.

Why, it's Ray and Kathleen!

Sorry, guys. This boat's full. You can wait for one of the buses. They'll be here any minute. You just wait and see.

Rider on the Storm
6/30/06

I've always thought a bicycle was the best way to get around, especially in New Orleans, where there are no hills to affront the ab-challenged.

I favor big, fat-tire, one-speed models for their comfort and ability to negotiate curbs, exposed streetcar tracks, potholes, drunks on the sidewalk, and the general curbside debris of New Orleans.

This is no town for thin tires.

Also, with a big, fat bike, I've never felt the pressure that many men my age suddenly feel to wear spray-on black shorts and bright yellow shirts with Italian logos on them.

But somehow I can still manage to feel nearly naked and overexposed. This happened to me last week when I was tooling around the Upper 9th Ward, where my presence on a bicycle prompted three people to ask me if I was from Common Ground, the hippieish volunteer organization set up over there, because who the hell else would be riding a bicycle around what used to be one of the most dangerous neighborhoods in town?

So there I was in the 9th, riding around and taking notes, when a speeding car broke the peace of the moment on a street whose only sounds were those of industry: hammers, nail guns, Skil saws.

As the car—a white sedan—whipped past me, two guys hanging out on the corner up ahead yelled out the driver's name and the car screeched to a halt. I was over by my side of the road, next to the curb, when the sedan driver threw the car into reverse and then plowed into me.

As I said, my bike is big and heavy. Real heavy, with tires like a Hummer.

The car hit my back tire and sent me shooting forward like a cowboy on a crazed rodeo bronc. Amazingly, I stayed on the thing. I ended up about ten yards from where I had been a second before, but I appeared to be upright and unharmed. Shaken, not stirred.

The driver looked at me and said, "My bad," and then hauled off up to the corner where his friends were waiting. Just like that.

You just hit me and all I get is "My bad"?

"Yeah, I guess so!" I yelled as he drove away, but I felt my response was lacking the fortitude the situation called for. Then again, big red bikes don't really pulse with auras of fortitude. In fact, they veritably shout: Poet aboard!

So. What to do? I have just been hit by a car and the driver drove away. He is up the block with friends. I don't appear to be suffering any injuries, and my bike seems fine. I am in an unfamiliar neighborhood. I conclude: Don't get involved.

Philosophically, this aggrieves me. But I am alone and unarmed, because the fact is: the pen may be mightier than the sword, but it's no match for a Glock.

So I am about to ride away in a cloud of angst when a very large man steps up from behind me. Turns out he is a cop. A very large cop, or did I already say that?

He saw the whole thing. He asks if I am all right. I tell him yes and then he strides up to the three guys standing on the corner. They all jawbone for a while and then the cop waves me to join them and I curse under my breath and now I am, indeed, involved.

Funny, at this point, the two guys from the corner fall all over themselves asking if I'm okay. I tell them yes and thank them for their sincere concern for my health—now that the heat has arrived.

The driver, though, he yells in my face, "You called the police? You want to call the po-lice?"

"How could I have called the police?" I said. "You hit me ninety seconds ago."

Everybody starts yelling. "You want to call the po-lice!" the driver keeps yelling. It's stupid. I am a guy on a bicycle in a place I shouldn't be, and this is what happens. But then I'm thinking: No, this is my city, I can be here. Dammit.

But why is the guy who just hit me copping attitude like I'm the bad guy? Where does this come from?

I keep marveling at how huge the cop is. I take comfort from this. He asks me if I want to press charges, I tell him no; in fact, it was a minor traffic infraction in and of itself. It was the aftermath of swagger and stupidity that, to me, constitute the bigger crime, but what are you going to do? It's not against the law to be an ass.

And what if it was? Man, you think our jails are crowded now?

The driver holds firm on his infallible alpha-male stance, but the other two guys do that thing that is probably one of the male species' most annoying traits. They keep shaking my hand. Over and over.

"We're cool, right?" they say and then the handshake. They won't stop shaking my hand. And when they stop, they say something else and reach for my hand again.

I tell the cop thank you and withdraw my hand from further assault. And I ride away, feeling somehow humiliated by the experience, though I'm not sure what I did to feel that way.

On my big red bike in this big mean world, sometimes I feel like Pee-Wee Herman.

But I'm not going to stop riding around town. Not gonna let the fools get me down. This is our town. These are our streets. I'm allowed to be here.

From now on, though, I'm gonna watch my back.

Car 54, Where Are You?
9/10/06

I see that Car 54's schedule this weekend included a town hall–style meeting Saturday with residents of City Council District B.

And here's the kicker: The residents of District B didn't have to go to New York or L.A. or Houston to meet with Car 54. He was actually coming to them.

Here! In New Orleans!

What a refreshing notion. I guess there's nothing else going on in any other American city this weekend or Car 54 wouldn't be slumming with locals in New Orleans.

Last weekend, while in New York, Car 54 explained that there was hardly any reason for him to be back here at home because "It's Labor Day weekend. There's not a lot going on in New Orleans."

Funny how it's interpreted, though. To you and me, "not a lot going on" generally refers to things such as garbage pickup, trailer delivery, insurance settlements, getting phone service, and street repair. I think "leadership" might fit under the "not a lot going on" banner also.

To Car 54, "not a lot going on" seems to imply that there were no good national R&B acts playing in town and no large gathering of the national press corps and, hell, even Al Sharpton was going to be somewhere else that weekend, so what's the point?

So while there was nothing going on here in New Orleans last weekend, Car 54 hosted an art opening of photographs of himself in New York City and I wish I had one of those photos because sometimes I don't remember what he looks like.

But the photos are a little outdated, because they all seem to have been taken in New Orleans.

They must be old pictures.

And while in New York, Car 54 nabbed ten primo tickets for himself and his fleet of lemons to see sexy crooner Usher perform in a sold-out performance of *Chicago*, and that's exactly what I would have done last weekend. If I could have gotten the tickets. And if I'd been in New York. And if I didn't have any other pressing business at home.

And if I weren't mayor of New Orleans.

But there was nothing going on here, really.

And that's true for anyone who wasn't gutting their house or reseeding their lawn or looking for a job or moving into their FEMA trailer or trying to get a FEMA trailer or filling out SBA loan forms that are more daunting than Fortune 500 corporate tax returns.

There was nothing going on if you weren't tallying gunshot victims or praying for customers to come shop at your small business or if you were struggling with child care issues because it turns out the school where your child was supposed to start classes on Tuesday wasn't going to open because it wasn't ready.

And supposing that none of your friends or relatives needed help with any of these problems, then, in fact, there wasn't a damn thing going on around here.

Unless, of course: There's that pesky new city ordinance, which mandates that you toil with all the life and blood you've got to get your house and yard up to the new aesthetic specifications the city demands lest it find you a blight upon the landscape, whereupon the city will gut or tear down your property with or without your permission and slap a lien on you for the expenses.

Never mind that scores of city-owned properties stretching from Hollygrove to Almonaster fail to satisfy the code. Never mind that just about every playground and school lot owned by the city has overgrowth that violates the code.

Never mind that the pothole at the corner of Tchoupitoulas and Calhoun—a pothole!—has been there so long and grown so deep that the shrubbery growing out of it is of the length that the new city code deems a nuisance and is in violation of the law.

Of course, someone as glib as Car 54 might dismiss this pothole as "just some hole in the ground," but to some folks, holes in the ground matter.

They matter very much.

I worry about the influence Car 54's famous new friends are having on him, all those folks from up north.

From Jesse Jackson he has learned: Blame it on somebody else.

And from George Bush he has learned: Pretend it isn't happening.

Of course, Car 54 swears his mission is to drum up business for New Orleans and I heard he did talk the coat check girl at the Usher show into coming down to Mardi Gras with some of her friends and the bell captain at his hotel is apparently genuinely interested in checking out a time-share in the Quarter so maybe it's not all wasted time.

I had a crazy dream: I was driving around downtown wondering what the hell is happening to my city and wondering who would save it, and I looked up and I saw a bright light.

The source of the light was the third floor of City Hall and I realized that city leaders were working there until midnight every night to hammer out the excruciating details of our recovery.

Then I drove into a pothole and woke up and realized it was all a dream. Because, in truth, there's not a lot going on in New Orleans, particularly when measured in conventional units of activity and time.

One hundred days, two hundred days, three hundred days, it's all the same. Time is a mere medieval contrivance—an anachronism, really—that leads to nothing more than unreasonable expectations.

The warranty on Car 54 says it's supposed to last four more years. But the first four years seem to have taken a toll on the old beater. Sure, it runs as smooth as ever—a sleek and shiny ride, to be sure—but there seem to be performance issues.

This baby is leaking gas all over the place. And I hear a lot of folks are ready for a trade-in.

Not in My Pothole
9/15/06

After I wrote about a ferocious pothole in my neighborhood the other day, a reader contacted me to see if I had ever peered directly into the chasm, which is so big and so old that it has developed into a nature preserve for several species of local flora.

I admitted that I had not approached the beast on foot, that I had admired the gaping street gash only from the comfort and safety of my automobile as I drove by.

"Check it out," she said. "Look inside. You won't believe it."

So I did some old-fashioned gumshoe reporting this week and got out of my car and walked to the edge of the abyss—a roughly ten-by-six-foot section of Calhoun Street that has caved in on itself at the corner of Tchoupitoulas—from stress, age, water, design flaw, or just because it was tired, I don't know— right in front of Children's Hospital, at an intersection favored by ambulance drivers.

And what I beheld in the depths of this rupture shook me to my very core. It reawakened in me all the horrors of the city's devastated landscape last fall.

Inside the pothole—there, in the dark and rugged underbelly of our city—was an abandoned kitchen appliance.

A friggin' dishwasher. Or maybe a washing machine, I don't know; it's upside down and overgrown.

The metaphorical implications of this spectacle are boggling, to say the least. But I will bypass all of them to get to the seminal question that comes to mind and it is this: Just who the hell was driving around Uptown trying to get rid of their waterlogged dishwasher and came upon a pothole in the middle of a residential neighborhood and said, Hey, this looks like a good place?

After absorbing the initial shock of this scene, I felt anger well up inside me. But upon further reflection—upon my repeated meditations on a pothole—maybe I'm misreading this.

Perhaps this is some kind of tactical urban guerrilla artistic statement, some organic art installation that ties together themes of isolation, loss, and the commonality of experience.

Or maybe there is a richer and more urgent message in this complex, weed-strewn tableau: technology versus nature, the rediscovery of the id, man's inhumanity toward man and the titanic struggles of good and evil.

Or maybe it was just the careless act of a common punk and now it's somebody else's problem, not his.

My first impulse, was, of course, to blame the mayor for this. But no, I don't see this rather generic and budget-conscious machine—a sturdy but all too standard mustard yellow—being either his brand or style.

For him, I see stainless steel. I see Bosch, not General Electric.

So it must have been FEMA, then. Or the president. Or the terrorists. Or somebody not from here, right?

It had to have been some bogeyman not of our world, because I ask you: Do we really live in a community with people who pull crap like this? Look out your window at the guy walking down your sidewalk and ask yourself: Was it him?

I mean, what the hell?

Then again, maybe we should thank this guy. Maybe he's just trying to help. After all, now, if you drive your car into this canyon, the dishwasher could save you three feet of vertical drop. Thereby necessitating just a new front end and not a new chassis.

Yeah, there are bigger problems in town and we've all got

bigger worries than a pothole with a dishwasher in it but . . . wait. No. In fact, we don't.

What it has come down to in this town is a struggle between the people who live here, who are busting their butts every day to make this a better place to live, and the people who simply don't give a damn, and I would suggest that dumping an appliance into a pothole on somebody else's street would be a quintessential—if somewhat unorthodox—manifestation of not giving a damn.

What we have here is, in fact, a battle between the kind of folks who clean up after their dogs on the sidewalk and bag their leaves—and the kind of folks who have picnics in the park and leave crawfish shells on the ground when they leave or folks who hire lawn maintenance men to blow their leaves and dirt into the street and leave it there.

It's somebody else's problem, not mine. And we have here nothing less than the titanic battle between good and evil. The battle for our city.

Survive This
9/20/06

Television is without a doubt the most influential medium, and its effect on New Orleans' recovery is no small potatoes. There have been great moments of enlightenment (Spike Lee's documentary comes to mind) and giant steps backward (just about every time the mayor speaks into a microphone).

Each image projected from here frames our story, gives the nation the information it needs to decide our fate.

And although the upcoming *Monday Night Football* extravaganza will provide a huge spike in presumably positive publicity, I can't help but feel we missed a golden opportunity by not luring CBS to bring its *Survivor* franchise here this season.

Survivor: Cook Island, the thirteenth edition of the landmark reality series, drew more viewers for its premiere last Thursday night than *Dancing with the Stars*, and if that doesn't speak to the profound dominance of its intellectual content, I don't know what does.

Its ratings were no doubt boosted by the risky gimmick to segregate the four "tribes" on the show into ethnic classifications: Black, White, Hispanic, and Asian.

The producers have gone to great lengths to tell us how difficult it was to draw these tribes from an application pool that was almost entirely Caucasian—white folks historically having a stronger congenital predisposition toward exposing their character flaws on television (see: Jerry Springer, *The Gong Show,* et al.).

But the producers would have had it easy if they'd come to New Orleans. They'd have found exactly what they were looking for without incurring the expense of dragging production crews halfway around the globe: a physical and emotional environment teeming with danger, adventure, and challenge, and a community already divided into four ethnic components, all eyeing one another warily, suspiciously, each trying to maneuver its interests to the fore.

Throw in the elements of questionable drinking water, a rodent population larger than its human counterpart, lots of mosquitoes, and the imminent possibility of getting capped by three teens in a stolen Range Rover and it's almost sublime: *Survivor: New Orleans.*

We're already the most interesting reality show on TV—except we're confined to the second half of the nightly news twice a week. Why didn't anyone think to get a major advertising sponsor and put us on prime time?

What are they thinking in New York and L.A.?

What an opportunity lost.

Imagine how the traditional thematic elements of *Survivor*—shelter, safety, nourishment, water, comfort, teamwork, mental rigor, physical toughness, and political acumen—would have played out here.

Survivor's appeal is to show how contestants—everyday people like you and me, except maybe a little stupider and better-looking—are able to withstand life without power, water, food, bathing, transportation, communication, government, and all other creature comforts for thirty-nine days.

You call that tough? I call it "home."

If you put the four Cook Island tribes in the middle of City Park, I bet it would take them a week to find their way out. They could boil lagoon water to quench their thirst and hunt raccoons for food. Imagine a moment of desperation—one of *Survivor*'s trademark emotional bloodlettings—when an inconsolable contestant finds out she's been living on the sixth fairway of a golf course and what she thought was a nest of edible egret eggs under an oak canopy were actually Titleists and Callaways badly shanked by investment bankers skipping work back in the summer of 2005.

They could have one tribe live in a pothole, one in a tent under the interstate, one in a FEMA trailer (it goes without saying that it has no utilities), and one in what remains of Fats Domino's house down in the Lower 9th and let them try to survive the tangle of living options and deprivations that we have come to know as routine.

Better yet, one of the tribes could be embedded with Uncle Sal and Aunt Judy in their two-bedroom rambler in River Ridge, along with Sal's two grown sons and Judy's ex, C.J., and his fourth wife, Tina, and their two kids and four dogs, Sal's nephew Gerald and his family of six and Gerald's son Tony's *parrain*, Sid, and his boyfriend, Jeff, and their two cats—and then they will know what "surviving" means in the post-Katrina landscape.

Admittedly, much of life in the suburbs has played out less like a reality adventure series and more like a prime-time sitcom pilot—*Look Who's Living Together Now!*—as extended families and their nagging ancillary units bunk together under the oppressive climate of contractor delays in Gentilly.

But I digress.

To test the mental endurance of the contestants, they could be forced to acquire building permits, driver's licenses, and the working phone number of a psychiatrist. Anyone who comes home without them is voted off the island. Back to civilization.

The tribes could comb the wild swamplands of eastern New Orleans in search of buried treasure—perhaps the lettuce crisper from William Jefferson's refrigerator—and whoever finds the wad of cash gets two nights' immunity to blow it all on Bourbon Street.

I see great potential for a supporting role for our mayor, who could appear as some crazed tribal voodoo warrior who makes crazy gestures and says crazy things and then presents a challenge: Haul away the trash! Secure an equitable insurance settlement! Build a casino!

The winning tribe gets immunity. And a bar of chocolate.

The tribes could commandeer some boats from people's driveways and sail out into Lake Pontchartrain to catch fish. Then, when they return, they could fight lawsuits against the boats' owners.

When real looters break through the CBS security barricade and overrun the set, the tribes could all take cover in local bookstores—the only retail outlets looters never visit.

Then, in a surprise ending season finale that trumps anything the writers at *24* or *The Wire* could ever come up with, the four tribes—Black, White, Hispanic, and Asian—could discover a fifth tribe in their midst, a morally impoverished group suffering from an identity crisis greater than the sum of the other four.

There, living in rough brush in the shadow of Tad Gormley Stadium, an undisciplined and wild-eyed tribe lives off the cadavers of New Orleans, sucking the blood from any living being in its midst, a primitive and unruly tribe bereft of a code of conduct, decency, or civility for the past three decades.

In the season's climactic moment, the New Orleans contestants could come face-to-face with the motley and desperate indigenous cannibal tribe that destroys its enemies without regard to race, color, or creed: the Entergy board of directors.

And because of their electric bills, all four *Survivor* tribes are forced to relocate to Houston to finish the game.

Love Among
the Ruins

September Never Ends

2/7/06

I'm standing on Iris Avenue, and it feels like last fall.

I look up and down the street at the fresh wreckage wrought by tornadoes that have no name, and all I can think of is that Green Day song "Wake Me Up When September Ends."

When does September end around here?

Buildings are shredded and power lines dangle like Mardi Gras beads off the oaks on St. Charles Avenue after the Bacchus parade, and stuff and things are just everywhere. It's a sheet metal jamboree.

There's a building at the corner on River Road that looks as though Jerome Bettis ran right through it, and I love this part: the front door is spray-painted NO LOOT ZONE.

Well, the good news is you weren't looted. The bad news is, five months after The Thing, a tornado came and knocked you flat on your ass.

Now, both the president of Jefferson Parish and our mayor have said a lot of crazy things over the past few months, but I don't remember anyone taunting the fates and borrowing a line from our president: "Bring it on."

But somebody done brought it on.

Some folks say it's God's work, some say the Hand of Fate, but I have to think it's because of all the trailers we've got around here now. It's a bad joke, but when you create the world's largest trailer park, you're going to have tornadoes.

That's true science. It's in the chapter right after fossils.

It was such a tough wind came down this neighborhood that it knocked over DeWitt's, the little vegetable stand that's been there on River Road forever, taking with it the big, faded HARRY LEE sign that somebody put there the first time he ran for sheriff in, what—1950?

I never thought that sign would go away. I thought it would outlast Harry Lee, in fact.

But nothing will outlast Harry Lee. At the End of Days: cockroaches, Harry Lee, and Johnny White's Bar.

I suppose there is a certain poignancy or entendre—double, triple, quadruple; I don't know—that one of the buildings that got clipped on Iris Avenue last week was the storage warehouse for Mardi Gras City.

There, in the middle of the street, was half a building, and left behind, standing in plain view from the street: boxes and boxes and boxes of beads. Neatly stacked. Ready for loading.

Is somebody trying to tell us something? Throw me something, God. Perhaps a colorful strand of baubles rather than a roof this time, if you please.

I have a co-worker, Renée Peck, who was among the first in her neighborhood in East Lakeshore to rebuild a house that was whacked by The Thing last fall.

Maybe you saw her story in Saturday's paper: her family was among the first to empty the contents of their house onto the sidewalk and the first to gut the insides and the first to get teams of roofers and carpenters and everybody else, and this week, the painters were due and they were going to move back into that house this month and plant one of the first flags in the Vanilla Wasteland, lay claim to a spot of land, and say: Here we are. This can be done.

I'm guessing you know where this story is going.

Wednesday night, when the torpedoes—er, tornadoes—came roiling through the area, one of them took out half their house. It imploded. Dust to dust. Bricks and rubble. A front-porch portico was found two streets away.

Wake me up when it's over.

You could hardly blame someone for waking up last Thursday morning and telling himself: I can't do this anymore. I won't do this anymore.

But we will.

I am listening to the car radio and it's WTUL and they're broadcasting out of the Rue de la Course coffee shop Uptown because they lost their studio, and when the deejays come on, you can hear the baristas pounding their empty espresso grinds on the counter and you can hear plates clatter in the background, but they're getting by. The coffee shop and the radio station, doing what they have to do to bring us the essentials of post-Katrina life: caffeine and music.

At the corner of Napoleon and Claiborne, Chill the Barber is set up between two gas pumps of the shuttered Shell station and he cuts hair there because the building marked CHILL'S FIRST CLASS CUTS around the corner is a literal shell.

Chill is just getting by, barbering with power supplied by his car battery. Come hell or high water, people will still need haircuts. Men will still need a place to talk politics and sports. Even if it's a gas station island.

I was with my family on the levee in Algiers Sunday afternoon, looking across the river at the city, and my daughter said, "That's where my new best friend lives." And I asked, "Where are you talking about?" And she pointed to a cruise ship docked at the Convention Center.

Her deskmate at school, a first-grader named Brooke, lives there on a big boat in the Mississippi River until, well . . . until when?

The ship is called *Ecstasy*, and I swear, if we gave it a chance, the irony around here could just kill us.

Because it's beginning to look like nothing else can.

Punxsutawney Phil stuck his head out of his groundhog hole in Pennsylvania last week and made the official forecast: six more weeks of September.

We can take it. Bring it on.

The Muddy Middle Ground
3/12/06

I went to Mid-City, looking for a friend.

There are still so many folks I used to run with whose fates and misfortunes I do not know since The Thing came down.

Every couple of days, I try to track one down, sometimes by phone, sometimes in person. Sometimes I find him, sometimes I don't.

I love Mid-City. I've always loved tooling around there. It has its own vibe and languorous pace and never seemed to be in sync with society's inexorable march to revolutions in retail, food service, upholstery, auto repair, and flooring.

You could still buy remnants in Mid-City. You could still get your car fixed by a mechanic named Sal.

Mid-City has its own alluring architecture—some Creolized version of the antiquated American cottage—and I've always felt that if I were transported blindfolded to the neighborhood and then was asked to divine where I was, I would look around and maybe smell the air and think: We're near Liuzza's.

You can just tell.

Mid-City seems like one of the (many) forgotten neighborhoods in the Aftermath. Not as rich as Lakeview and not as poor as the Lower 9th and not quite as whacked as either but very much whacked, indeed—soaked, sodden, gutted, and blanched in the sun like a dead fish.

Not black, not white. Not so easily categorized and labeled and affixed in the political order we are being force-fed, the notion of Us and Them.

That's probably one reason I like it.

The brown line, the watermark, the stain of our national disgrace—sometimes it's over your head here.

Sometimes I'm in my car and I look at the line and realize I would be completely submerged where I am driving if it were six months ago, and this is so hard to fathom, to process, to make peace with.

I try to picture the corner of Banks and Carrollton as some sort of lake, but I don't see it. I look at a building now and think: It looks fine. Where is everybody?

Over a few blocks, Mandina's is a shell, not to open for many, many months, but at least it will reopen and that's important because when you break things down to their very basic fundamentals, you'd have to question whether living in a New Orleans without Mandina's would be worth living at all.

Mid-City was always so full of classic neighborhood joints with lively and eccentric crowds day and night. Venezia, with its beehived waitresses and "sit anywhere ya like, dawlin'," and, down the block, the gray men whose elbows were permanently affixed to the sticky bar top at the Red Door, smoke from their unfiltered Camels streaming from tin ashtrays straight into their listless eyes.

I spent much of the night of Hurricane Andrew in 1992 at the Red Door, grabbing buck-ten-cent Carlings and going out on the neutral ground on Carrollton with friends and grabbing tree branches and letting the wind lift us up.

Young, wild, free, and stupid. My friends and I greeted Andrew with a game of bourré, a bottle of Pinch, and mud slides on the neutral ground until one in the group got covered with red ants and, later, got out of sorts and hit another in the group with a baseball bat.

Paul Sanchez, from the band Cowboy Mouth, wrote a song about it, "Hurricane Party." I'm guessing they're a thing of the past now—hurricane parties, those homages to the bravado and insouciance with which we used to greet the news of impending hellfire and destruction.

Now it's not so funny.

The Red Door is whacked and Venezia is whacked and Liuzza's is whacked and the barest few Mid-City businesses have been able to limp themselves back into order, now six months later, seven months later, time marches on.

The New Orleans writer Jonathan Hunter recently lamented his favorite neighborhood's state of disrepair with a hopeful paean: "I look forward to the return of the Liuzza's waitresses yelling 'Draw one!' over the buzz of the crowd drinking frozen schooners of beer on a Friday afternoon. A plate of fried pickles was only a dollar. They were weird but good. And I certainly hope that my barber continues to interrupt my haircut to take bets on the phone: 'Gotcha covered, babe.' "

We will be part of what we were and a part of something new. Maybe Sal will fix your car. Or maybe you'll have to go to Jiffy Lube on Vets.

I was in Mid-City looking for my friend Tracy Jarmon, a waiter at Mandina's and a painter of lively abstracts that I started collecting about two years ago. A man of interminable—even borderline annoying—good cheer, he was one I had wondered about.

I called recently, but couldn't find him. So I went to his rented raised double, where I had been twice before to buy paintings right out of his garage where he worked and struggled to make an artist out of a waiter; no easy task, that, particularly when the canvases are given away at a hundred bucks a shot.

His house on Bernadotte Street was empty. Cleaned out. No trace of life. No paintings. No interminable cheer.

I'm assuming that all his work was destroyed and his Mandina's gig is gone and whatever. Thing about Tracy is, he's probably laughing it off somewhere. He's got that New Orleans thing crawling all over him, the good stuff, that We Are the Champions, to hell with the rest and I'll just start over kind of attitude.

There was a neighbor on a cell phone on the sidewalk on Bernadotte, and I asked if he knew what happened to the painter down the block and he said, "Oh, that guy? Yeah. I don't know what happened to him."

This guy and I on the sidewalk, we did the obligatory small talk that has become so surreal attendant to what happened here. I did what I hate doing, what I swear I won't do anymore, but that I continue to do: I asked a stranger how he is doing. How his block is doing.

The guy paused a long time. Then he said, "We're doin' all right."

Isn't that the way? You can either tell the truth or you can say "We're doin' all right" and keep the stiff upper lip.

That's what I have taken to doing. When someone asks me how I'm doing these days, I ask them back, "What are the choices?" It's sort of my personal joke that no one gets. But either you beat this thing or it beats you.

Pandora's snowball stand has reopened on Carrollton and shirtless boys from the Jesuit cross-country team run through the rubble of the neighborhood every afternoon and there's your metaphor: not a sprint, but a marathon.

Snowballs today, fried pickles tomorrow, Mandina's ever after. Gotcha covered, babe.

Misery in the Melting Pot
3/22/06

It has been seven months.

I am walking down Toledano Street, the wide pitch from Broad to Claiborne, ten blocks of classic urban American landscape: sad grocery stores, chicken, pig's feet and dirty rice to go, brick revival churches, funeral homes, auto parts stores, and ramshackle row houses.

There was a time when optimistic paint jobs — orange sherbet, burnt sienna, and sea foam green trims, posts, and porches — did their best to cover the age and decay, but it's all laid bare and painful now. The optimistic veneer here — everywhere — was stripped by the water.

Seven months ago.

The corner of Broad and Toledano once marked a turf war for customers between Cajun Chicken and Cajun Seafood, two catty-corner carryouts owned by Asians in a black neighborhood.

Welcome to the melting pot.

But the war is over; both stores have been shuttered. For seven months.

Just down from the corner at Broad, there's a sign that says, NO DUMPING: $5oo FINE.

That's almost funny. Eight feet above the ground, the crooked sign has the brown watermark across it. And there are, about every hundred paces, big piles of debris, like a dump—carpet, plaster, furniture, and televisions, lots of televisions.

You have to figure the local Nielsen ratings took a beating in this hurricane. The revolution was televised, but all the TVs are broken.

This is one of those puzzling neighborhoods where you look at some of the houses and you tremble at their altered states of decline but you sometimes realize: this one or that one was falling down even before The Thing.

The Rhodes Funeral Home anchors this unwieldy boulevard, all stately, grand, and white, looking like nothing more than a mausoleum itself. It is gutted now, and masked workers are removing the floor with shovels.

You don't want to think about what happened in the funeral homes. The only consolation is that at least the people inside were already dead.

But still.

In the middle of the afternoon, there's a wan ghost town feel to Toledano, with weeds gone wild and power lines dangling and swaying in the breeze like electric spiderwebs and Styrofoam cups and potato chip bags drifting this way and that as motorists speed by on their way to or from Uptown or the interstate, destination always someplace else—anyplace else but here.

It's easy to fall into a listless state after a while out here on Toledano. You get an irritation in your throat, or maybe that's just your imagination—that Katrina cough that people talk about, but is it real?

The work crews around here are spotty and slow-moving; there seems to be no urgency.

Many houses have been gutted, but that's as far as the work goes in most cases while the residents wait to learn the future of Broadmoor, this neighborhood, designated "green" by many specialists who suggest that low-lying areas such as this should be returned to their natural state and their natural state didn't include crawfish egg rolls or jazz funerals.

Or Bible study or happy hour, so both the Pleasant Zion Baptist Church and Tapp's II are gutted and waiting. Capt. Sal's Seafood is cleaned out and cleaned up with shiny stainless-steel counters in place and a fresh paint job, but there's no one on the premises, hardly ever is, all boarded up and waiting.

Inside the storefront window, on a tabletop: work gloves, industrial wipes, small electrical fixtures, and a book, *Your Best Life Now: 7 Steps to Living at Your Full Potential.*

Indeed. Talk about self-help. Best of luck to you, my friend.

There's an unmarked green tin building down the block, the parking lot still full of drowned cars, but life and commerce stir around them.

This is Dooley's Auto & Wrecker Service, but you'd know that only because that's what's printed on the brand-new shirt that the man named Dooley wears in the office.

There's no actual wrecker visible on the premises, but gospel music blares from the back auto bay, where Dooley's grandson-in-law—the only current employee—busies himself with auto repair.

Dooley sits at his desk eating lunch out of a Rally's bag with *Guiding Light* blaring on a TV against the wall. After losing every tool and every machine seven months ago—to say nothing of the eight cars he was working on at the time and all the old mechanics' uniforms with names stitched on the pockets—he's been back in business for three weeks.

New uniforms. Some new tools. Still need new machines, but can't wait forever.

"Need to get back to work," Dooley says. He's cobbling this thing back to life with no help from FEMA or the Small Business Administration or anything else that's government-related or spelled by acronym.

"I don't fool with that," Dooley says. "Just doin' it myself."

Doin' it with no sign and no phone; there is still no land-line service in this part of town. Seven months later.

A customer walks into Dooley's shop. Broken headlight. Dooley loses interest in his conversation with a stranger and attends to the customer and the gospel music in the back bay blares and the sound of tools—new tools—clatters in the shade.

Moving down the block, more piles of debris. Big and small. A pile of riding lawn mowers stacked up on the sidewalk speaks of the loss of a small business. One small story. Many small stories make the big story.

Other places, little things, cosmetics, bedding, toys, small appliances. It's just stuff. Possessions. But it was *somebody's* stuff, and it took a long time and some scrap to get this stuff, and in a lifetime, this stuff amounted to somebody's comfort zone. Their home.

We are Humpty Dumpty, laughing on a wall one minute, then cracked and flat on our back the next.

A work crew is gutting a home, its debris spilled out onto the traffic lane and marked off with police tape. A man in a mask delicately lifts and tucks strands of Christmas lights that hang from the aluminum awning on the front porch to keep them from getting tangled in the floorboards the workers are ferrying out. It's as futile and loving a task as you could witness.

Let there be light. Let there be life.

Most houses here on this stretch of Toledano are one-story and empty, but some folks here are living in the rare upstairs and there are some trailers dotting the landscape, though not much sign of activity in them.

Clara Hunter watches this world from her front porch. In a housecoat and plastic hairnet, she is the only resident in view this afternoon, one of the first back.

"I was in Metairie, but I didn't like it," she says. "Didn't like paying rent. So I came back home. There is nothing like home."

Her front lawn, all twelve square feet of it, holds two new azalea bushes and one gardenia, the only living plant life other than the menacing, spiky weeds you see up and down this street.

She regards the boulevard before her, silent but for speeding, anonymous drivers seemingly oblivious to the stirrings out their windows. They've got their own problems.

A retiree, Hunter has lived here for thirty-five years. She says most of her neighbors own their homes. From what she has heard, the neighborhood will rise again, but she doesn't hear much these days because there is no phone service and she can't afford a cell and there's no one on the stoop next door or next door to that or next door to that.

"I can't talk to my friends," she says. "But the lady up the street says some folks say they're coming back here soon. And some folks say they're not coming back at all.

"You got to be patient, I guess. You're not patient, you get a stroke or a heart attack."

Words to live by. Seven months in.

The End of the World

4/4/06

There used to be a sign at the end of the road in Delacroix, at the termination of Highway 300, that said END OF THE WORLD.

The official state Department of Transportation and Development map identifies the endless expanse beyond this point as simply "hunting and trapping."

Of course, that sign and that map predate August 29, 2005.

On that date, the sign disappeared, washed away like just about every man-made structure in lower St. Bernard Parish. The End of the World went from being a commentary on geography to a statement on what happened here on August 29. The sign itself washed out to sea. Obliterated.

Some other time, some other place.

And the landmass that reaches forever southeast to Black Bay and Breton Sound—next stop, Cuba—is currently of indeterminate quality as the famous pristine Louisiana sporting grounds it once was.

Standing at what was once the End of the World, a commercial fisherman named Cap'n Rocky Morales, a brick house of a man, gestures toward the horizon—the hunting and trapping—and says, "It was marshland before. Now it's just water."

Indeed, as far as the eye can see, mostly water, with lumps of land trying to rise up, trying to break through, trying to dry out. Trying to exist. Kind of like St. Bernard itself.

The tidal surge that Katrina's brutal storm bands pushed into this land took everything, including the sure footing, geographically speaking (and perhaps psychologically as well).

There are boats where they shouldn't be and no houses where there should. And in the trees, everything, crazy stuff, it makes no sense: furniture, appliances, tires, clothes, ice chests, a toilet— all of it hanging like some nightmare vision of Christmas in the Oaks.

Katrina in the Oaks.

And there are blue trawler nets everywhere—everywhere— fanned out in branches like spiderwebs across the expanse for miles, and it's impossible not to think of Bob Dylan's song about Delacroix: "Tangled Up in Blue."

The whole damn place is tangled up in blue nets and just trash. An unholy mess. Coyote ugly, and there's not enough beer in the world to make it look pretty.

"It's not so good," Cap'n Rocky says. "I was leery about coming back here at first. But I was born here."

That explains a lot, particularly why he would try to carve a life here out of the matchsticks that remain. The inexorable lure of a sense of place. Home sweet home. A man's trailer is his castle.

Cap'n Rocky was born half a mile up Bayou Terre Aux Boeufs, and in his forty-two years he has moved only this far—third house from the End of the World.

Funny, sort of, but he doesn't even know how to spell the name of the bayou he has lived on all his life. Apparently no one has ever asked him to spell it before.

It has been a life uncomplicated and on his own terms, and this is where he will stay, despite the fact that his house vanished and everything in it is a memory now.

"When most people came back here, the only way they found their houses was by the steps," says Cap'n Rocky. "That's the only way we knew."

And it's true. All that seems unmolested by the fury are the steps to the doors of the houses that aren't there, stairways to nowhere.

Lined up and down the highway, they call to mind that macabre joke about the little black boxes on airplanes that always seem to survive a crash: Why didn't they make the houses out of the same material they used for the steps?

Delacroix, it's just wreckage and steps and ghosts. No ice, no fuel. Hardly a way for a man who makes his living on water to carry on, but carry on he will. His life is the water. Give Cap'n Rocky a boat and some bait, and he will make it.

And not necessarily alone. "Let's see," he muses over the question of who else has come back to live at the End of the World. "My uncle is up the road; he's back. There's my other uncle. And there's that old man up there; I guess there's four or five families."

But more will come back, in that prideful and insolent Louisiana fashion that The Thing has carved into our hearts.

You can see already at the End of the World at least two dozen stacks of new crab traps set out on empty lots where people used to live. Local fishers have delivered them down here and will get busy with them when they can clear the channel and if they can get new boats and if they can find a place to live and if it doesn't all happen again this summer then, well . . . then everything will be just peachy in Delacroix.

"It doesn't pay to worry about it," Cap'n Rocky says. "Whatever's going to happen will happen."

I don't suppose Bob Dylan will get down here to Delacroix when he comes to town to play the JazzFest in a few weeks. It's just not a song anyone wants to hear right now.

Moving up the road, up toward civilization on Highway 300, there is smoke on the horizon to the east, off toward Chandeleur Sound. No one knows what it is. Grass fire is everyone's guess. Natural causes. Probably methane. What doesn't drown burns.

This area is supposed to be the region's natural defense against hurricanes, and if it were a dog, someone would shoot it. It's flat, clear-cut by winds and water, and you look at it now and you'd almost think God took the sixth day of Creation off and turned over the job of Louisiana's natural barriers to the Corps of Engineers.

It's scary is what it is, all tangled up in blue.

Over in Yscloskey, at the foot of Lake Borgne, there are lots of trailers and tents and fishers who look as though they're still wiping the unbelievability of it all out of their eyes.

Dazed and confused. It's all rust and incongruity. And more steps to nowhere.

In Violet, there's a sacred place called Merrick Cemetery. The caretakers of the place don't know how old it is; just that it's nineteenth century and that there are slaves buried there.

The flood came through like stampeding water buffalo, plowing, piling, and stacking the simple white above-ground tombs like toy blocks. When the water receded, it left a jumble of concrete that looked like bad modern sculpture all tilted this way and that.

Scores of vaults broke open and the caskets inside them broke open and the bodies—those that were found—are unidentified. Add to the indignity that the cemetery records, in a nearby house, were destroyed.

So much for eternal rest.

There is a long line of new gray tombs that look as if they were hurriedly made of pavement and they're lined up along the length of the west side of the cemetery.

A man tidying up the grounds with a weed whacker explains, "A lot of 'em came out and they don't have any names so they put them there." On them are markings: ME 12-00001, ME 12-00054, ME 12-00107, and so on.

That's who they are now.

Some families have come back and tried to locate where the tombs were before August 29. In one case, someone has stuck the end of a yellow kitchen broom—bristles up—to mark where a headstone should be.

Just past here, past the house that's painted MAW MAW, CALL CHAD and the trailer that says WE SHOOTERS LOOTERS, the road to Plaquemines Parish is washed out.

This area has the distinct air of a place you'd call the middle of nowhere—unless, of course, you lived there. In that case, it's home.

In the Story Park subdivision, in the lost suburbia halfway between the middle of nowhere and Chalmette, three teenage boys skateboard through empty streets piled shoulder high with debris.

The voyeur accustomed to the brown watermark of New Orleans and Metairie—the line that measures our misery index—would be confused here.

The houses were clearly flooded, but there are no watermarks. The riddle is easily solved by the appearance of a tree and other debris that settled on a rooftop when the water went back to where it came from.

It's just as bad as it gets; it's the Lower 9th but with low brick houses that refused to budge. Painted on one: DESTROY THIS MEMORY.

On another, a homeowner has painted a one-finger salute to Allstate.

There are several FOR SALE BY OWNER signs up and, way up close to the 40 Arpent Canal, the rear door of St. Bernard Parish, there's a guy laying new sod.

On a sad long cul-de-sac that cleaning crews have yet to clear a man is carrying hope—or is it delusion?—onto his yard, one strip at a time.

It's hard to know what to say to this guy. So I offer, "Good luck, man."

"Thank you," he says and toils on while the skateboarders down the block rule their street without fear of oncoming traffic or a cranky neighbor telling them to cut out all that infernal racket.

No question about it, nature and the Corps opened a can of whup-ass on St. Bernard. It's impossible not to wonder about its future, not to worry about its precarious location between the river on one side and the ruinous man-made Gulf Outlet on the other, and then the lakes and the sounds whose shores move closer day by day, week by week, the disappearing coastline now more famous than the hunting and fishing grounds.

There's little doubt: it can't possibly take another hit like this.

But the hustle of the streets is constant, traffic off and running on the main streets, Chalmette literally pulsing with commerce and cars as people forge ahead—that Louisiana insolence: This land is our land. No one is going to take it away.

No one trusts the Corps, and no one trusts the government. Nature, they'll take their chances with. Live free or die trying.

Sitting at a table at the busy Flour Power Confectionery on Paris Road, one of the few commercial lunch joints open in the parish, Nunez Community College history professor Ron Chapman lays out the hard truth in one chilling statistic.

"Our soil is soft," he says. "A cubic foot of water weighs sixty-two pounds. Do the math. The entire infrastructure of St. Bernard was compromised by the weight of the water. The flood literally compressed the parish."

He pauses, sips, then says, "Think about that."

I think about that guy I saw laying sod in a battered subdivision. And I think again about the only thing I could say.

Good luck.

A Huck Finn Kind of Life
4/9/06

After witnessing the chaos, confusion, and clutter of last summer's massive evacuation and displacement from New Orleans—
people wandering from town to town with everything they
owned in a shopping bag while carting pets and octogenarians
halfway across the country—my wife and I decided that our life
wasn't complicated enough.

But we don't have any octogenarians in New Orleans to haul
around with us. So we got a dog.

She's a freaky-looking yellow mutt who was abandoned near
Lafayette during Hurricane Rita and was on the kill line in a
temporary euthanasia clinic in Acadiana when a friend of ours
stepped in and rescued her.

She has one blue eye and one brown and her name was
Luna but my kids wanted to call her Biscuit so her full
name is Luna Biscuit, which I like, because that's French for
"Moon Pie."

Sort of.

But this story is not about my dog, not really, but about the
landscape and horizon she has allowed me to revisit here in this
city I love and that she has introduced to my children.

We're river rats now. We hang out down by the water with our
dog. On the banks of the Big River, the Mighty Mississipp, that

brown serpentine of lore, legend, mystery, romance, mythology, literature, song, and history.

And, yes—of cliché, hackneyed antebellum commercialism and volumes of bad poetry.

But still. What a grip it has on the American imagination, character, and identity.

And it's strange how, even though the city's economic livelihood depends on it, both for industry and tourism, it is so often unseen, unnoticed, in our day-to-day living.

It seems very few of us around here actually interact with the river on a regular basis—on any cognizant sensual or emotional level—other than to drive over it, drop kids off to play soccer near it in Audubon Park, or absorb its majesty from inside the hermetic glassed-in cocoon of a tall office building.

But it is us. It is everything, really.

Over twenty-two years and at seven different New Orleans addresses, I have never lived more than eight blocks from the river. But still, there have been periods of time—years at a time—when I have lived in nearly total disconnect from it.

I've had my occasional dalliances. I remember, in my younger and more vulnerable years, heading to the levee with friends after the Uptown bars closed at daybreak, and we would open our trunks, fetch our golf clubs, wait until tankers came by, and then try to drive balls and hit them.

This was stupid, and not just because the tankers are a half mile away (their immensity on that watery chimera makes them seem so close) but also because it is a perfect waste of $2.50 with every swing of the club.

Once, while I was drinking with a prospective girlfriend on the river many years ago, she took off all her clothes and went swimming and that freaked me out beyond words and reason and she wound up contracting some kind of wicked skin rash.

Let's just say we eventually drifted apart.

When I was single and had two dogs—and a hell of a lot more free time—I used to frequent the popular Uptown dog levee, the long patch of open space where Leake Avenue meets Magazine Street, right by the Corps of Engineers headquarters.

It's a busy social scene where legions of dog owners gather daily to let their charges run free and wild off leashes—a practice that is not quite legal but that the authorities have mostly allowed to exist over the years.

Dogs run crazy with play on the levee and tire themselves to their core and the pet owners hang out and talk issues of the day or gossip about regulars who aren't there at the moment.

But most of the dog walkers don't venture down to the back side, to the rugged and brambled shoreline, and it is here that the adventurous go and this is where I take my kids and my dog now, every chance I get.

It's not a pretty place, not by a long shot, at least not in any conventional sense. Some folks who frequent the area—I'm not sure whether it's kids or homeless folks—seem to revel in breaking their empty bottles here.

And the water, of course, is almost always a thick, muddy brown and all manner of random maritime debris floats ashore: empty gallon jugs, plastic rope, hard hats, chunks of Styrofoam, tires, work gloves, etc.

Watching the massive tankers churn up and down the river allows me to teach the kids about the three staples of Louisiana industry: petroleum, agriculture, and pollution.

Nevertheless, we love it here. It is an area largely primitive and ungoverned and probably no proper place for a dog or children, but it is there and we are drawn to it.

My dog runs through the thicket and splashes in the water with other dogs and my kids seek out their secret places and conduct treasure hunts and climb the small trees and I am teaching them, without success, so far, how to skim stones.

There is a rope swing, and when we are feeling particularly daring—when I have my protective daddy guard down—we explore several old rusted barges nearby, run aground and rotting for what looks like decades.

The kids' imaginations run wild in this environment, and they play out a thousand pretend scenarios of danger, rescue, and travel. "You're the wolf," my daughter tells the youngest boy, and the three of them are off and running, ducking and climbing to magical places—castles, pirate ships, and jungles—that I can no longer see at the tired age of forty-five.

Watching my little Huck Finns and Becky What's-her-name at vigorous play on the banks of the river makes me feel so . . . I don't know. Southern?

I have taught my kids which way is upriver and which way is down and what there is in each direction. As spring has progressed, the beach area has shrunk dramatically and I have told them about melting snow in the upper Midwest and I'm pretty sure this is an abstract concept to them other than the fact that the rope swing has, in the past few weeks, become inaccessible due to the swollen tide.

I tell them they can swing on it again at some time in the future, depending on the precipitation on the Great Plains this summer, and, again, we're a little over their heads on this one.

A lot of it is over my head, too. I don't pretend to understand all geographical and hydrologic underpinnings at work on this river and their relationship to our city and my house, but, like everyone else around here, I have learned a hell of a lot about it in the past year.

I do understand that man's mercantile and arrogant determination to control this river over the years—to control nature itself—is a big part of the problem, as the river has been restrained from seeking its own course over the centuries and is confined within unnatural boundaries we have set.

And I know that to reverse this march of progress and engineering would surely spell our doom as a community—if the river left us, as she surely would if left to her own devices, we would be left with nothing.

At the same time, its containment prevents it from building the protective barriers and wetland masses we need to sustain our very physical presence. Here on Earth.

Talk about a conundrum.

I don't know what's on all those barges and container ships and tankers that go by, but I know that our nation's economy would be ruined without it—all that food and fuel and petrochemical whatnot and whatever, all going this way and that.

People from out of town ask me since The Thing: Do you think New Orleans will survive?

I tell them: America has no choice.

Sometimes when I say that, I feel like Luna Biscuit howling at the moon. I am haunted by mortality issues as never before.

Sometimes I look at the river while my kids are off on their nature walks, and I ask it: Will you kill us one day? Is that your plan?

I get no answer I can brook. The river, it just runs by silent and mischievous, in swirls and eddies that I swear sometimes look like the Devil's smile, and seems to whisper to me: That is for you to find out, my friend.

Only time will tell.

Our Very Scary Summer
5/30/06

I was riding in the back of a cab recently through a wasted neighborhood full of damaged and abandoned houses, pick a neighborhood, any neighborhood.

The driver and I were talking about the future, the immediate future. Specifically, we were talking about June 1.

You don't need me to tell you what day that is.

Taking the pulse of the town and its citizenry, the driver told me, "I've never seen or felt anything like this. I'll tell you, brother: I'm scared. I'm real scared."

Now, let me preface here by saying that I have spent much of my adult life in the backs of cabs disagreeing with their drivers on basically every premise we've ever discussed, whether it be sports, politics, or culture.

I have worked hard in life to become the antihack; I am doggedly optimistic, nonreactionary, and deodorized. But I admit, I fell right in line with this guy.

If I had to try to gauge the mood of the city right now, I'd venture that it's not good—no matter whom you wanted to be mayor. There is the unmistakable odor of malaise in the air.

The five classic stages of grief (anger, denial, bargaining, depression, and elections) have taken hold of this city in menacing waves—constant, undulating, nauseating, relentless waves—to the point that there have been sixty, maybe seventy stages of grief since The Thing.

The high points have been easy to define: Mardi Gras, French Quarter Festival, JazzFest. The unequivocal success of these events and the community pride they ignited were the surest signs we've seen that (A) we can indeed be saved and (B) we are indeed worth saving.

Then came the sweep of high school and college commencement exercises across the region these past few weeks, annually joyous rituals to behold, but this year each one a small miracle of survival, endurance, resilience, and determination to plant our flag in this soil, our weak, peaty soil. Our home.

But all that is over now. The high holy holidays are past us and the celebrations are muted and what lies ahead is . . . well, truthfully, not much.

It's going to be hotter than hell around here this summer, and the convention and tourism industries aren't exactly booming. Small businesses and frail marriages are going to take a beating, and many flat-out won't survive.

I know several families who are choosing to get out now—now that school is over and before the houses of cards come tumbling down. They're packing and bailing. And it's not because of Ray Nagin's reelection—as many suggested would be cause to pull the trigger—but simply because there are better jobs and happier people elsewhere.

You know how you can feel around here, walking the afternoon streets in the thick of the summer—you feel like the walking dead, only the dead don't have any worries and aren't waiting for a call back from Entergy, Allstate, and FEMA.

The dead don't need flood insurance to buy a new house, and for that you almost have to envy them.

The malignant vestiges of the Jefferson and Morial machines are stinking this place up worse than old refrigerators. Our levees aren't ready and the government is in gridlock and street crime is picking up a frightening head of steam and it's impossible—no, unreasonable—not to look in the mirror and ask yourself: Is this how I want to live?

What are you going to do the first time Bob Breck comes on the TV screen with that crazed Armageddon look in his eyes and the Super Doppler shows nothing but a big red swirl in the Gulf and—admit it—you still haven't gotten all your vital paperwork in one place as you've been promising yourself, and maybe you've got a generator now and maybe not, but what the hell difference does it make?

What are you going to do now? Other than telling yourself that you're not going to Houston this time no matter what happens—just what is your plan?

Whoever thought there would be a day of dread more wicked than April 15? But here it is, two pages ahead of us on the calendar. The feds could drop $80 billion in our laps right now, but what's that going to do for you in June, July, and August?

That's why the cabdriver is scared. That's why I'm scared.

And I'm just thinking out loud here. I'm not trying to lay out some doomsday scenario or send you running to the local Walgreens to re-up your meds.

I'm just saying: It's going to get tough around here this summer. Real tough and you can count on it, so you better dig in. The real fight is just beginning; prepare to defend yourself against the psychological plunder.

I recommend comfortable clothing, lots of water, and an ax in your attic.

Our ranks are in delicate balance, but there is something profoundly rewarding, uplifting even, in living in a community where the majority of folks are in civic lockstep. For whatever reason—because you're artistic, eccentric, or alcoholic or simply because your mama was born here—you have chosen to remain.

I've never been in the military, but I think I understand now what it's like to engage in battle and know—unhesitatingly and unwaveringly—that the guys beside me and behind me have got my back when the hammer comes down.

Semper Fi and all that. I get it now. And I've got your back, neighbor. You can count on that.

That cabdriver I was talking about? After driving in silence for a while, he said, "You notice all the sunflowers growing all over the place?"

Funny thing is, I have been noticing all the sunflowers popping up in random locations.

"Maybe that's a good omen," he said.

The other day, my kid's grade school principal said to me, "The magnolia trees around here are amazing. They're so broken and battered, yet they're blooming like crazy."

There are your metaphors, if you're looking for some. Flowers. Those time-tested symbols from art and literature of hope, beauty, youth, and rebirth.

Let's hope they're not all false promise. Let's hope they're telling our story. Let's hope we've got what they've got.

Songs in the Key of Strife
6/6/06

All I wanted was a piano. I did not seek a reality check or a meaningful moment or a story to tell in these pages.

I just wanted a lousy piano, that's all.

My editor had said: You need a break, take a day off from Katrina; go do something to forget.

He recommended gardening—digging dirt and pulling weeds— for that's what had cleared his head of the malaise that had stalked him the weekend before.

Indeed, my yard desperately needs attendance. But I'm not as interested in yard work as I used to be, or golf or cooking, and I realize that losing interest in your hobbies is a bad sign, but I reasoned that replacing old hobbies with new hobbies would be a sure way to end-run the case of the mean reds that hunts me.

Fool the mind to save the body.

Several weeks ago, I sat down at a piano at a friend's house with a resolve to learn it and within an hour realized that I had found a new salve.

I was terrible, of course, but the ease with which I coaxed out a few simple melodies delighted me. A natural? Far from it. But, like Stella, I just want to get my groove back. A piano, I thought, would help.

I had no idea where to get one. I wanted something simple and compact. A modest electric model would do.

In the yellow pages I came upon the Bitsie Werlein Piano Company in Metairie.

Surely you know the name. The Werlein family opened their first music store in New Orleans in the mid–nineteenth century, and there has been a store operating under their name—first on Canal Street and then on Veterans Memorial Boulevard—ever since, with only one interruption for the Civil War.

When the family closed the Vets flagship store three years ago, Bitsie started her smaller operation around the corner on Severn Avenue.

I guess I am still sometimes fairly naive about the scope and distance of the flooding that occurred in Jefferson Parish—and in other places, actually. It seems that you can drive and drive and drive in all directions and never find the end of it.

But I didn't realize until I pulled into the parking lot of the somewhat nondescript shopping center that housed Bitsie Werlein's shop on Severn that her pianos had marinated for weeks in Katrina Stew.

The store was vacant and closed.

I stood there looking through a storefront window at empty space. First it took the Civil War. Then, 140 years later, it took a fierce wind coupled with government incompetence to shut Werlein down. Cue Joan Baez: "The night they drove ol' Dixie down . . ."

I tracked Bitsie Werlein down. I wanted to know what had become of her. I apologized for bothering her at home.

"That's all right," she said. "My customers, they find me. Even when I was evacuated, they managed to find me. You know, when most of my customers leave my store," she added, apropos of nothing, "they usually kiss me good-bye. That's the way the piano business is."

She said her longtime staff is scattered to the wind but she will open—alone—sometime, some place, down the road.

"We were like family, but things aren't the same anymore,"

she said. "It's been a long haul, but I am finding my way anew. I will be re-established."

When? Who knows? Where? Who knows? Like everything else around here, it's a work in progress.

I hung up the phone. Stared into windows. I came for a piano and instead got a sad song. So I went back to the phone book, where I found the Hall Piano Company on David Drive.

The Hall Piano Company was not affected by the wind or the water. I just wanted to get inside the air-conditioned showroom and bend my head over some keyboards and forget, to lose myself into music and otherness.

I was in the digital piano studio in the back when another customer pointed out to the salesman, "That's the one! It was just like that. That's the one she used to have."

Good God, it's following me, I thought.

I looked at the customer, the man. He wore the vacant and pained expression of the tribe we all belong to—the Elders of Loss. This guy was here, in a piano store, trying to put back the pieces of his family's life, and one of those pieces was a piano.

And then I realized, or wondered, actually: How many pianos? How many were destroyed? Thousands upon thousands, I suppose.

Like everything else.

Watching the dynamic of the Hall Piano Company, I suddenly realized you can drive around enough to get away from the brown waterline but you can't escape the storm no matter where you go. Welcome to the Hotel California.

Here, inside this pristine showroom, a bunch of guys in shirts and ties who simply used to sell pianos now have a new job description: grief counselors.

"Everyone who walks in here has the same story, but it's a different story—if you know what I mean," sales manager John Wright told me. "I mean, there's always a twist to it."

It starts with the piano, of course. It was the grandmother's, back in that old house she had in Gentilly, and then she moved to Chalmette, gosh, back in the '60s, and then she died, and, well . . . it was in our house in Lakeview when, you know . . . when it all happened . . .

Then come the stories of everything that happened around that piano for the past fifty years, and wrapped inside the small story of a piano are the larger stories of lost homes and scattered families and dreams torn down and everything just . . . sorrow.

Watching folks buy pianos at Hall's, you'd think they were selecting a casket in a funeral home, so filled with grief and remembrance they are.

"Pianos are like members of the family," Wright says. "They've been part of the family forever, a centerpiece of their lives. Even if it just sits over in the corner against the wall, it's always been there, usually longer than any other piece of furniture in the house."

So the guys at Hall Piano listen to the stories, as all of us—postmen, pharmacists, waitresses, barbers, UPS guys, meter readers, coffee shop clerks, real estate agents, reporters—listen to the stories. That's all of our jobs now, because all anyone really wants—all anyone really needs around here—is to have someone listen to their stories.

The same story, but different.

"People really get attached to their pianos," Wright says. "I'm willing to guess that when someone walks into Best Buy to replace the fifty-four-inch plasma TV they lost in the flood, they don't pull out pictures of their old TV to show to the salesman. We get that all the time."

Me, I just wanted a piano. And so I got it and, obviously, much, much more. It's a Yamaha P-140. It's nice. Nothing fancy.

At night, I stare at the keys, try to look inside the machine, to see if I can find a song, a melody, even just a slight phrasing that's not about all this. I sit at my new piano and try to remember how to tell a story about something else.

And nothing comes. Not a single note.

The End of the Line
6/25/06

Every day is a matter of taking stock. Ten months after The Thing, you still look around to see what is here and what is not here anymore.

Every day, it seems, you can find something missing. While following the ongoing financial drama of the New Orleans transit system, I discovered that the city's most (in)famous bus line is defunct.

The bus named Desire is no more. It ran its last route on Sunday, August 28. When the Regional Transit Authority rolled back to life last winter, the Desire route was not among the resuscitated lines.

With last week's announcement that the Feds will pick up the tab for limited bus service until November, it's unlikely Desire will roll anytime soon, if ever again.

And so goes a small and curious piece of the city's history.

The New Orleans Railway & Light Company debuted the streetcar named Desire in 1920. The Tennessee Williams play *A Streetcar Named Desire* opened on Broadway on December 3, 1947. The real streetcar ran its last route in New Orleans almost six months later, on May 30, 1948.

The bus that replaced it more or less followed the same route, from the vast 9th Ward residential sprawl to the Quarter via Decatur Street. Legions of restaurant and hotel workers relied on it for decades.

A few years ago, Desire's route was shifted and its traditional route through the Bywater, Marigny, and French Quarter was streamlined into a straight shot from the 9th Ward to Canal Street via Claiborne Avenue.

I decided to retrace the route of the final bus named Desire this week by foot and bicycle. I don't really know what I was looking for. Maybe a glimpse of history, or maybe just to see what's out there in the city now that everything is different.

Maybe I was just taking stock.

The bus named Desire's official departure point was the corner of Elk Place and Canal, the nexus for a huge portion of the RTA fleet; buses headed Uptown, to the East, to Kenner, and to the West Bank all stop here.

There's a statue on the neutral ground at this spot where all the buses converge. It was made by the New Orleans sculptor Enrique Alferez in 1943. It's a tribute to the women of war, called *Molly Marine,* and she is one tough broad.

But no one ever seems to notice her. She's just so much landscape, like the untended shrubbery and the busted marquee of the Downtown Joy Theatre or all the pay phones on the wall that nobody uses anymore. Invisible.

The bus named Desire would head west on Elk, then right on Tulane Avenue to Claiborne. It passed under the shadow of Charity Hospital, another institution gone with the wind and water.

The first thing you notice at the corner of Tulane and Claiborne are the waterlines on the walls. On Desire's outgoing route, the water was thigh high. Across the street—a stretch of dead zone under the interstate—it's at shoulder level.

The second thing that strikes you, heading down Claiborne past Canal and into the desolate stretch between the auto pound and the back of the old cemeteries, is the litter.

Everywhere. Every five feet, within every rotation of the bicycle wheel, within every step.

It's not storm debris. It's litter. Trash. A discarded hardpack of Kool menthols, an empty bottle of Bacardi, a bag of Doritos, a Styrofoam takeout container, napkins, envelopes, on and on and everywhere, the ubiquitous tumbleweed of downtown New Orleans.

You wonder: How can people contentedly settle into a life surrounded by their own detritus? It's a sociopathy I have never understood.

It's June and it's hot and most of the activity on the streets, sidewalks, yards, and rooftops is repair crews, fixing what Katrina hath destroyed. The sounds of jackhammers and generators and that ubiquitous pneumatic *tat-tat-tat* of roofing nail guns; this is the music of the summer of 2006, the sound of a city putting itself back together.

Down Claiborne, I pass a couple of indie hip-hop record company offices and hair extension salons and Club Fabulous and Ernie K-Doe's Mother-in-Law Lounge, where six freshly glazed cast-iron bathtubs full of newly planted flowers line the sidewalk.

I pass two old men sitting on their stoops, one white, one black. Their imperceptible nods—the slightest tilt of the jaw—are the only signs that they are alive.

Rounding the bend on Claiborne at St. Bernard Avenue, I pass the old classic rounded facade of the Circle Food Store and I get the first—and strongest—of the powerful whiffs of decay that will assault my olfactory sense on this journey.

The Circle Food Store, it smells like last October, and if you were here you know what that means and if you weren't, be thankful you don't.

The old route of the bus named Desire went past the newly opened Family Dollar Store at Claiborne and Elysian Fields and it is positively bustling, a beacon of commerce here at the entry point to ruin.

Across Elysian Fields, then Franklin, the road begins its climb up the overpass that shadows the railroad tracks below. Off to the right, in the train yard below, there are two sheet-metal

Mardi Gras dens all blown apart by the storm and you can see from here the hallucinatory papier-mâché smiles of the jesters and mythical characters of several wrecked floats.

The Easter Bunny and Little Red Riding Hood—or is it Dorothy from *The Wizard of Oz?* it's hard to tell from here—have fallen out of the front of the float dens and tilt toward the train tracks, greeting the conductors upon their arrival to New Orleans.

From atop the overpass, you can see back over the city skyline, downtown. From here, it looks just like a regular American City.

As the Claiborne overpass descends into the 9th Ward, there at the bottom of the ramp, on the right, is the unassuming brick facade of the New Light Baptist Church. As I pass by, the Reverend Gregory Davis is out in the churchyard spraying citrus wood cleaner on a 1954 Hammond C-2 organ. It's a classic model, the staple of Southern Gospel church music.

With Davis is David Tarantolo, who stands next to a white van marked THE ORGAN DOCTOR. Together, they are bringing the organ, which was halfway submerged for three weeks, back to life.

"The electrical components work; they missed the water by just a few inches," Davis says, his eyes shaded by a ridiculously oversized sombrero that his wife picked up once at a Chevys Fresh Mex restaurant but that does the job it's supposed to do. "We're working mostly on appearances now."

Davis's flock is largely scattered, from Houston to Atlanta and everywhere in between. He figures about a third are here in town but the church has had no services yet, so he can't be sure. The church's drum set, sheet music, and Bibles are stacked all around him in the yard and he works every day, getting it fixed, getting it ready.

"You know, when I first came back here [in November], it seemed that there was no hope," he said, and that's a serious problem for a man who makes his living dispensing hope.

"But looking at it through the eyes of faith, I see that there is progress. Just to see a red light function, I rejoice. A gas station opens, a grocery store opens—I rejoice. I rejoice at the small things. They give us hope."

On the second Sunday in July, Davis is going to send a brass band into the neighborhood to gather the people and lead them back to the church. Then he will conduct the New Light's first service since August.

Now there's cause to rejoice. For hope. For new light, indeed.

Tarantolo—the Organ Doctor—mostly smiles and says very little. Finally, I say to him, "Organ Doctor? You must hear every stupid joke in the world."

"I've heard some good ones," he tells me. Then he pauses. "But not in the presence of a minister, please."

When you're on a bike, you notice all the other people on bikes. At the corner of Robertson and Desire, where the bus used to take a left into the flatlands of the Upper 9th, I ask a fellow rider where the closest place is to get a cold drink.

I have a feeling—which would prove to be true—that once I head toward the lake, there will be no open businesses.

He sends me on a detour down to St. Claude, and then he rides up alongside me, asks if I'm from the neighborhood. I tell him no and ask the same of him.

"I'm from the Lower 9," he tells me, "but I'm staying by here since I got back to town. I was only one block from where they blew up the levee, and if it wasn't for a Bobcat tire, I wouldn't be talking to you right now.

"I can't swim—couldn't swim from me to you right now to save my life. I was trapped in an alley, and a Bobcat tire floated up and I grabbed it and floated out and then saved two other people with it. We got to a rooftop and then got out."

Everybody here has a story. New Orleans was always a place where people talked too much even if they had nothing to say.

Now everyone's got something to say.

As we part, the man asks me, "Got fifty cents?" I reach in my pocket, find seventy-five, and give it to him.

Back on the bus route, riding up Desire, more wasteland. You know the drill: Piles of household debris. The occasional FEMA trailer. All the houses bearing the inscription of our loss, the Xs and Os, like morbid football plays, painted on the weatherboards and doors.

It's third and long. Very long.

At the improbably named Bunny Friend Playground, two federally contracted security officers—one from California, one from North Carolina—sit in lawn chairs under a makeshift shade cover.

They tell me the job is pretty easy. The California guy tells me, "We heard this neighborhood used to be pretty bad, but it's all good now. All the trouble is Uptown these days."

Bunny Friend, like so many other playgrounds in the city, is paved over with stones. It doesn't exactly exude neighborhood warmth, no family-friendly vibe from all these pristine trailers crammed together like cell blocks.

Not much of a place to raise kids, but it is what it is. There's a brand-new playground set in the corner of the lot. That's a start, I guess.

At the corner of Desire and North Miro, Georgiana Mitchell sits on her stoop finishing off a cheeseburger and a Coke. Her nephew is gutting her house.

"It used to stop right here in front of my house," she says of the bus named Desire. She rode it for thirty-one years, as the dining room manager of Le Pavillon Hotel and also as a salad maker at Antoine's restaurant.

She's retired now. Trying to get back in, get back home. Thieves recently made off with what little survived the flood.

"My crystal, my mama's china," she says. "They took it off the porch." She pauses. "We thought we had lost everything anyway—before we found it—so I guess it doesn't matter."

She gives me a look that says: It matters.

Her family, all of whom lived within three blocks of this corner, have spread as far as Hammond, Houston, and Atlanta. They're not coming back. But she wants to.

"I just love New Orleans," she says. "It gets into your blood. I'm seventy years old, and I thought at this point in my life I'd just be out here in the yard fooling with my sunflowers and rosebushes and going to the Wal-Mart. That's what I was going to do."

And now, this.

"Look at my grass. I can't believe there's no Saint Aug at all! Let me tell you: when you come by here someday and see all the pretty grass and all the pretty flowers, you will know I am back."

Further up Desire, there's a boat on the side of the road, right where the flood deposited it. It's a Scottie Craft, about fifteen feet long. It's called *Zombie*.

Perfect.

A shirtless, heavily tattooed guy with a Billy Idol haircut, rocker shades, and pierced nipples is gutting a house. He's the only white guy on the block—in the whole neighborhood, for that matter.

His name is Eli. He's a general maintenance man at the tony Bombay Club in the Quarter, and he tells me, "I'm the only one around here who's not related by blood or marriage. But it's a good place. Historically, it's not a bad neighborhood. It's a poor neighborhood, and crime tends to gather in poor neighborhoods. But it's pretty quiet now. That's for sure."

He cooks on a wood fire in the front yard and had been sleeping in a tent there until the woman across the street got power and now he runs an orange extension cord across the street to power a fan so he can sleep.

"I went from having $200,000 worth of material possessions to what was in two duffel bags," he tells me. "I had my pity party, but you dust off and say, all right, it's time to rebuild. The family that lives on this block, they're all coming back. You can see: it's the only clean block around here. We're going to turn this little block into a Garden of Eden in the middle of Hell."

It does get hellish up the block, toward where the big Desire housing development used to cast a gloom over the whole area until it was torn down. Now it's all empty fields and empty hair salons and juke joints and grocery stores; that smell.

The rats have become legend around here. Someone tells me the firemen come by and shoot the rats with paint guns, but I don't know if I believe that.

Here at Desire and Florida, the bus used to head down to Mazant Street and start its loop back downtown.

At Mazant and North Galvez, a stunning spectacle breaks the pale and dusty horizon. A man has moved himself and what few belongings he has left onto an abandoned corner lot, and, in the process, he has become a bona fide Southern Gothic art installation.

He has positioned broken cars, trucks, and barrels around himself as a perimeter. Yard umbrellas and tarps make his shade, and flags and mirrors and stuffed animals and plastic flowers and just plain stuff, lots of random stuff, are scattered throughout, making for a strange oasis.

It's a junkyard, but an artful junkyard.

The man says, "I am Willie Gordon, sixty-four years old, 1425 Egania Street." He says this as though he says it a lot, and from the Superdome to Houston to a series of Texas hospitals to FEMA to the Red Cross and everybody else, he has.

He says to me: "That's *Egania*. Do you know how to spell that?"

I tell him I do. He pauses. Says, "You know, I lived there for eighteen years and just learned how to spell it six months ago."

He's a truck driver by trade, an eccentric by birth, and, from the look of all the empty bottles on the premises, a drinker.

"I'm the Special Man!" he tells me.

Egania is in the Lower 9th. His house is still there, but he says he's afraid to go back.

"The water . . . ," he begins, and he tells an hourlong story about the water rising around his car and his long walk through it and the surgeries for the infections he got from it and the cabdriver in Houston who scammed him of his money, and the story, which began as a mirthful exposition, takes him from playful wisecracker to the depths of human sorrow and he begins to sob.

It's hot outside. Hot as hell. I don't know what to say to this guy. "I'm shook up," he says. "I'm scared. I'm sixty-four years old, and I am alone. What am I going to do?"

He has big gold earrings like a genie would wear. He was wearing boxers when I arrived, but he has put his pants on now.

A guy in a muscle T-shirt rides up on one of those too-small bicycles that gang-banger types favor and he starts to sing: "Dun-dun, DAH-dah! Dun-dun, DAH-dah-dah-dah-dah."

It's the theme from *Sanford and Son.* The guy on the bike asks, "What's up, Fred?" and Willie Gordon gives a good-natured howl in response. The guy looks at me and asks, "Where y'at, Lamont?" Then he rides away, his laughter echoing in the canyon of broken houses.

A man across the street, on a cell phone, yells into it, "What do you want from me?"

Willie Gordon looks at me and says, "Women."

The bus used to roll down Mazant, which matches Desire in its presentation: the good, the bad, and the ugly. The route turns right on Claiborne to head back downtown, and along this stretch, volunteers from Common Ground are gutting houses.

On the street, folks around here tell you they trust white people more than they used to because of all the help from Common Ground and groups like it. It's kind of weird, but almost all the volunteers you see working in the 9th Ward—upper and lower—are white.

Young and white, from out of town, dressed in space suits, and doused in patchouli, gutting out the ruins of a city they never knew.

The route runs past the recently refurbished Stewart's Diner, where the mayor, the governor, and the president stopped for lunch one day in March. Bush had red beans and rice with potato salad, smoked sausage, veggie.

On the menu, it's called the President's Special now. Served five days a week. $8.50.

I ride my bike, my big red bike, down Claiborne and under the interstate where a million cars are waiting to be carted off. The tires are missing off a lot of them. Those are just about the only salvageable parts on the waterlogged auto farm, and in a town where everyone gets a flat tire once a month, they are no negligible commodity, those tires.

I ride by the newly opened Cajun Fast Food To Go, operated by Asians and patronized by African Americans, and isn't that a New Orleans story?

Back at the corner of Elk and Canal, the bus named Desire would have finished its run. But it doesn't run anymore, so I look at the buses that are here, loading and unloading passengers, and I see on the marquee scroll on the front of a bus, in those letters made from green dots of light: SULLEN.

This bus goes to Algiers. To Sullen Place, to be exact. And I am astounded.

The bus named Sullen instead of Desire, and what is there to say?

Taking stock of things, that's pretty damn funny.

We Raze, and Raise, and Keep Pushing Forward
8/29/06

I drove down Louisville Street in Lakeview the other evening, one of the Avenues of Despair that I have incorporated into my regular rounds of the city as I seek out the progress of our recovery.

I have several friends who lived here. One of them had not mucked out or gutted his house since it soaked in its own sewage last fall and, rather than take offense at the disaster tourism phenomenon that abounds in our region, he welcomed visitors—friends and strangers alike—to enter his home and experience the full sensory shock of what happened here.

To walk into this foul and infected house and gaze upon the domestic carnage was, in many ways, a more effective storytelling device than driving past miles and miles of wretched and abandoned exteriors. The eyes burn, the breath shortens, and the weight of lost history, memory, and family is crushing.

"Imagine if you came home to this," I used to tell my visitors.

This week, my friend James had that house—where he had lived for fourteen years and raised two sons—torn down. He left work one morning to witness the act with his wife. He bought sodas and ice cream from a passing truck for the work crew, went to Subway for lunch, and then went back to work.

Three blocks down Louisville, I drove past my friend A.J.'s house. His block was nearly pristine, having been recently mucked, weeded, and scrubbed out by one of the legions of young-volunteer groups who have come from elsewhere to aid our city in its distress.

Across the street from his house, a woman and her daughter were sweeping the sidewalk. They have already moved back in. She asked me for A.J.'s phone number and called him right then—he's in Covington now—to invite him to a neighborhood get-together, a gathering of souls and survivors to commemorate just being alive.

Next to A.J.'s house, I was taken aback by the spectacle of a house in transformation; it had been raised that afternoon on giant piers, looming above the shoulders of a profoundly cheerful woman who stood in her yard, planted her hands on her hips, regarded me, and asked, "Whaddya think?"

What do I think? I think she's crazy. Bonkers. Stark raving mad. That's what I think.

But what I wanted to tell her was that I loved her. I wanted to hug her. And what I said was "Looks great!" and I continued on my journey, strangely comforted by what I have come to consider the nearly delusional optimism of our populace. Life gives you lemons? Make icebox pie.

The Corps of Engineers gives you eight feet of water? Raise your house eight feet. Move on. Move up.

Not all stories around here are so cheery, so full of equanimity and can-do. Far from it.

One of my favorite local stores, Utopia, a funky Magazine Street boutique, closed a week ago because of lack of business. In one of the mayor's ever-increasing public gaffes—his pronouncements on race, progress, and politics have gone from comic to weird to just plain alienating—he recently dismissed the concerns of business owners who say the economic and political climates are driving them away from the city. He said he'd send a postcard to those that leave.

Mr. Mayor, Utopia's forwarding address is a shopping mall in Houston.

And so it goes.

This isn't Sudan. It's not Lebanon. There are greater hardships all across this planet than living in New Orleans. But by American standards, by the standards of those families who lived side by side in the same voting precincts for the past sixty years in Chalmette, Gentilly, and the Lower 9th, by the standards of those who worked their asses off to get a nice house, a nice car, and a picket fence in Old Metairie, well . . . it pretty much sucks here.

But we move on, move up, our faith in government washed out to sea with all that floodwater and our hopes for recovery rooted in our reliance on one another and the triumph of the human spirit. They are our best and only chance.

Folks from other places must think we're out of our minds when they see pictures of the ruination and hear about all the stress and depression and hear the crazy stuff that comes out of our mayor's mouth, and maybe they're right.

It will be decades before we sort through our post-Katrina housing landscape while psychiatric journals write about our post-Katrina emotional landscape.

Most of us have visited other places this past year, where sidewalks are clean and parks and playgrounds are pristine and schools are progressive and city government is efficient, but still, this is where we are.

We stay. We raise our houses and we raze our houses and we get up and go to work—the lucky ones—because this is home and no word has a stronger allegiance in the English language.

I'm not going to try to lay down in words the lure of this place. Every great writer in the land, from Faulkner to Twain to Rice to Ford, has tried to do it and fallen short. It is impossible to capture the essence, tolerance, and spirit of south Louisiana in words and to try is to roll down a road of clichés, bouncing over beignets and beads and brass bands and it just is what it is.

It is home.

I have a friend permanently evacuated to Chicago who confirms my belief that, as bad as it is here, it's better than being somewhere else. To be engaged in some small way in the revival of one of the great cities of the world is to live a meaningful existence by default.

You can't sleepwalk here; you will fall into a pothole.

My Chicago friend told me over a crawfish boil this spring that the only person he has in the world to talk to about all this—this Thing—is his third-grade daughter.

At night they talk. No one else understands the thousand-yard stare and the apoplectic frustration of not being here to be a part of this. It's that song: "Do you know what it means . . . ?"

Yes, we do.

As Ernesto wobbled its precarious path over the weekend, my wife and I secured our papers, discussed our options, made our evacuation plans.

"Is this how we're going to live?" she asked me. I don't think I answered her directly but instead offered only a shrug—not of disregard or defiance or even determination, but a simple motion of the head to look around the room, our house, our home, and absorb what we've got here.

It's not another day in Paradise, not by any means. And I am tired of the trash and the theft and the blame, just like everybody else.

But there's something about being here that makes you feel alive. I mean, if offered a chance to be one of those guys who raised the flag on Iwo Jima, you'd take it, wouldn't you?

That's kind of what this is. A shot at glory.

There are tough hours, tough days, tough weeks at a time, but underneath all our sorrow is the power of community and the common good.

I remember sitting on my front stoop near the end of the first week of September last year when a disheveled and seemingly disoriented guy pulled up in front of me in his pickup truck. He had Michigan plates and was pulling a boat behind him.

"Which way?" he shouted to me. "Who's in charge here?" he said.

I had to laugh at that part. No one's in charge, I told him. But if he wanted to put that boat to good use, I said, "Keep going straight and you'll hit the water."

He nodded. And then he started crying. "I'm sorry I took so long, man," he told me. "I got here as fast as I could." And he drove off.

I saw him two days later on Canal Street, looking fresh and invigorated. He had been rescuing people and pets ever since I'd seen him.

From time to time, I talk to a retired New York City fireman named Jim Kearney on the phone. He has made several trips here and to the Mississippi coast to give free massage therapy to first responders, rescue workers, and volunteer house gutters.

He says that every time he goes back to New York, he flounders with a sense of loss of purpose and direction. He says his friends who have volunteered to work here feel the same way.

"They go through their own grieving hell when they leave New Orleans," he said to me. "It's like leaving the *Titanic* for a safe distant shore—and leaving all the people behind. There is such a dissonance between what's going on down there and everywhere else in America. Everyone in New Orleans is going around with a spike stuck in their heads, and they don't know how to get it out."

He paused and said, "You all are amazing people to be doing what you're doing."

And he's right. We are.

Tens of thousands of other volunteers like him have discovered this, too. They have come by the bus and plane load to help us help ourselves and the ship is far from righted, but, one year into this, we're trudging forward.

Moving on, moving up.

It's impossible to thank all these people who have come from faraway places. It's impossible even to know who they are anymore, so many have come and gone and they come still and again.

There is only one way to properly express our gratitude to the masses, to show them that what they have done is not wasted time and effort. To show them that we are worth it.

And that is by succeeding.

Echoes of Katrina
in the Country
8/8/06

I went to the Mississippi woods for the weekend and did what country folks do on a Saturday afternoon: went to a baby shower that was capped off with riding lawn mower races.

Baby shower/riding lawn mower race. Like shrimp and gravy, bathtubs and Virgin Marys, and the colors purple, green, and gold—there's just some things that nature meant to go together.

This was up near Picayune, at my in-laws' neighbors' house. The only vehicle with which I could enter the event was my father-in-law's golf cart. It was faster than the lawn mowers, but it didn't rev like they did and I felt so . . . city.

Like being on a Vespa in a convoy of Harleys. Except for the "faster" part. I was the only male over fourteen who didn't have a tattoo.

At one point I looked up and saw my seven-year-old daughter driving an off-road four-wheeler and I don't even know how to drive a four-wheeler myself and you turn your head for one minute in the country and somebody teaches your kid something.

It's like that.

After the completion of three lawn mower races, one of the

riders opined, "You know you're a redneck when . . .," and he didn't finish the phrase because we all knew it and it truly was a moment, families gathered together, dogs barking, fish frying, barefoot kids running all over the place, the sun setting on Saturday-afternoon America.

But it's not so country as it used to be in and around Picayune these days, in and around the entire north shore and Louisiana/Mississippi border region, actually, and on that long stretch between New Orleans and Baton Rouge.

As the southern Louisiana and Mississippi coastlines disappear—literally—residents' fear rises proportionally and only a thrill seeker would want to live near the coast now.

People, people, everywhere inland now. And you can see them all so easily because it seems that half the trees in Dixie were swept away in the wind and twisters of a year ago.

I was with my kids and my nephew tooling around the country roads in Picayune and we stopped at a cul-de-sac by a pond where we used to hang out and do nothing and all the boys—three kids and me—got out to whiz at the end of the road, a place we have whizzed many times before in privacy.

I guess I hadn't noticed that a house had been built right there by the pond—it happens that fast—and the view out of that home's living room window at that moment was the backsides of a bunch of boys relieving themselves on the side of the road and I guess you've got to be mindful when new people start moving in, when a place starts to get crowded and everything changes and the comforts of privacy—this land is my land—begin to disappear.

When I started going to Picayune twelve years ago, my in-laws lived in near isolation in the woods. They began selling off pastureland to build houses about two years ago.

They got in on the pre-Katrina building boom of Hancock and Pearl River counties, favored destinations for folks from St. Bernard and St. Tammany parishes who found their neighborhoods too crowded, too city, for their tastes anymore.

Since Katrina, the market has soared, and now there are homes going up all over what used to be woods and meadows.

Land is being cleared at an astonishing pace as the area becomes home for folks who were pushed out of or gave up on
the New Orleans area but who want to stay close to the mother
ship nonetheless—it's only an hour away—on land that won't
flood.

With the influx of New Orleanians comes change, of course.
The top story on page one of this past Sunday's *Picayune Item*
newspaper ("Serving Pearl River County Since 1904") began
thus: "Petitions have been circulating in Pearl River County to
allow the sale of liquor in Pearl River County, and to allow the
sale of beer and light wine county wide, but religious organizations are rallying in an effort to defeat the petitions."

Troubled times, they have come. To your hometown.

It's an economic issue, a county revenue issue, a restaurant
issue, and, of course, a lifestyle issue. The newspaper speculates
that the possible vote on the November ballot could swing on
how many "additional people in the county" register to vote in
time.

"Additional people." That's us. The new kids on the block, all
across America. It's a better term than "evacuees," which sounds
so temporary and fraught with emergency.

And I guess the additional people could accurately be figured
to constitute the swing vote because, of all the people I know
who have moved away in recent years—and I know many, both
before and since Katrina—they have cited many reasons for leaving New Orleans (crime, education, politics, opportunity), but
not one of them ever told me it was to get away from all that
beer and wine.

It's funny, but out there in the Great Elsewhere that is America, New Orleans seems to get most or all of the focus of the national media. As if this whole thing happened only in a place
called the Lower 9th Ward. As the memory and images and
impact of Katrina fade in the national consciousness, so, too, it
seems, does the geographical and emotional scope of its damages, not to mention Rita's. From the Texas border to Mobile Bay,
a huge swath of America took a grenade. And everything changed
everywhere.

And we muddle through the changes, geographical, cultural, political.

In Mississippi, I suppose it's only a matter of time before someone squawks about that infamous sign at the entrance to the town on Memorial Boulevard right off the interstate, the one that proclaims, "Jesus is Lord over Picayune."

It looks like one of those green, government-issue signs, not a private billboard bought by a church, and that's going to bug someone, eventually.

The times, they are a-changin'. Or maybe not. Will there be rush hour in Picayune one day? A Daiquiri's drive-through?

Jesus drank wine, we all know that part. Maybe everything comes full circle, becomes part of the whole. Everyone's in this together, right?

So saddle up the lawn mowers and grab a bottle of easy peace—purchased in Louisiana, of course, for now—and forget about your cares. Gather near your loved ones and let the party start. Let the good times roll. Let the music play. Let the wild things run.

It's Saturday afternoon in America.

The Purple Upside-Down Car

Second Line, Same Verse

3/21/06

It has always been the greatest allure of this city that you could travel a very short distance and completely disappear into somebody else's life and culture and, generally, that somebody else would welcome you or—at the very least—tolerate your presence.

Back in the late '80s and mid '90s, I was all over the map. My Saturday nights would be spread from the rough-and-tumble biker joints of Fourth Street in Marrero to the Vietnamese billiards halls in the East to the Latin dance clubs in Kenner to evangelical tent revivals in Bridge City to the Cajun roadhouse scene down in Crown Point.

I've always had a fascination with hanging out in places with large crowds of people who are nothing like me. A culture vulture? Yeah, I suppose.

I remember an amazing and nearly mystical dance hall in the shape of a green pagoda off Canal Street in what amounted to the city's teacup version of Chinatown—now long gone—where Asian Madonna wannabes imported from L.A. used to seduce massive, sweaty crowds.

I remember Dorothy's Medallion on Orleans Avenue, watching Walter "Wolfman" Washington back up Johnny Adams while he warbled love songs that could change the world.

This, I used to think. I like this.

When I first stumbled onto the second-line scene down in the Treme and Central City, my life was energized. I was hooked from the moment I fell into my first snaking street parade of horn players and revelers bumping and grinding through neighborhoods I had never seen before—or at least had seen only through my car windows.

This was about twelve years ago, right after I met the woman who would become my wife. In fact, much of our early courtship took place on the parade grounds of this city. Kelly and I would bounce along the streets to the blockbuster vibes of the city's brass lions on Sunday afternoons and duck into dark corner bars to check out the score of the Saints game and we'd nod and shuffle in the way that white people who are dressed all wrong do when they're hanging out with a bunch of black folks who are truly tripping the light fantastic.

We danced, we got drunk, and we were long, long gone into the unbearable lightness of being in New Orleans. We became part of the scene, made friends, shed our self-consciousness, and just blended in.

Occasionally, there would be a menacing character or two—or more, quite frankly—lurking around the edges of these celebrations, particularly at the end of the parades, when massive street parties would form, streets would clog, and evening would come.

But we never felt personally threatened. Ever. We'd introduce friends to the scene, telling them: You gotta check this out. But mostly, we realized that big chunks of our social circle had no particular interest in joining this ritual of ours.

Then one afternoon, about ten years ago, Kelly and I broke a run of many, many consecutive weeks of second-lining to do something else on a Sunday afternoon; I don't know what, but it must have been important for us to skip out on our favorite pastime.

That afternoon, in August 1995, the second line we missed ended in gunfire, lots of gunfire, two dead and six wounded on St. Bernard Avenue. We didn't go the next Sunday, either. Nor the next. Somewhere in there, there was another shooting at a parade.

At this point, we felt personally threatened. As weeks and months passed—or am I embellishing this out of frustration?—it seems the Monday-morning paper would too often carry a story about a shooting or a stabbing on or very near a second-line route the day before.

These clippings litter the files of *The Times-Picayune*, leaving a bad smell.

We had kids now, Kelly and I. A part of this city's culture that I desperately wanted them to know and understand and embrace was out of our reach. It was not an option. I wasn't going to lead my kids into danger simply because Daddy thinks they need to be dialed into the fundamental currents of my city.

With the exception of a few high-profile events—Ernie K-Doe's funeral, the Mardi Gras Indians on Fat Tuesday, or Super Sunday—the second-line scene was dead to me.

Then, earlier this year, word got out about the big homecoming second line in the city and it was said that thousands of folks were coming from exile in Texas and Mississippi and that the Social Aid and Pleasure Clubs were going to replant their flag in this city and take back their streets and bring back what is among the most vital and enduring traditions of New Orleans.

I told my wife that Sunday afternoon: Things are different now. The city is different.

Let's take the kids.

And we did. We didn't catch as much of the parade as I would have liked; we caught up with it on the very busy and inhospitable Rampart Street, where car traffic was all backed up, instead of a cozy side street where the walkers rule.

But we saw it. My kids saw it. I have no idea if it registered with them, but I didn't care because now I knew: We can do this again. We can go back to the second lines and our kids can understand this city in ways others don't and—let's cut to the chase here—I can dance in the streets again and not give a damn how stupid I look.

There is a tangible freedom in dancing in the street. I ask you:

What better public expression of joy exists? Where else in the world do horn players and drummers just wake up in the morning, strap on their instruments, and start wandering around making an unholy racket and then hundreds, thousands of dancing lemmings fall in and follow them to the sea?

Well, you know how that second line ended. Gunfire. Blood. Sirens. A thousand people there and no witnesses to the crime, police would later report.

It was a day of profound disgrace for this city and one that probably would have had greater impact and provoked very heated and very uncomfortable public discourse had not our mayor given a famous speech the next day that completely distracted the citizenry from the violence at hand.

We focused on the Chocolate City instead of the Killing Fields.

No matter. My wife and I decided not to go back to the second-line parades again. It's not for us, I thought. There is such a disconnect between my value system and the culture of guns that permeates our streets that I don't even have the words to make sense of it.

My kids don't know what happened at the end of that parade, and I'm not going to tell them. We do other things on Sunday afternoons because the odds of their getting capped at the zoo are pretty slim.

And then there was this weekend. Hundreds of folks in from Texas and Mississippi, trying to regain their footing and traction here, trying to get back into the New Orleans life cycle, and here comes a gang-banger bent on revenge and willing to put his entire community at risk to prove he is a man worthy of respect.

Nobody of reason wants this. Black, white, no one. And in the same news cycle a guy walking in the Frenchmen Street music district takes a bullet in the chest—after surrendering his wallet to a thug.

So here we are. Back where we were before, when locals and visitors alike cowered in fear of the predatory generation we have loosed unto our community.

You can't care about this city and then read about this crap and shrug and say either (A) It's not my problem or (B) That's just the way it is.

That's not just the way it is. It is perversion and error.

And it *is* your problem. Our problem.

Our city lies in such delicate balance that the return of indiscriminate killing ranks right up there with another hurricane as a compelling reason to pack your bags and get the hell out of town while you're still alive.

The psychic toll of Sunday's police blotter is immeasurable. And it is fodder for the New Orleans haters, the tolerance fighters, and the racial jihadists—of both colors—who think that murder is what this city is about.

I reject it.

It's not us.

Don't Mess with Mrs. Rose
2/21/06

As I loaded my two sons in the car to head off to the pet store Sunday afternoon, I saw a guy walking on the sidewalk across the street.

He wore all the trappings of generic urbania: oversized jacket, big baggy pants, all in black. He was traveling alone, with very busy eyes, taking in the details between houses on my street.

Before Katrina, I was a fairly attuned city dweller; I've generally had a good nose for trouble. So I was dialed in on this guy.

As I pulled away from the curb, I thought about making the block, doubling back just to make sure everything was copacetic. That's what I would have done in the past; I've done it many times.

But I have developed this profoundly naive notion that if you are in this city right now, living in this mess, you are one of us. I have this delusional optimism that we're all in this together.

Of course, this doesn't make sense, because not one day goes by that I don't hear from people in Lakeview, Fontainebleau, Gentilly, and the East who tell me that their houses are getting looted. Repeatedly. Still.

But I didn't make the block. I told myself this cat just happens to favor thug fashion regardless of how people may react to him and treat him as a result, and that's his business, not mine.

I guess I'd sound like a cranky old fart if I suggested he dress like—I don't know—me?

So it turns out that, two minutes after I pulled away, my wife saw my bicycle flash by our living room window. She ran to the front door to find this guy mounted and ready to roll.

The purpose of this theft can only have been a joyride, an easy way home for a lazy thief, because there is absolutely no black market for my bike. It is a rusted, dorky dad bike, one speed—but not retro—with a bulky child seat mounted on the back.

I've always had a particular fascination with people who steal stuff that obviously belongs to kids.

Anyway, my wife, she's like me: a little raw. A little roughed up by all of this. With all that can go wrong around here on a minute's notice, she's in no mood to let her day be ruined by a punk, a bad guy, part of the problem.

So she unfurled a bloody tirade against this guy, who may or may not have been armed but was so stunned by her fury that he babbled some lie about "That guy said I could borrow it" and she continued with her furious but rather persuasive diatribe.

She grabbed the bike. He got off and walked away.

"Moseyed," she tells me.

Since I moved to this city twenty-two years ago, I have been stolen from more times than I can count on both hands. I was burglarized three times in my present home before I got an alarm system and a crazy dog. In my former house in the Marigny, I was burglarized twice.

I have been cleaned out, literally. One thief was apparently a 40 regular, because he stole my clothes in addition to everything else. And never mind the litany of bikes, weed whackers, garden tools, and other small stuff that has walked off my property for the past two decades.

The same thing has probably happened to you, a lifetime of petty aggravations—some not so petty—that amount to a constant assault against your peace of mind.

Amazing, how you can adapt to a life surrounded by thievery. How you can accept as part of your lifestyle the fact that a huge number of people you live near would steal anything you've got lying around if you turned your back for just one moment.

The post-Katrina looting is still the most disturbing thing to me about this whole Grand Catastrophe: how some citizens of our community turned on their own, using the devastation as an open call to Christmas in New Orleans.

Everything for free. The wasted homes of Lakeview, Fontaine-bleau, Gentilly, and the East? Just take what you can find in the ruins.

I ask you: What kind of man picks over the bones of a destroyed life?

I am not naive enough to believe in a theft-free city; a few junkie burglars are inevitable in any society, even the most civil. But a town teeming with opportunistic predators is not in my job description anymore.

We don't have to suffer the ills of our past. You know, Dawn of a New Day, and all that. And this ragged sumbitch is lucky I didn't make the block and come back and find him coming out of my backyard.

I'm pretty sure I would have run him over.

Yes, for a stupid bicycle.

I'm not going to take this crap anymore. I'm not going to let two-bit predators get inside my head—and yard and car and house. I'm not going to secure my psyche with a lock and chain as I have for all these years.

I shouldn't have to put up with this while my city tries to put itself back together.

And if you think I'm all worked up about this, trust me: You do not want to cross my wife when she is walking on the edge.

You will rue the day. This I know.

Shooting the Rock
8/6/06

Me and my new friend Shaq were shooting hoops this week at Wisner Playground, Laurel and Upperline Streets, 13th Ward Uptown.

I used to play softball here. I remember a guy on my team once crushed a home run so far that it cleared the right-field fence and cleared the basketball court behind right field and hit a car parked on Upperline.

That's a mighty swat, let me tell you. A thing of beauty.

But the poetry of the moment was broken by the discovery that the car belonged to one of the guys playing hoops that night and a near riot (I kid you not) ensued as we all figured out—in a not-so-civil fashion—whose responsibility the damage was.

The local hoops players didn't invest much authority in the city recreation league softball umpire, who declared all vehicles parked in the area to be inherently at risk.

The incident ended with baseball bats brandished as weapons but no blows struck. It was stupid, really, the way these incidents always are, awash in clouds of race and class and distrust and a supreme failure to communicate.

That was a long time ago.

The basketball court is still there. The softball field is not. There are brand-new backboards on the court, with bright green

Sprite logos on them, so I guess the soft drink folks are under-writing what little passes for recreation around this town these days. The softball field has gone the way of just about every other once-wide-open space in this city: now paved over in stones and all fenced in, home to rows of gleaming white trailers that look like nothing more than isolation cells in a modular prison yard. I look at this and wonder whose bright idea it was to put all the FEMA trailer parks on the city's playgrounds rather than around the city's playgrounds.

You don't have to be forward-thinking to realize that putting the trailer parks around the playgrounds instead of on them would have created common green spaces that would have served as de facto community centers and kids would have had places to play other than on debris-strewn streets and sidewalks filled with rotting garbage, roofing nails, and rats.

We're a city that never seems to tire or even despair of doing things simple, dumb, and cheap and—as a father in this town—I can tell you this: kids are pretty much the last consideration in just about every public policy decision around here.

It boggles. I went to Wisner to do my therapy. Nothing gets me out of my head more than going outside at the hottest point of the afternoon and finding a basketball court on which to run up and down, doing layups all by myself.

I came to Wisner a lot last fall, in the dark days, and I would always pass a dead guy on a bench on the front porch of a house in the middle of the block next to the playground.

He was there for three weeks before anyone came and took him away. His name was Alcede, and it got so I started saying hello to him when I passed by.

If you were here in the days of pain, everywhere you go now, there's some memory staring you in the face. What it used to look like. But that's another story for another time.

At Wisner, I was shooting hoops when two little kids rolled up and asked if they could play with me. Some older kids were play-ing at the other end of the court and it's a free country so I said yes even though what I really wanted to be was alone and banging the ball hard and working up a sweat and forgetting everything about Alcede and what they did to the playgrounds in this town. But what are you going to say? Scram, kids?

One of them was slender and quiet, said his name was Shea, or something like that. The other kid, full of vinegar—but with a set shot to match his trash talk—introduced himself to me as Shaquille O'Neal.

Shaq just about never shut his mouth for the hour we played, but he didn't hog the ball or act the fool and so the time passed pleasantly enough. I'd shoot and jump and sweat and then roll the ball off to them for some shots and we rotated around like that, talking and shooting.

Shaq's basketball shorts hung low, down below the cheeks of his rump in the back and down to midthigh in the front and his boxers flared up and it just about drove me crazy and all I could think was: You're ten. You look stupid.

But that's not what you tell a kid. Not what you tell a kid you don't know. In his neighborhood, not yours.

So I just filed the shorts away with the trailers and Alcede and everything else. Not your problem. Nothing you can do about it. Breathe.

"You the *po*-lice?" Shaq asked me at one point, and I'm not sure why, other than I guess not a lot of middle-aged white men play ball in this park and maybe my presence was . . . suspicious?

"No," I told him. "Not the police."

My shot was on the mark that afternoon, and this probably helped my street cred with Shaq and Shea, even though these kids are ten and why am I worried about street cred?

We practiced dishing off to one another and high-fived on good plays. When I retrieved my ball in the high grass once, I found a Spider-Man basketball hidden there and Shaq sheepishly admitted it was his. Then Shea volunteered that he has a Scooby-Doo ball at home.

We talked and played and the kids cut up and acted silly and talked endlessly about "booty."

My kids do that, they talk a lot about "booty." It cracks them up.

They did not get that from me. I swear, they did not get that from me.

I told Shaq, "You guys are just like my kids."

"You should bring them here to play," he told me.

I said they're too young still, too small to shoot at a regulation basket.

"They could swing," Shaq offered, and we both regarded the sorry-ass situation that appeared before us: the swing set at Wisner is just about the saddest piece of paint-peeled steel you ever laid eyes on and the seats are all tangled and there are two feet of grass growing under it and, twenty-five feet away, there is a mound of black garbage bags that has been sitting there since who knows when.

"I can't bring my kids here," I said. "Look at that grass."

"Yeah," Shaq admitted. "Nobody plays there."

This kid, he's ten. But he knows. He knows the city is dogging. The city can't deliver. They can't cut the grass for the kids.

How stupid is that?

When we started playing again, Shaq grabbed my hand while he was dribbling the ball. He took hold. He was holding my hand. I instinctively held back while he made a layup but then thought in an instant: Whoa, cowboy! This kid is ten. Not your kid. If you drove by a playground and saw your son holding hands with some guy who looks real out of place on a playground, what would go through your head?

I shook his hand off. I didn't want to. He didn't want to. But I had to.

"Last call, fellas," I told the kids and said I had to go. Shaq challenged me to take a shot from half-court before I left. So I did. And it went in. Just one of those days, I guess.

The kids just opened their eyes wide and checked me out.

I was thinking: Now's your chance. Now is your only chance, I told myself.

So I said to Shaq, "Pull up your pants." And he looked at me and bundled up his pants and pulled them around his waist. Just like that.

And I walked off the court.

And I was thinking: I am my dad.

The City That Hair Forgot
11/7/06

A friend of mine had been telling me, "If you want to experience a nice New Orleans moment, go to the Oak Street Cafe for breakfast. There's a piano player there and he plays for tips while you eat and it's a great scene."

So I went to the Oak Street Cafe for breakfast. I was thinking I could use a good New Orleans moment and can't we all. I was also thinking I could use a haircut. Only my immediate family knows what my hair really looks like; that in its natural state it assumes an Afro shape that rivals that of former mayor Marc Morial's famous high school yearbook picture, the only difference being that he was a teenager when he had his and it was the '70s.

And oh, yeah—he's black.

At night, I tease my hair up into a fright wig that looks like those old troll dolls we used to play with and I scare the pants off my kids, which seems like a warm-and-fuzzy domestic portrait until the dawning realization: My hair scares my kids.

So before I went to the Oak Street Cafe, I went to the barbershop down the block because another friend had told me that if I wanted to experience a nice New Orleans moment, I should go to the old barbershop on Oak Street because the guy who cuts hair there has been there for something like ninety years and he's a character.

I figured that anyone who went through the Marc Morial high school years and the Beatles era and then Flock of Seagulls and all that would not fear my hair, so I went to visit him before going to the Oak Street Cafe, with the idea that I could just stack up a full morning's worth of nice New Orleans moments there on old Oak Street, so architectural and antiquated, lost in time, where movies set in the '50s come to film street scenes because they hardly have to change a thing.

But the barbershop was closed. It's closed a lot, according to the sign on the door, and I guess I'd be closed a lot if I had been cutting hair since the Teapot Dome Scandal.

I was dressed in my usual post-Katrina daytime attire, which is torn, paint-covered jeans and an array of sweatshirts from the Contemporary Homeless selection at Thrift City and my hair looked as if lightning had just struck the side of my head and that's how I presented myself to the counter at the Oak Street Cafe for my breakfast and my New Orleans moment.

The piano player was there. The energy was just right, soft and languid, diners slowly leafing through newspapers, the tinkling of spoons in coffee cups, sleepy-eyed conversations.

I was behind three women in line. I spied an exotic dish called Eggs Beauregard on the daily chalkboard and was ready to order when the first woman in line turned around, regarded my presence, and said, "You look like shit."

That's what she said. Just like that. And in a town that refuses to filter itself, I suppose it was in itself a small New Orleans moment, but I'm thinking, well, she's right—but what the hell?

The two women with my fashion critic turned and looked at me and kind of nodded in agreement and then turned back to the counter to gather up their food and utensils.

Then the woman who had addressed me turned her attention to a woman wearing one of those generic white institutional uniforms that everyone from a nurse assistant to a cafeteria worker wears and she inquired into her life and the customer said she worked at a salon just up the street.

As the woman in white was leaving with her meal in a Styrofoam package, I stopped her. "Does your salon do men?" I asked and she said yes. "Ask for Lynette. Lynette Boutte, she's a master barber."

Now, this woman in white was courteous and professional. But she was also black, and I was wondering if I should make sure we were on the same page by explicitly asking: Do you do white men with poofy, thinning, dried-out dead limbs of hair? A follicle hard case. A desperate man, with hair like Beetlejuice dipped in volcanic ash, asking strangers in a diner if they'll cut his hair?

But I didn't ask. So, after my Eggs Beauregard (exquisite) accompanied by boogie-woogie piano (sublime New Orleans moment) I wandered up Oak Street to where I thought the woman in white had told me her salon was, and as I tried to walk in the door, two thin, beautiful caramel-colored young men blocked my way, rendering unto me a look nothing short of horror.

I'm pretty sure one of them was about to ask me if I was there to fix the broken heater vent.

I had indeed walked into a hair salon, but not the one I had been directed to, and the *über*-hip stylists with their tight shirts and fashionable shoes quickly pointed out the error of my ways, leading me down the banquette to a decidedly busier, noisier, messier salon than theirs and I wanted to sneer at them, "Hey! I was metrosexual once—before the storm!" but I figured it was a lost cause.

And so I walked into the salon where the woman in white works and it was bustling with women of all ages, doing what women do in salons all day, which is talk a whole lot, mostly about men and food, but it kinda got silent in there when I walked in.

It's amazing how you can be wandering the streets around here in your comfort zone and you walk through a door and you're in somebody else's world and I was picturing that scene from *Animal House* where all the white rube frat boys walk into a blues roadhouse and I wanted to call out, "Otis, my man!" but there was no Otis and I was alone.

A woman broke the discomfiting silence by saying to me, "You must be the man my daughter met at the restaurant. I'm Nettie. C'mon in."

Everyone in the joint laughed when they heard I had tried to get into the salon in the front of the building and Nettie said to me, "Honey, they don't have customers that look like you," and I'm sure she meant that in the best possible way.

I sat in her chair. "Can you make me beautiful?" I asked her.

"No," she said, "but I can cut your hair."

So, amid the chatter of women and the smells of exotic hair products I have never heard of, Nettie Boutte cut my hair.

She is one of the ten Boutte siblings and extended family members (the Vaucresson sausage folks, for instance) whose imprint on New Orleans is immeasurable, all those singers and chefs and artists. She had a salon in the 7th Ward but it got whacked and she spent three days on the overpass after Katrina ("Don't get me started!"). She now drives an hour from the Northshore to get to her temporary business on Oak Street, and she stopped cutting my hair at least fifty times to direct her employees or answer the phone or greet customers, one of whom actually said to her, "How's yo momma?"

Sometimes I forget that people really say that here.

Athelgra Neville walked in while I was there. She is the Neville Brothers' sister and a singer in her own right, and she was asking everybody, "Did you see Aaron on *The Young and the Restless?*"

With my belly full and sitting there in the overpoweringly nurturing warmth of a room filled with women at work, I was indeed having a New Orleans moment and I vowed to start dressing better, but I was just caught up in my reverie and that probably won't happen.

I left Nettie's salon with decidedly less frightful hair. Nettie is an artist, if you ask me . . . taking into consideration, of course, the raw canvas I gave her to work with.

In my car, driving down Oak Street, I turned on the radio. It was WWOZ and there was a song by the Bob French Band and the vocalist was Sista Teedy—aka Tricia Boutte, one of the legion of far-flung kin—and she was singing "Do You Know What It

Means to Miss New Orleans?" and I couldn't have contrived a better transition if I were directing a movie.

It really happened that way. It had been a somewhat awkward journey, but I had gotten my New Orleans moment, and it was staying with me as I drove away, locked into New Orleans in my head and on my radio.

I said to myself: Don't touch that dial.

A Rapturous Day
in the Real World
12/5/06

Living inside the Katrina Bubble and never getting out, one tends to be consumed by the bad stuff; at least that's how it seems when all anyone talks about is crime and trash and politics and insurance companies and No Road Home and progress seems just to slog along in the day-to-day. It's practically insufferable unless you set your iPod on "Motown's Greatest Hits" and just keep telling yourself: Think happy thoughts, think happy thoughts, think happy thoughts.

Of course, then you wind up not paying attention and driving into a pothole and busting up your front end and now you're more pissed off than before you started thinking all those happy thoughts—Ice cream! Kittens! New Britney photos!—in the first place, so this method comes with a surgeon general's warning.

I find the best way to get an optimistic sense of recovery around here is to leave town, go observe life somewhere else, and then come back.

When you've been outside the Katrina Zone for even just a short while, you can get a fresh perspective, and when you come back, you tend to notice more changes, improvements; the brown caterpillar slowly—very slowly—morphing into the colorful but-terfly.

Even if I haven't been out of the city for a while, I ask friends who have just returned from vacation or a business trip (or rehab) what they noticed when they got back, and most of the time they actually come up with some positive stuff that con-firms my purely anecdotal theory.

That's why this past Saturday was such a grand experience for me. Without leaving town or setting out on a contrived mission to look for signs of recovery (and cranking up the Supremes), things jumped out at me all day long. The butterfly spreads her wings.

That morning, I was driving down Prytania Street and noticed a line outside the Bluebird Cafe and I know there's probably always a line there on weekends because it's such a popular break-fast spot, but everyone looked happy to be there, chatting with strangers around them, and it looked like the Bluebird of old.

Shortly after that, I passed the old familiar sight of movie trucks and trailers and lights and there were scads of self-important young people rushing around with headsets and clipboards, and this is a welcome sight—at least to anyone who can muster enough civic spirit to prioritize the city's long-term economic recovery over his own personal parking hassles, and I am aware that not everyone can.

Minutes later, I passed by Mother's on Poydras, and again, there was a line down the block. Not long after that, I drove past Port of Call on Esplanade, and same thing. Customers, lots of customers, waiting to get in for lunch.

These three sights compounded to lift my spirits. Commerce! Activity! A living, breathing community!

Continuing about on my errands, I dropped off a friend at the airport and had assured him that he'd get to his plane in no time because there was never anyone at the airport. But in fact, the cars dropping folks off at curbside were two deep all the way down the concourse level.

Of course, these cars represent people leaving town—arrivals are downstairs—but presumably the great majority of them came from somewhere else to visit or are from here and will return. It looked almost like the airport of old.

Down in the Central Business District and the Quarter, there were pedestrians all over the place, some of them showing off the visiting 49ers colors, and outside Anne Rice's old house in the Garden District (it's been years since she lived there) the crowds still gather to gawk, take pictures, and search for ghosts.

The weather Saturday was, as you know, profoundly clear and crisp, and Sunpie Barnes was singing about Creole tomatoes on WWOZ when I got stuck in traffic because there was a caravan of Mardi Gras floats bouncing up Rampart Street behind tractors, headed for who-knows-where and who-knows-what, but obviously somebody was having a big party somewhere with all these strange and beautiful indigenous means of transportation.

Saturday evening, a friend of mine went to Brennan's to eat, but they told him it would be an hour's wait so they went to Galatoire's instead. At the Galactic gig at the Maple Leaf, David Letterman showed up in the crowd and Paul Shaffer sat in with the band. Over at Rock n' Bowl, Jimmy Buffett showed up at the Sonny Landreth gig and joined in for a few numbers, and, funny: it's December, when, even before Katrina, there wasn't usually that much going on around here.

There seemed to be people everywhere, a city—what's left of it, at least—jumping and alive.

At Tipitina's that night, Lusher, my kids' elementary school, held its annual winter fund-raiser. The music for this event is generally supplied by the school's jazz orchestra, which is positively phenomenal. They are young members of the true cultural elite—the very future of this city's musical heritage.

Music is also supplied by the parents of students who happen to be professional musicians, of which there are plenty. There are Iguanas and Imagination Movers and members of $1,000 Car and various jazz singers and more and it was crazy to see the mothers of my kids' classmates, women who generally look pretty frazzled and hurried just like me when I drop off my kids at school in the morning, suddenly wearing cocktail dresses and singing torch songs and transformed and what is it about this town that everyone is an artist of one kind or another? Every-body's got something happening on the side.

Last year, the fund-raiser seemed to be a somewhat forced affair, held a few weeks after the school reopened in January and muddied by the still-humid aura of shock and uncertainty.

But Saturday night, it was a rocking affair, and I realized it felt that way because now, fifteen months into this thing, everyone who showed up to support the school—although we are mixed incomes and religions and ethnic backgrounds and philoso-phies—all had one thing in common: We're here. And we're likely staying. And by our very presence, we're obviously com-mitted to making this a better community for ourselves and our children.

Some of the folks I knew and some I didn't, but I looked around the room at people laughing and dancing and living here in the center of the universe because, in case you haven't heard, that's still what New Orleans is.

Like my travel theory above, this opinion is based purely on anecdotal evidence. But wheeling all over town Saturday with the windows down and WWOZ rolling out one New Orleans chestnut after another, I couldn't imagine anywhere else in the world I'd rather be. When we've got our game face on (insert ap-propriate Saints metaphor here), there is no place like it in the world.

Now, I realize that at that very minute I was having a golden moment, other people all over this town, this region, were star-ing at hollowed-out houses with glassed-over eyes and their hands on their hips, wondering how they'll ever find their way back to peace of mind.

I know there is plenty of bad stuff out there. Good and plenty, to be sure. But I didn't see any of it Saturday, and maybe it's good not to see it every now and then, to get away, whether by airplane or simply by cranking up the radio.

It's the ever-present and always alluring possibility of this type of near-rapturous experience that I had Saturday that makes people want to be here, I guess.

I swear, if some loathsome creature had accosted me and axed me where I got my shoes, I could have transported myself to a dream state where you could almost believe that the things that have happened here were all just a bad dream and in fact, life is groovy.

But despite the insistence of some to the contrary, we live in a reality-based world and what happened happened and that's that, but it is mighty damn refreshing once in a while to feel as if we're crawling out of the hole.

Even with a flattened landscape and so many challenges ahead of us, I don't remember a single person on Saturday asking me how I made out in the flood, and if that's not a change for the better, then I don't know what is.

Big Daddy No Fun
6/18/06

My family went to Ye Olde College Inn for dinner Thursday night.

This local institution has a new look and a new menu since The Thing—heck, it's even in a new building—but it still verily throbs with local charm.

You look around at the patrons at the bar and in the dining area, and whether you recognize them or not, they just exude that strange and familiar essence of this place. I don't really know the proper words to describe it—the exact metaphor escapes me (in fact, it has escaped every writer who tried to find it)—but you know what I mean if you've ever walked in the door of College Inn or Uglesich's or Domilise's or Dunbar's or any other of a million places where the talk is too loud and the calories too high and the energy is that just-right, impossible stew of languor, insouciance, comfort, and anticipation.

Ah, this place.

We were told it would be twenty minutes until we could get a table, and we understood in the New Orleans lexicon that meant it would be forty-five minutes until we could get a table so we decided to take a walk rather than try to rein in our kids amid the hungry and waiting masses.

They were drawn immediately to the scene down the street, a wasteland of rubble that covers an entire city block, that stretch of Carrollton between Claiborne and Earhart where those huge brick mansions all burned to the ground—or should I say to the waterline—back in September.

All that stands today are steps and chimneys, and otherwise it's a blackened potpourri of ash and bricks, glass and appliances. You can make out the charred skeletons of bicycles and hot-water heaters and bedsprings and a few other things.

To you and me, this scene generally evokes horror and anger and sorrow, but then again we see it every day so it also strikes a chord of the familiar—as familiar as walking into your favorite old restaurant, I suppose.

It is part of our life. A New Orleans thing.

To the kids, it's something completely different. "Where are the bathtubs?" my two oldest shouted from the sidewalk that borders this mess, and this was a strange question since my kids don't spend much of their time or energy in their own home seeking out the tubs.

Quite the opposite, in fact.

But it's what popped into their little minds and they actually wanted to go prospecting in the rubble for bathtubs but Big Daddy No Fun put the clamp down on that idea.

We did walk the perimeter of the block, hunting bathtubs, and even walked up a few front stoops to get an "aerial" view.

We found two tubs.

For my kids, this was a game and for me some sort of cautionary lesson/observation period: Let the kids absorb this. Let them keep absorbing this.

But then you think: This was someone's house. Someone's life. Someone's stuff. Hopes, dreams, memories, and probably lots of not-so-pleasant things also, the grist of life, reality and struggle—even before it all burned down and washed away.

I guess I've kicked around so many busted houses that it's easy to lose sight of that—lose the proper sense of respect and perspective. I hope I haven't crossed the line, but if the reason you do this—to gawk at all the ruin around here—is to learn and to never forget, then is it okay?

Is it okay that my kids played here on the site of someone's extreme loss? Even if the larger aim—in my mind—was a lofty ideal of understanding?

I don't know the answer to that. I suppose whoever owns these properties can tell me some day.

Across the street, directly behind the restaurant, someone had obviously just gutted their house; that ubiquitous mountain of wasted domesticity was piled up six feet high on the curb.

Such a familiar sight. A New Orleans thing.

It's amazing how free and unburdened little kids can be in this stark environment. There was a huge stuffed Snoopy in the maw in front of this house and my kids asked if they could keep it and I don't have to tell you how Big Daddy No Fun responded.

My kids have seen the depths of the devastation here. One Sunday afternoon, we drove them down to the Lower 9th for reasons that elude me now other than it seemed like a good idea at the time.

They spoke very little and I didn't even try to narrate our driving tour but let the landscape speak for itself, a vista unlike anything they've ever seen in movies or on TV.

My son Jack—four years old at the time—looked out his window and said, "Purple upside-down car."

That's all he said, and in those four words of simple declarative observation (there was indeed a purple upside-down car), I realized that maybe Jack will be the next writer in the family, for so perfectly did he capture the metaphor that has eluded me for all these months.

New Orleans is the Purple Upside-Down Car. A bright color with no sense of direction. A stalled engine. A thing of once-beauty waiting to be righted and repaired. Something piled up on the side of the road.

I am a father and my kids are riding shotgun in this purple upside-down car. We drive the streets of the familiar and the horrible. We use the seat belt. We live our life. We move on. We do the things that make us feel comfortable in these discomfiting times.

At the College Inn, I went with the foot-long fried oyster, melted Havarti, and bacon po-boy, drenched in mayo and Crystal Hot Sauce. A wondrous spectacle to behold. A truly ludicrous thing to eat.

Such a New Orleans thing.

Peace Among the Ruins
2/3/06

Those first hours and minutes, they stay with you forever. The
very first time you rolled back into town after The Thing.

I was dropped off at my house by another reporter. I had a car
parked there, but it was out of gas.

So I retrieved an old rusted bike that I had inherited from a
neighbor and I was going to hit the streets, see what was here,
what wasn't here, absorb the meaning of it all.

It had a flat tire. I didn't care. I took it and started walking it
down the middle of the deserted street, having become—after
just ten minutes in town—one of those zoned-out, postapocalyp-
tic zombies doing things that make no sense.

I had joined the tribe.

The first two guys I met—you remember the first living people
you saw—were good Samaritans sent my way. They pulled up
alongside me in a pickup, and I had met them before—a friend-
of-a-friend thing—and we went through these strange reintro-
ductions and the thing is: I can't remember today who they were.

But I remember what they had: a bicycle pump.

In what would become a season of strange and inexplicable
occurrences, this was the first. Here I am, feeling like the only
living soul on the planet—with a flat tire—and the first guys I
meet say, "Do you need some air in that thing?"

Even at its lowest hour, New Orleans has the capability to surprise you with her penchant for serendipity and delight. The human element.

We parted ways. I was, for the moment, a little less frightened by The Thing, having been rescued from my first physical plight so quickly, easily.

Then I ran into Terrence Sanders, and he was the first to smooth out the mental rumples in my head, to make me feel — even on that first day back, a time when New Orleans still smelled of death and rot and panic — that one has many choices to make in life and one of those choices is simply to carry on.

A New Orleans credo: When life gives you lemons — make daiquiris.

That's not what Sanders was making, though. He was making art.

He was sitting crouched in front of a massive canvas in the Magazine Street gallery that bears his name — and where he lives — and he was putting the finishing touches on a bold, colorful painting and listening to the radio.

At this point, my mental images of New Orleanians — not so mental really; they were from TV — were people dangling from choppers and dying of thirst in front of the Convention Center, and here's this dude, painting.

I was thinking more about foraging for fuel and food, maybe fending off the roving gangs I had heard about — and here's a guy making art.

I need to talk to this cat, I thought.

So we talked. We talked about the city and we talked about art and this guy was so rock steady — or maybe he was flat-out nuts — that he settled me.

Like many of the more eccentric characters in this city, he's not from New Orleans (born in Pineville, actually) but settled here about a year ago after a young life traveling the globe because it feels like home. He's been here a year, just kind of muddling along; an unknown in local art circles, just trying to make a name.

And here's the thing about the painting he was working on: It was the final panel of a series he had been working on for four years, a commemoration—of all things—of the September 11 disaster. It was a list of the names of the dead.

Well, if you're a fan of irony. . . .

I glibly remarked that he shouldn't have any trouble finding subject matter for his next project.

"Yeah," he said. "Disaster can be like that. It makes death, despair . . . and art."

He told me this week, all these months later, "I felt like an obscure guy in a lost place. There was all this hell going on. I was just trying to find some inner peace."

At age thirty-eight, Sanders is throwing his own New Orleans coming-out party tomorrow night, announcing his arrival on the local art scene with a show about September 11 and Hurricane Katrina and some things in between.

The work that emanated from his quest for inner peace is colorful, passionate, political, and New Yorky. He used to run in Basquiat's crowd in Gotham City; maybe that's an influence.

There's lots of text, for those who like to read their paintings. There are stark photos he took of passengers when he was a cabdriver in Baton Rouge. He's showing a movie he made, projecting it onto the front of his building.

Every time I drive by that building now, I remember what amounts to the strangest day of my life so far, and I will always remember stopping there to talk to a stranger and feeling better.

I will always remember that building and the moment of humanity I found in its doorway and how I pedaled away thinking: We can do this.

Artful Practicality
3/31/06

One thing the Aftermath has proven is that if you are not an adaptable creature, New Orleans is no place for you.

Staying in New Orleans necessitates redefining oneself. Marco St. John would be a good example.

St. John is a "decorative painter," which means he does commercial murals, trompe l'oeil paintings, and fine-art restoration.

But in the post-Katrina world, there's not much demand for $8,000 billboard-sized reproductions of Michelangelo's *Creation*, fine art being one of the final frontiers of discretionary spending, and "discretionary spending" being one of the final frontiers of the current New Orleans vocabulary.

There is, however, a huge demand for housepainters.

"It's almost funny," St. John muses in the bright yellow living room of a freshly restored home on Palmer Street Uptown. "I was finally getting the kind of clients I wanted and I was booked for a whole year. And then."

And then.

"I quickly realized I had to be as utilitarian as possible. And this idea kept resonating with me: people can't buy paintings if they don't have walls to hang them on. So I decided I would help them get walls. And then it suddenly clicked with me that I could band a lot of my artist friends together to do this."

Thus, St. John is now managing three full crews of interior housepainters who were visual artists left unemployed by The Thing.

And with such a gesture—hiring photographers, mask makers, graphic designers, and landscape painters to restore a home—comes inadvertent slices of comedy and unintended character studies of the methodology of the artistic temperament.

"They're all wonderful artists," St. John says. "But they bring a level of craftsmanship to the job that, quite frankly, doesn't belong here. I am learning how to run a business, and I have learned: Time is money."

The foibles of a team of meticulous aesthetes attacking the job of refurbishing a flood-ravaged community almost plays out like some weird reality TV show on Bravo.

To wit: "The photographers seem to understand how to do this because they're used to the immediacy of the artistic process," St. John says. "The mask makers, they're used to such meticulous work. When it comes to filling in little nail holes, they excel at it, but faced with the huge expanse of a living room wall, they pick up little brushes and just start dabbing.

"And the realist landscape painters! They can get fixated on a piece of rotten baseboard and you can't get them off of it. They could spend hours caulking and recaulking the same spot if I let them, and I can't afford that if they're on the clock.

"There's no question that we're very good at what we do," St. John says. "Fast is what we've got to get."

Korey Kelso, a former illustrator at the Lionel Milton Gallery on Magazine Street, is one of the artists St. John was able to bring back to New Orleans.

He was waiting it out in Massachusetts when St. John called. "I wasn't sure what I was going to do," Kelso said. "I wanted to come back and be a part of all this, but I didn't have the means to do it. This allows me to be functional on my own again. It gives me a chance to make a living while I put a portfolio back together again."

And there are subtle rewards to it all.

"I don't see an incredible nobility in painting houses,"

St. John says. "But we're the last ones in during the renovation process, so we're here when the families start moving back in, carrying their children's furniture back into these houses."

He pauses. "I'm proud of that. I don't envision being a house-painter for the rest of my days, but we're doing something good here. And rest assured: once we've got all these big blank walls finished, we're not shy about letting them know who to call if they need something to hang on them."

"She Rescued My Heart"
9/14/06

At the same time Hurricane Katrina was making its way across the Atlantic Ocean last August, Katie McClelland was attending a seminar in Atlanta on animal rescue techniques.

The instructor, Meredith Shields, a rescue specialist with the American Humane Association, had been closely following the storm's track and asked the class, "If this turns into something serious, who's interested in helping out?"

McClelland put her hand up.

At twenty-nine, McClelland had recently switched careers from television reporting to working for the Atlanta Humane Society. "I wanted to get out of the hustle and bustle and work with animals," she said.

When Katrina took out the southern coasts of Mississippi and Louisiana, McClelland said, she went to her supervisors at the Atlanta Humane Society and asked for a leave of absence to help. They said no. She went anyway.

"I don't know," she mused. "I just felt this was something I had to do. I had just come out of a relationship and my life was in flux and I wanted to get involved in something that wasn't about me."

So she signed up with Shields and the American Humane Association as a volunteer and headed to New Orleans.

At the same time, across the country in Eugene, Oregon, a pharmaceutical sales rep named Paul Dyer got word that his National Guard unit was activating immediately for deployment to New Orleans.

At twenty-eight, he was floundering also. He felt static, as if he wasn't moving forward. Like McClelland, he'd been thinking about a career switch and had also just extricated himself from a bad relationship.

Getting called up for emergency Guard service was almost a relief, freeing him from introspection and locking him into his autopilot, duty-bound role as a captain in the U.S. Army.

In the immediate aftermath of Katrina—with no central command to guide them—military, medical, and humanitarian organizations fanned out across the Gulf Coast, looking for dry, safe areas from which to stage their search-and-rescue operations.

Dyer's 186th Infantry Regiment set up camp on the campus of Delgado Community College in Mid-City. Their tasks included clearing Esplanade Avenue for passage, powering up and securing the New Orleans Museum of Art, searching for survivors by airboat in the City Park area, and stemming the rising tide of looting activity from Esplanade Ridge through Gentilly.

Several days later, the American Humane Association showed up at Delgado and set up camp in the same parking lot.

"We were two independent organizations; we didn't know quite what to do with each other," Dyer says.

But one thing was clear in the lawless environs of New Orleans: the animal rescue folks were going to need security.

Dyer was handed supervision of the security details. He assigned himself to Team 6. That was McClelland's team.

And so began a story of love among the ruins.

For three days they worked side by side, nonstop, breaking into homes whose owners had contacted a national hotline for help.

At night, he slept on the roof of a classroom building in the open air; she bunked down with her team in the parking lot. They spent what little free time they had hanging out in the college courtyard, getting to know each other.

"Her dedication was amazing to me," Dyer recounts. "I mean, I was in the Army and they called me and told me we had to do this. I just got shipped here. I didn't make a choice. Not her. She gave up everything and came here to help. That's a real volunteer. She's the real hero in all of this."

It was September 19 when they met—one year ago today—but three days later, the impending arrival of Hurricane Rita sent their outfits in different directions. They talked every day by phone as they continued their respective missions into October.

As they headed home to their respective coasts—without ever having shared as much as a kiss—they made a promise to each other: the first one who could find a job in the other one's town would move.

By Halloween, McClelland had dusted off her television résumé and landed a job as a ten o'clock news anchor with the Fox affiliate in Eugene. Duly motivated, Dyer enrolled at Portland State University to study for an MBA in hospital administration.

When it came time to plan a wedding, it was a no-brainer: the courtyard at Delgado.

So, this past Sunday night, McClelland, Dyer, and two dozen friends and family members gathered for the event.

Though the bridesmaids wore matching linen gowns—a sign that at least some planning went into the affair—the postceremony "reception" consisted of flowers purchased from Sam's Club in Metairie, a lemon cream cake from the A&P on Magazine Street, and four bottles of champagne from a downtown liquor store, chilled in four ice buckets "commandeered" from their hotel rooms in the CBD.

A nondenominational New Orleans minister, Don Bohn, performed the service. His wife, Samantha, did the photography. McClelland and Dyer had found them online.

As the bridesmaids and groomsmen lined up and McClelland walked into the courtyard from a nearby parking lot, the crowd took up an improvisational a capella version of "The Wedding March": "Dum dum, da-dum . . ."

During the brief service, a visibly nervous Dyer pulled a sheet of paper out of his pocket and read this:

One year ago my life changed in a way that only poets can dream. I was shipped to a city in ruins to help others recover from a terrible disaster. The funny thing was: My life, much like the city of New Orleans, was a disaster.

I had little direction, little guidance and little confidence I would ever find what my life was meant to be. Then, on a muggy afternoon in this very parking lot, I was introduced to a woman who, unlike me, volunteered to help rescue helpless animals with no home, no food and no water. Little did she know, but she rescued my heart that day as well.

My life has changed. Like the city of New Orleans being rebuilt, my life is being rebuilt in a way that I can be proud of. To everyone here as my witnesses, I share with you this: True love is real and oftentimes it is found where you least expect it.

The only sounds were sniffles and crickets. They were pronounced man and wife.

Asked about the difference between this moment and when they all met a year ago in this same spot, bridesmaid Colleen Porth, a pet rescuer from Austin, Texas, said, "We smell better now."

Said McClelland, "It seems like everyone we worked with here changed after they left. Everyone either got divorced or changed jobs or moved to a new state or just started over again in some way because of what they saw here and what happened to them here.

"We went into these homes together and we would find clothes laid out on someone's bed for work the next day and the people were now a thousand miles away and it made you realize: you never know when it's all going to be over. New Orleans changed all of us so much. It will always be a part of us."

Once the cake was cut and the champagne poured, Walter McClelland, the father of the bride, raised a plastic cup as the sun set over the courtyard and said, "Paul, welcome to our family."

A sentiment to which I would like to add, if I may, to Paul and Katie, and your friends and family: Welcome to our family.

The Family of New Orleans.

Miss Ellen Deserved Better
12/3/06

As far as crimes go in this town, the incident in the parking lot
on South Clearview Parkway outside Marshalls department store
on October 26 was hardly a blip on the screen.

An elderly woman was walking with an armful of packages. A
couple of guys pulled up in a car. They grabbed her purse, knock-
ing her to the ground. They drove off with a haul that amounted
to forty bucks.

Witnesses ran over to help the victim. The cops came. A report
was filed.

In an era of brazen daylight shootings, horrific gangland exe-
cutions, and postdisaster fraud schemes that run into the millions of dollars, this was just a petty annoyance, a piece of
paperwork, a statistic. Except for one lingering detail.

The victim, eighty-five-year-old Ellen Montgomery, broke her
left hip when she hit the ground. She had an emergency hip re-
placement operation at Ochsner Hospital and spent three days
in postop and then nine days in rehab.

Her son Jamie picked her up and brought her to his house in
Gentilly. By mid-November, she was making good progress with
a walker; despite her age and injury, Ellen Montgomery's life had
been marked by an unbending will to get by on her own.

But on Friday, November 17, she complained of shortness of

breath and had trouble with her balance. Sunday the nineteenth, she collapsed in the kitchen. An ambulance rushed her back to Ochsner, where doctors tried to revive her. But in the end, she died of a pulmonary embolism—a blood clot in the lung.

The Jefferson Parish coroner's office determined that the blood clot was a result of the hip surgery and therefore a direct result of the purse snatching, and thus she became another member of the mounting murder victim roster in Jefferson Parish.

The muggers have never been caught.

Ellen Montgomery was my friend and, at times, my muse.

In the Days of Pain that followed Hurricane Katrina, she was my only neighbor, and it's funny; I guess as a result of some sort of ageism on my part, during the weeks we spent together last fall, I always had this self-delusional notion that I was taking care of this old and eccentric woman, helping her get through the traumatic aftermath of Katrina, when, in fact, she was taking care of me.

But I bet she knew it the whole time.

We had first met shortly after I bought my house on Magazine Street in 1992. Her house had the classic pack rat/cat lady look to it, all paint-peeled and overgrown, hidden from the street by an iron fence and tangled trees that conjured Boo Radley or some other kind of weird or scary resident therein.

She lived there alone—unless you count her thirty-three cats.

Our single encounter way back then wound up being a small, life-changing event for me. I was single, reckless, and in a world of financial and legal trouble. My car was wrecked and my phone service cut off for months because I couldn't make the bill.

My home had been burglarized three times in a six-week period, pretty much relieving me of all my possessions and distractions. I think I can say with certainty that it was the roughest patch, both personally and professionally, that I had ever known and would know until the fall of 2005.

I was thirty-two years old and welcome to any new idea or direction that might drag me out of my self-pitying ways. Miss Ellen had heard about me—the troubled soul on the block—and she offered what she thought was the key to happiness: a stray dog.

Lord knows where she got the thing, but its presence in Miss Ellen's house was none too welcome by the feline masses that had been living there for years. The dog needed a home and I needed something, anything, and that's how I wound up adopting an exotic silvery-blue mutt of some sort of husky derivation whom I named Alibi and who taught me the notion of unconditional love and who gave me something to do, something to love, and something to look forward to in an otherwise bleak time.

Alibi left a lasting impression. In the years since, I have adopted four more homeless dogs.

After that, I rarely saw Miss Ellen. Truthfully, she had made a great impact on my life, but in my typically self-absorbed way, I never really kept in touch with her. She had her life, I had mine, and there weren't many opportunities for a shut-in cat lady and a gregarious party boy to commune.

And that was my loss, not hers.

I first returned to my home near Audubon Park on Monday, September 5, one week after the hurricane. There was no one anywhere—desolate, messy streets, debris and glass everywhere, and few signs of life other than police cars, Army Humvees, heavy-equipment trucks, and pickups pulling boats up and down Magazine Street.

I ran into my neighbor Martin as he was pulling up stakes and getting out of town after riding out the storm. He told me the area was basically abandoned except for Miss Ellen and her cats.

He had checked in on her and told me her stash of pet food and canned goods looked ample enough to sustain her until the city came back to life, and he had given her a radio and batteries, but that if I could look in on her from time to time, that would be helpful.

She had refused to evacuate and stowed away in her own home for the week because she feared that the police or the military would force her to leave. Then there would be no one to look after her cats. She told me she'd rather die with her cats in New Orleans than live elsewhere without them.

She was neither scared nor delusional nor lonely. In fact, in many ways, the near-total evacuation of New Orleans—the people, not the animals, that is—created a veritable Utopia for this self-reliant, literary, and poetic lover of animals, nature, and solitude, a woman of the simplest means imaginable with no need for modern technology and all of its noise and intrusions.

She was a woman of uncommon serenity and quiet devotion, living on the very margin of society, nestled among her modest but plentiful belongings—mostly books and paintings—in a nineteenth-century bungalow—more of a cabin than a house, really—with no cable, no air-conditioning, no shower, no lawn mower, computer, or cell phone, no ungainly attachments to the material world other than a beat-up old blue sedan for her occasional outings to the grocery, the pet store, the doctor, or church.

To her, the aftermath was an unfortunate circumstance, to be sure, but it was almost Paradise. Imagine a day, a week, a month—a whole season—with nothing to do but read dusty old novels, write poems about the weather and nature, and tend to her magnificent brood of felines, her family, some affectionate and playful, some aloof and nocturnal, all of them beloved and cared for with the patience and attention of a mother.

During daylight hours, she would often scurry about the neighborhood, literally ducking behind cars and between houses when the National Guard drove by, collecting slate roof shingles that had scattered all over the streets and yards of Uptown.

She had been a dilettante but extremely prolific painter for years and had filled her house, floor to ceiling, with her work. But she had run out of canvases and no art stores were open and she thought the slate tiles would make a base for lovely pictures—the color just jumps off them—and so she began to fill dozens, then hundreds, of other people's rooftop debris with impressionistic paintings of trees and oceans and wind and sky, the night sky that shined so brilliantly last fall over a city with no working lights and that she often admired for hours in her backyard alone at night with her thoughts and her cats.

And so I took to looking after her in those days, making sure she was comfortable and content, and, of course, she always was, though she lacked a few luxuries that she dearly wanted. She was not the type to do what other members of the Resistance were doing—entering the darkened Circle K, Whole Foods, and Winn-Dixie, scouring for food, water, booze, and whatever else they needed to survive.

So, each day, when a supply truck from Baton Rouge would deliver supplies and food to the team of *Times-Picayune* reporters and photographers working out of the city, I would scavenge through the care packages for the things that Miss Ellen told me she desired: coffee, sugar, creamer, batteries, and, of all things, peanut butter.

She loved peanut butter.

And so I began my routine early last fall, bringing small care packages to Miss Ellen, and when the newspaper started appearing in the city again, I would bring her a daily copy.

She read me her poetry—she wrote dozens of haikus a day, dreamy meditations on quietude, dappled sunlight, the sounds of birds returning to the area, things like that. She would tell me what book she was reading that day—she had returned to a collection of Beatrix Potter's work that she had read many years ago—and she tried, in vain, to tell me the names of the cats as they wandered out of hiding, one by one, to check out the strange visitor.

In turn, I would tell her the most recent news and events of the city—the water finally receding, the military putting down the clamps on looting, all that stuff. I painted a mental picture for her of life in the city. She always greeted the news with a knowing pause. "Well, I suppose it will get better," she would always say.

I realize now, all this time later, that I was living in my own little *Tuesdays with Morrie*. Miss Ellen was my one window into real life, the simple life, the beautiful life of just being, reflecting, and creating. Of living life in the moment, never complaining because what's the use. She's the only person I knew who could look at the violently jagged tangle of fallen trees in her yard and not see loss and anger but just smile and say, "It's very interesting, isn't it? The shapes."

I also realize now that, despite the nagging notion I always had that I was simply humoring a simple and lonely cat lady, she might have been one of the smartest people I ever met.

Much as I tried to latch on to her Zen-like appreciation for the beauty, power, and grace of life and all its capricious fury, I was pretty much a wreck in those days. I had virtually stopped eating or sleeping, and my hands had begun to shake uncontrollably. One day as I stood up to bid Miss Ellen good-bye, I felt a dizzy rush hit me with the force of a speeding train.

I tripped over a recycle bin on her porch as I was leaving and she asked if I was okay and I said yes, just a little tired and stressed out, and I ducked and climbed my way out of the obstacle course of trees in her yard and turned to walk down the sidewalk to my house and I blacked out.

I pitched face-forward on her sidewalk and snapped my glasses in half and opened a gash on my head and spent the next several hours drifting in and out of consciousness on my back. I have written about this episode before, how I lay there on the sidewalk of a major metropolitan city for several hours but no one came to help me, no one passed by; it was just me and the sky above, burning into me.

The only thing I remember during that period—three, maybe four hours on the ground, I don't know—was the sound of Miss Ellen in her house singing to her cats. Her voice drifted out the open windows like a gentle piano sonata, lilting and calm, and it added the sense that maybe I was crazy or dreaming or dead or all three.

It was the voice of a guardian angel.

I realize now, all these months later, that Miss Ellen was the closest thing to sanity that I encountered for months. And I was so embarrassed about what happened leaving her house that day that I did not again return to her house until after she was dead.

I had once again taken benefit of her inherent healing touch, her natural grace, and then I walked away from her life, just as I had done when I leashed up Alibi and walked away all those years ago.

She had her life and I had mine. After the storm, her old friends returned to town. Her church reopened. The local grocery stores reopened. She didn't need me for peanut butter anymore.

My family came back. My kids and my work consumed me—and we adopted a new stray dog!—and life went on and everything around here changed every day but I thought there would always be one constant: I thought the Cat Lady would be there for me if I ever needed her again.

I never got around to introducing her to my kids. I never got to tell them: This is Daddy's teacher.

I'm going to ask her family if I may have one or two of her slate paintings to remember her by. I guess that will be enough to remind me that the simple things in life are what get you through the day, and that fear and loneliness are but self-contrivances, and that life's great moments are just what Tennessee Williams always said they were: the kindness of strangers.

Things Worth Fighting For

Rebirth at the Maple Leaf

8/25/06

I am sitting in my office at home. I'm feeling an attack of the mean reds coming on. I need medicine. Now.

To my wife I say, "I'm going to hear Rebirth at the Maple Leaf." I ask her if she's ready to go out and party and this is our private joke, because she is already in bed, comfortably settled with a book for the evening.

I like knowing that when reasonable people are turning in for the night around here, some places haven't even fired their engines yet. My usual bedtime coincides with the hour when scores of bar backs across the region are just beginning to slice limes for the midnight rush of Coronas and gin and tonics.

I don't take advantage of this social phenomenon very much anymore. My need to bring sunglasses with me when I go out on a Saturday night has long since expired.

All the same, there's nothing like walking out of a bar after a night of shooting pool and dancing to a jukebox, into the vengeful glare of the morning sun, to remind you that you live in an alternate universe, that alternate universe being here, New Orleans.

Though I rarely indulge, I have always found a strange comfort in living in a town that never closes. I never want a drink at four in the morning anymore. But I like knowing that I could get one if I did.

And that I wouldn't be alone.

The Tuesday-night Rebirth gig at the Maple Leaf has iconographic standing in the lore of New Orleans nightlife, like the Thursday-night zydeco stomp at Mid-City Lanes or the Sunday-afternoon *fais do-do* at Tip's.

Something you can count on. No need to consult a schedule.

Long before Katrina, the Rebirth shows at Maple Leaf were where I'd drop in from time to time to remind myself why I live here, why I love here. Why I am here.

For the uninitiated (and if that's you, shouldn't you ask yourself why?) the Rebirth Brass Band is one of the veteran standard-bearers of the New Orleans brass-band renaissance and I realize that if you ask me what that means, well . . . I don't know. What is New Orleans brass-band music? Got me.

Jazz, I guess, in its basic DNA. Layered with rock influences. Smothered in hip-hop beat and attitude. All rolled together in a scary marching band.

It is an explosion of sound, just drums and horns—who needs anything else, really?—and it is the sound of Mardi Gras, of second lines, street parades, and house parties. Of New Orleans.

The Rebirth Tuesday-night gigs have been colossal draws for years, crowded, sweaty, throbbing, disorganized affairs packed with Tulane students, downtown hipsters, stiff-collar types, and soul brothers.

It is so energetic, so in the groove, so diverse, and so perfect that it almost looks contrived, like if a director wanted to create the quintessential bar scene for a movie, this is what he would make.

But Hollywood could never make this. Not on a Tuesday night. And not in any other town.

It's organic. Sexy. Maybe even mildly dangerous—all that sweat. In the ultimate act of self-absorption, I'm going to quote myself, from a tourist guidebook I wrote several years ago, trying to capture a moment at one of these shows: "Loud. Fast. Free-falling. Funky. You've got 10 new friends. The girl in your arms—what's her name? Who cares? Dance. If you saw yourself in a mirror at this instant, you wouldn't recognize yourself. And that can be a good thing."

I couldn't say it any better myself. And this past Tuesday night, that's what it was. Good medicine. As I knew it would be.

"Bounce" is the name of another kind of New Orleans music, our unique and commercially successful ghetto rap scene, but it should be the name for brass-band music, too. Because that's what you end up doing. Bouncing.

It's impossible not to. If you can't dance to this, you are on life support or maybe already dead.

If I don't feel better after doing this, I told myself on the way to the Maple Leaf, then I am irretrievable.

But I did. In the thick of a too-hot crowd full of strangers and old friends, watching ten, eleven, maybe a dozen guys packed on a too-small stage under bare lightbulbs and a pressed-tin ceiling, feeling the release of the fist-thrusting call-and-response, staring into a wall of horns whose music is so muscular that it almost takes on a physical manifestation and reaches out and beats you about the head and grabs your collar and screams in your face, "You are *alive*, boy! *Do you understand?*" And I do. And I am home again.

Melancholy Reveler
2/19/06

So the season is upon us.

In some pockets of town, I see the banners, flags, bunting, and lights with the colors that speak to my spirit, and I hear Al "Carnival Time" Johnson on the radio calling me to fall in.

By this time of year, I have usually wiped down the ladder that has been stowed in the shed for a year, making sure the safety straps, bead hooks, and cup holders—especially the cup holders—are tight and secure.

Sometimes I'll have added a fresh coat of paint.

But it's still in the shed as I write this. I'll get it out. Soon.

I see the empty stands down on The Avenue, waiting for the revelers to come. For some reason, I have always been rendered wistful by the sight of deserted stands and stadiums, and this year it's a small hole in my heart.

Even though they're at least a mile away, maybe more, sometimes in the afternoon if the wind blows just so, I can hear the St. Aug marching band—what's left of it—merged with St. Mary's and Xavier Prep, practicing their grooves in the streets of Uptown.

It is music from Heaven. If Heaven had a lot of trash on the sidewalk.

I see those roadside carny food trailers parked down by Lee Circle, and even though I have never bought a corn dog from them and probably never will, for some reason, as I drove past those monstrosities the other night, I felt . . . happy?

That's not the word for it. Happy is a tough place to get to these days. Especially with no street signs.

And "normal" isn't the word, because this Mardi Gras certainly won't be.

Comforted? Maybe that's it. I don't know.

Who can't use a little comfort these days? Who doesn't want their momma to hold them tight and tell them everything is going to be okay?

Maybe Mardi Gras is our chicken soup this year. For the soul. For the heart.

Will the first post-K Mardi Gras serve to reinvigorate civic pride and community cheer and our sense of esprit and renewal? Or will all the parading about on the only remaining sliver of habitable ground in a larger desolate wasteland only serve as a disjointed reminder of just how out of whack our lives have become?

Will the Carnival season, traditionally so full of rollicking good-time music, crawfish boils, and paradegoing throngs, remind us of how good it feels to be in a crowd of like-minded souls—our irrepressible community—or will it more resemble one of those painful New Year's Eve parties full of forced cheer and false promise?

I hate those parties.

In the relentless tides of emotions that batter us about in these hard times, I waver these days between dread and wistfulness, wistfulness and longing.

It's like getting stuck on some girl you knew in high school. Really stuck, for some odd reason, maybe because things aren't going so well at home, and you Google her late at night when no one will know.

You want to know what happened to her. Where she is. It becomes a strange fixation and you keep looking, even though you know you probably shouldn't. It can't lead to anything good.

Well, I just tried to Google my Mardi Gras of the past, and I got no hits.

I am so thankful I have little kids right now. I can perch myself on the backs of their ladders and make it all about them. The kids are who I always tell people it's about, but in truth, any parent (hell, any adult) knows that it's really about us and that the kids are just a necessary impediment to our unvarnished search for Total Joy.

It goes without saying that this Carnival season shall be like no other.

Several parade krewes had heavy water damage to their floats and some went to great lengths to obscure the flood stains, but others have purposely left the water damage in view.

I know of at least one krewe that will have a dark and riderless float this year as a reminder. Of what has happened. Of what is not here anymore. Of who is not here anymore.

A reminder that we are changed now and will be changed forever, maybe until the day we're all old biddies who talk about how we made it through Katrina like the old biddies around here used to talk about how they made it through Betsy and Camille.

Well, you don't hear them talk so tough anymore.

But we carry on. We deal.

My family will find a new street corner on The Avenue this year.

Our friends who hosted us for so many years—storing our ladder for three weeks, putting up with our kids and out-of-town guests, cheerily suffering through our overstayed welcome, year after year—well, they've sold their house and moved away.

I will miss them. But I miss a lot of things. Some are big and some are small and here's the weird thing: it's the small ones that can make you cry in your car when you are all alone.

I mean, Mardi Gras hasn't really gotten into swing, so I don't even know what it is I am missing—but I am missing something.

Ah, but aren't we all?

We've got other offers, other street corners we can go to. Our little perch at the corner of Milan and The Avenue is now but part of our scrapbook of family memories.

We'll plant our ladder in a new place and make new friends with the folks who've been there forever—as we used to be at our corner—and we will deal.

Who knows? Maybe a change of scenery will be refreshing. After all, it's just a parade, for cryin' out loud. Such a little thing, really.

Sweet sorrow. Mardi Gras, Mardi Gras, home again.

I hear Al "Carnival Time" Johnson calling my name, and I shall answer the call.

I gotta go get that ladder.

They Don't Get Mardi Gras, and They Never Will

2/2/06

I have decided to free myself of the yoke that burdens me. I am removing the boot heel from my neck.

From now on, I don't care what THEY think.

THEY think we're drunk, insouciant, lascivious, and racist. So be it.

THEY show the images of revelers flashing for beads on Bourbon Street as some sort of distasteful microcosm of the libertine life of New Orleanians—our callous dancing on the graves of the hurricane dead at Mardi Gras.

And the people in the Great Elsewhere watching these images in their living rooms are horrified at our behavior, but is anybody going to point out that 98 percent of the people flashing and taunting for beads on Bourbon Street are from THEIR hometowns?

That THEY are watching a mirror of THEMSELVES, not us?

Do they know that we don't actually hang out on Bourbon Street? That karaoke and cover bands and Huge Ass Beers are not where we're at, culturally speaking?

Not that there's anything wrong with Huge Ass Beers.

Bourbon Street is of great local value, don't get me wrong; it employs hundreds if not thousands of locals and serves as a licentious call to Middle America to come down here and forget your cares and maybe even your clothes.

But that's not us. That's not where I show my wits, so to speak. But if you watch cable TV coverage of Mardi Gras, THEY would have you believe that's US.

So be it. I can't bring myself to care about that anymore.

If you watch the news and read the papers in the Great Elsewhere, you will see Mardi Gras framed in simple, easy-to-grasp terms: it is rich people in Uptown drawing rooms, dressed in gilded capes and gowns that look like Liberace and waving scepters and wands at one another over the heads of their debutantes, the lily-white chosen few.

And then it is profoundly destitute black folks who are pushed to the margins of the celebration, left out, dismissed, forgotten, and trod upon.

Never mind that the story line leaves out several hundred thousand of the rest of us.

It's a journalistic device, and it works. National coverage of the flood has largely been played out to pit the rich white folks of Lakeview against the poor black folks of the Lower 9th, never mind that the flood itself ignored such devices and claimed lives, property, and peace of mind indiscriminately and equally across race, class, and gender lines and across hundreds of square miles.

The failure of the Corps of Engineers was true democracy in action. Or would that be inaction?

I have a friend, a citizen of the fallen nation of the Lower 9th, and she tells me that she is fed up with the reaction she gets when she tells someone that's where she is from.

"They immediately think I am poor, uneducated, have no car, no job, and was too stupid to get out of town when a hurricane comes," she says. "I was in Dallas; I'm not stupid."

Nor poor. Nor unemployed, nor, well . . . what the hell am I telling you for?

I live in a dreamworld.

That comes from living in New Orleans, of course, where

healthy doses of denial and delusion are as vital as food, water, and prescription medicines just to make it through the day.

I assumed that the flashy cable outlets would stick with the "tits and beer" story line but that, all in all, New Orleans would shine at this monumental crossroads: the first Mardi Gras after . . . The Thing.

I figured the thoughtful news organizations (yes, there are such entities, rare though they are) would "get it." But I would lump the *Chicago Tribune* into the "thoughtful" category (maybe I'm a newspaper sentimentalist) and I was pretty bummed out to read its recent front-page take on the matter.

It was a long story. Nicely written. But, in the end, it came down to this subheadline: CARNIVAL'S 2 FACES REFLECT CITY'S DIVIDE.

It's the story line that has played out ad nauseam across the globe. Rich white folks pitted against poor black folks. No shared interests or goals between the two.

Rex versus Zulu. The whole story.

I suspect it is too much to expect them to understand that this is probably the most complex ethnic and cultural port of call in America, that many Islenos of Plaquemines Parish have darker skin than many African Americans and that St. Patrick's Day is commandeered by rowdy Italians in green pants and that the cowboys of the prairies of southwest Louisiana don't look like John Wayne or Heath Ledger but are French-speaking black men with blue and green eyes.

There's the Quarter, of course, where men are men and women, too. Our canines, black and white, march together in parades. A metaphor?

I don't know. I live in a gold mansion and flew in teams of Israeli commandos in Black Hawk choppers to protect my silver and china when the looting broke out.

Okay, maybe I'm too sensitive. Maybe I'm too defensive. Maybe I have lost my path. Maybe it's I who don't "get it."

The city editor of this newspaper recently addressed a National Press Club banquet in Washington, D.C., and when he mentioned that Mardi Gras was viewed here in New Orleans largely as a nightly festival for children, he was greeted with snorts and guffaws.

By the men and women who are covering this thing, making the words and images that the Great Elsewhere consumes for dinner.

Whatev. It is what it is. We are what we are. No apologies necessary.

There are two days left before our season of atonement, remembrance, and renewal.

Live it.

Reality Fest
4/28/06

Take them to the ruins.

It's important. It will always be important.

This many months in, maybe you're tired of giving your relatives and friends the misery tour or maybe the city's wreckage is not what you want to dwell upon as you prepare to soak in the rays and revel in the sights, sounds, and smells of JazzFest.

Maybe you'd like to take the opportunity to step out of the darkness and into the light, if only for a weekend. Maybe you'd just like to kick your feet up and cut loose with your out-of-town friends and talk about things that people in other places talk about: baseball, gas prices, and what's the deal with Tom Hanks's hair in *The Da Vinci Code*?

Fine. Talk about those things with them. Talk about those things while you drive them around the city and show them what happened here.

It's important.

I have more visitors coming to stay with me this JazzFest than I have had in fifteen years—back when I was single, immortal, and had three million friends and a freezer filled with vodka bottles.

They're coming this year because they love this place and want to support this place and because of the general realization in the Great Elsewhere that any dollars spent here in New Orleans are a contribution to a good cause.

And it's quite possible that many visitors will want to witness what this city looks like right now—witness what it really feels like; they'll want to see the breaches, the brown lines, the Lower 9th, and the cloud of emotional dread that hangs over it all.

They'll want to understand what happened here, the scope of human suffering that occurred before and occurs still.

Then again, many may not want to see that. Quite frankly, they'd prefer to stick to Dylan, the 'dudes, and Fats, thank you very much. And my answer is: If you want to see Fats at the Fair Grounds, you've got to see his house on Caffin Avenue first.

You must pay to play.

No one who visits me this year is going to get to the festival without seeing Lakeview and eastern New Orleans first.

Yeah, even just a regular drive to the Fair Grounds from any point in the city is a strong cup of coffee, an unfiltered look at the damage done, and evidence enough of what went down here. And though I don't intend to bring my guests down, I think it's a small crime of negligence not to put this festival into context for them.

In that way, really, it actually becomes a bigger celebration than usual. A rebirth. A return. A claim to our heritage and our future. A testimony to the triumph of the human spirit.

The New Orleans spirit.

I think JazzFest visitors can collectively be considered among the most intellectually curious and influential visitors we'll see in the course of the year.

They will probably drink, yes, but they're not here for the liquor. I'd wager that the Bourbon Street strip clubs do not experience any great spike in business this time of year. But the record stores, music venues, art galleries, and bookstores do. These folks matter. They want to get it. So give it to them.

Undoubtedly, the spectacle of legions of video-toting gawkers in florid print Hawaiian shirts and straw hats and wearing socks with sandals and shorts will present a disconcerting sight among the colorless wreckage of the Lower 9th.

But it means no disrespect. It is no disrespect, any more than wanting to see where the Twin Towers once stood or the city of Pompeii.

From history, we learn.

Teach them. Teach yourself. Remind yourself, because we forget. We get used to it.

I recently drove a TV news producer around town and was down in the 8th Ward and remembered so painfully what it had looked like in September, so I was provoked to nod my head at the transformations since then and I offered, "Lookin' good!"

The producer, from New York City, looked at me as if I were out of my mind. "It does not look so good," he said.

Gut check. Correct. It does not look so good. It looks as though a war was fought here and we lost the war.

So never forget. And never surrender.

Love Fest
4/29/06

Arriving at JazzFest long before the gates opened Friday morning, I headed for the nearby Fair Grinds coffee shop for a cup of joe, to begin my personal celebration of JazzFest, beautiful JazzFest and not just another JazzFest, if you know what I mean.

And I think you do.

The Fair Grinds has not reopened since The Thing. But it has been giving free coffee to the neighborhood since October, providing a service of importance just a notch below that of the first responders.

Think about it: Once you put out the fire in my house and fix my head wound, please—may I have a cup of coffee?

Fair Grinds proprietor Robert Thompson says it may be another month, maybe two, before it opens again, because of hangups, bang-ups, and delays.

"We're in the New Orleans quagmire," he shrugged. "We're swimming in molasses."

That's a beautiful way, when you think about it, to describe a terrible thing. And more proof that when you get down to it, everything is about food.

Beneath our cheery demeanor this weekend as we greet our guests and our grandiloquent cultural gathering, the fact remains that we are a community largely held together by duct tape and delusion.

And truthfully, as I entered the festival grounds, I fully expected more of the ignominious weeping attacks I'm prone to that make everyone around me avert their eyes in embarrassment, but, in fact, I held up.

You try and you try and you try to get into the zone where you stop mourning what we aren't anymore and start celebrating what we are and what we will be one day. And I got there. I got a new attitude. A new set of clothes.

We told our kids they were playing hooky, and we rolled out. Oh, happy day.

The kids, they behave on days like this. After all, if they're getting on your nerves—if they whine too much—you simply say: Okay, you're right, this sucks. What say we just take you back to school for the day?

That usually works.

I wanted them to be there on the first day JazzFest played in the year 2006, with the idea that I will tell them when they get older—when they're teenagers—that they were here for this, were a part of it, part of something bigger than them and bigger than Mommy and Daddy and part of something important and even though their likely response will be "That's great, Dad, but can I use the car tonight or not?" I will still shoulder this burden for them and with them until "this" is them.

We waited in line a really, really, really long time to get into the Fair Grounds, and it's nice to know some of the festival's charms haven't changed despite the storm.

We grooved to the New Orleans Jazz Vipers. Anders Osborne laid out at least three new Katrina-themed songs, but they were neither maudlin nor sad but just good. I had managed to get this far in my life without ever hearing Johnny Sketch and the Dirty Notes and now I have and now I have a new favorite band.

They sang a song about St. Bernard Parish that was neither sad nor maudlin but just good.

Funny, the announcer who introduced the Dirty Notes did one of those "Let's hear it for our sponsors!" routines that

283 Dead in Attic 283

nobody ever listens to and he laid out Southern Comfort and everyone clapped and then American Express and then Shell and people clapped and you just couldn't imagine such a thing a few years ago.

Or ever, really, from your typical anticorporate JazzFest crowd. But everyone clapped. Because everyone realizes that without the big money—the guys in suits—this would likely be just another April weekend in New Orleans. Just another spring Friday.

Among the many lessons we have learned here in our little town is humility. Generosity and giving are hard enough, but this receiving thing can just knock you flat on your ass.

And so the day rambled along, and despite the occasional political T-shirt and the occasional Katrina ballad and the occasional thank-God-we're-here exhortations from stage emcees, it had all the flavor of, really, just another day at JazzFest.

A really good day at JazzFest. To hell with The Thing. Let's party.

And then the set by local rockers Cowboy Mouth provided just the right ominous poignancy, and isn't ominous poignancy really what you're looking for when you walk out your door each morning?

Drummer/singer Fred LeBlanc preached to the masses: "Some folks say we shouldn't talk about the elephant in the room today. Some folks say we shouldn't think about it. I say don't avoid it. I say dance all over the son of a bitch."

It was a point taken to heart, and the crowd danced all over the son of a bitch.

Then, the weirdest thing. It came during one of their signature concert sing-along songs that they were forced by circumstances to quit playing this past fall.

It's a chestnut: "Hurricane Party," a rollicking (and true) story about giving the finger to hurricanes in that insouciant and mildly charming way we used to do around here until, well . . . you know.

So they stopped playing it this fall as they toured America even though fans called for it. They stopped out of respect. Out of mourning. Because it just didn't work anymore.

But when Cowboy Mouth played the reopening of the House of Blues in December, they decided what the hell, let it rip, and they've put it back in their repertoire since, much to the delight of the Mouth faithful.

A flirtation with the fates and furies? Maybe. But it's only rock 'n' roll.

Or is it?

In the middle of the song Friday, the power went out at the Southern Comfort stage where Cowboy Mouth was playing. In my twenty-two years of JazzFest attendance, I've never seen this happen, a colossal technical glitch that ground a performance to a halt.

Total silence. Right in the middle of "Hurricane Party."

I mean, that's a coincidence, right? Please say yes.

After about ten or fifteen minutes, tech crews got the power back. Cowboy Mouth came back onstage.

Chastised by meteorological hoodoo? You better believe it. Rather than finish "Hurricane Party," they restarted their show with "Over the Rainbow" from *The Wizard of Oz.*

I'll leave it to you to decipher the symbolism therein. I've had enough of it myself for one day.

O Brothers, Where Be Y'all?
5/12/06

JazzFest 2006 can be regarded only as a huge success; the muses and the weather teamed up for a sublime celebration of Louisiana music, food, and culture.

And you don't say—even some jazz.

It was more evidence that the triumph of the human spirit is the engine running this city.

But there's no question that the festival's final moment allowed for a flood of conflicting emotions and—for JazzFest veterans—poignant absurdity.

For as long as I can remember, the festival's "closing ceremony" has pretty much followed this script: All the other stages shut down, the concession stands close, and all that remains is the encore on the Big Stage—Fess, Ray-Ban, Acura—whatever it's called in any particular year.

And that encore is imprinted in the New Orleans canon: As daylight fades to dusk, Aaron Neville sings "Amazing Grace" and then the First Family of Funk jumps in with a rousing version of Bob Marley's "One Love" or some other anthemic sing-along and fifty thousand people in the crowd fall all over themselves with tears, laughter, group hugs, and the general righteousness that attends the realization that you are, for one brief moment, at the center of the universe.

This moment has always spoken so clearly to the power of music, togetherness, community, love, and all those other squishy ideals we're afraid to speak of anymore but that still stand as worthy goals nonetheless.

If you have ever witnessed this glorious moment—where exhaustion, drunkenness, and aria mix their sultry stew—it stays with you forever. And I mean: forever.

Bereft of that annual emotional capstone, this year's festival was kind of like witnessing a grand opera without its finale.

For various reasons—Aaron's asthma, Cyril's sense of embittered entitlement—it's clear that the Neville Brothers, as a family unit, are not going to lead any part of the rebuilding of their hometown. Each brother has participated in benefit concerts outside the city, and that's, well, that's great.

So we move on. The landscape has changed, and we adjust to a new paradigm and that paradigm doesn't include the family band that has provided the sound track of our lives for the past thirty years and so be it.

But what a sound track. We will love them forever. But, as a T-shirt I saw at the Fair Grounds said, I guess we can call them the Never Brothers now.

The substitution of Fats Domino to fill the huge void of the closing act was brilliance on the part of festival producers, but Fats is always a no-show risk and he stayed true to form by bowing out at the last minute, showing up nattily dressed but also claiming ailments that would prevent him from performing. And so, in a quick stage rearrangement, we got—for that sweet, palpable group love moment—Lionel Richie.

To the JazzFest snob—and that seems like most everybody, because most everybody takes the appropriate sense of ownership from this event, our event, *my* event, dammit!—this news was nothing less than heretical.

The master of cheesy 1970s dance tunes and unbearably maudlin '80s ballads was going to lead us into the sunset? Into the future? Sure, there were the obligatory final jazz, zydeco, and gospel acts—but the visceral closer, the curtain call, the group therapy, the massive teardrop moment is always at the Big Stage. But Lionel Richie? It was so Not JazzFest and so Not New Orleans and probably anything but the cathartic moment that the thousands waited for, but I'll tell you this about Lionel Richie: he rose to the occasion.

Yeah, it was real Vegas-y, but the man sweated and he said the right things and he gave all and what more can you ask—especially when some dear to our hearts give little or nothing?

The man gave all. And God bless him for that.

He rolled out the hits, an embarrassingly large portfolio of familiar songs, the lyrics of which are imprinted into the cerebral cortex of every American between the ages of thirty and fifty-five, at least, and probably more like fifteen to seventy-five. So with a shrug the crowd said bring it on, and what the hell, and the hits rolled out and everyone kind of looked at one another and asked: Is it okay to dance to this? What if anyone from work sees me?

But of course it was okay to dance to this. This is our festival, so let's dance. All of us.

But you go first.

I guess somebody finally went first because everybody fell in and everybody sang along and what are you going to do? Instead of "Hey Pocky Way," "Yellow Moon," and "Sister Rosa" we got "Brick House," "Dancing on the Ceiling," and "All Night Long."

A friend next to me plopped into her folding chair and said, "I don't know if I'm going to make it. I'm running out of irony."

I told her: We're alive. Embrace the Lionel Moment. Seize the Lionel Moment. *Be the Lionel Moment.*

Truthfully, at that moment I would have danced to the sound of a fluorescent lightbulb humming. Because it's our moment and because we were there and even though it was a somewhat imponderable moment—no Neville Brothers at JazzFest?!?!—we did what we do because we are us.

The JazzFest had run out of beer and it went thirty minutes overtime and we danced. In the mud. In our hearts. On the ceiling.

The man gave all. And we gave it back. That is our obligation to any who will sing us a song and lift our spirits in this time of our unbending sorrow.

Sing to us, Aaron. We miss you.

Funeral for a Friend
5/5/06

A jazz funeral during JazzFest celebrates the life of yet another soul lost in the storm.

In this space last Friday, I made the case that New Orleanians should take their out-of-town visitors this week—or any week, for that matter—on a Misery Tour so they would better understand what happened here.

I followed my own advice Saturday morning and took two friends from California and my brother from Maryland—along with my three kids—to Gentilly and the Lower 9th for a look around before heading out to JazzFest.

They'd already seen Lakeview and Mid-City the day before. More than anything else, the emptiness of it all is what stirs the soul. That's what tells this story. Eight months later, the question still hammers home: Where the hell is everybody?

While we were tooling around the 8th Ward, we turned up St. Roch Avenue and got stalled behind a gathering in the street and, unaware of what was going on, I backed up and took a circuitous route around St. Roch Cemetery and then ended up in front of the crowd.

It was a funeral. A jazz funeral, of all things.

It was small. A hearse, one limo, and maybe forty people following. Several men with matching T-shirts followed close behind the hearse, with their hands on the back of it and their heads bowed. A ragtag band played a slow dirge.

Unlike the big and brassy processions that follow the passings of famous musicians around here, this one was off the radar. It was just some family and friends and none of the attendant video and camera crews that can turn these intimate gatherings into culture vulture documentaries rather than unique spiritual reckonings.

The St. Roch area is still so blown out and desolate that this pocket of humanity and color lent a haunting quality to the landscape. It looked like an apparition in the hushed grayness.

"Is this for real?" my guests asked me, and I told them yes, this is what happens here.

I felt intrusive—pulling over and opening the car doors for my guests—but how could you not stop and watch? I took off my hat, my one pathetic gesture of respect for those gathered, most of whom took no notice of us as they passed by.

As they turned a corner, the band shifted from mournful to mirthful—to that "Oh! Didn't He Ramble" sort of street jig they play when a jazz funeral turns its party switch on. And we watched from behind as the men cut, shuffled, and buck-jumped and took their brother home sweet home glory hallelujah.

"It's like a movie," someone in our group said, and that is indeed what it felt like. But real movies make events like these look so contrived and clownish that I suspect most people outside of New Orleans don't think there really are such things as jazz funerals but here it was, in its lonesome, wistful reality.

This spectacle told my guests so much more than my words ever could, so I turned on WWOZ and headed for the Fair Grounds and we set about the business of celebrating the life and survival—albeit somewhat tenuous—of this profoundly soulful city and its culture.

And then this week, in a moment of downtime, I rifled through some old papers stacked in my living room and found a death notice from last week announcing that a "Celebration of Life" would be held for Derrick Arthur Brown at Our Lady Star of the Sea Church on St. Roch Avenue last Saturday morning. And that's what we witnessed: a celebration of life.

I read more of the death notice and found out that Derrick Arthur Brown had graduated from McDonogh 35 and played football at Jackson State and used to mask with the Cherokee Hunters Mardi Gras Indian tribe and was once employed by a place called B-Neat Cleaners.

He was forty-seven, with two daughters and three grandkids, when he died.

And it said this: "Derrick Arthur Brown passed away on or about Aug. 29, 2005."

Eight months later, to the date, he was sent to his final home, and the measure of this information leaves me stupefied.

What to say? We're still burying them. Still burying us.

I don't have the words to comment on this, to lend any clarity or perspective. It just sits in your head with everything else.

Where was he all this time?

It fails to shock or stun because the bar on shock value around here has been raised so high. It just is what it is. And if nothing else, we find in a back-of-town street on a cloudy Saturday morning a small act of celebration, defiance, and closure for one more death in our family.

Thanks, We Needed That
8/15/06

A severely injured Kirk Gibson is sent out of the Los Angeles Dodgers dugout to pinch-hit in the ninth inning of the opening game of the 1988 World Series, a truly desperate moment; watching him walk to the plate, you doubt he could even run to first base if he hit the ball, which he probably won't do because he's facing arguably the greatest relief pitcher in history.

Then, amazingly, improbably—impossibly!—he homers and limps his way around the bases, fist pumping in triumph.

It's 1998, and Michael Jordan cans a jumper as time runs out, clinching his final championship with the Chicago Bulls. His victory leap becomes an iconic image of success. Nike's stock price rises 23 percent.

The 2000 World Golf Championships, eighteenth hole. It's not that daylight is fading; it's actually nighttime. Tiger Woods takes a literal shot in the dark with an eight-iron, 158 yards, and the ball somehow finds its way to within inches of the cup. Tiger taps it in for a win as flashbulbs explode to capture the moment.

It's 2006. Reggie Bush takes a handoff left and sees what Saints running backs have been seeing all their careers: the broad backs of their teammates' jerseys being pushed back at them.

So he cuts a hard right and, while twenty-one players on the field are moving in one direction, he is moving in the other and he gets 44 yards before anyone can catch him. The Reggie Bush era begins.

Okay, three of these are considered among the greatest moments in contemporary sports history. But only one was truly important.

I think you know where I'm going with this.

Truth is, no one outside New Orleans will ever remember what happened the other night. First of all, it was not only a preseason game, but it was the preseason *opener*, not just football's—but the entire world of sports'—least meaningful event.

If anything memorable happened at the game Saturday night—something that just might make the history books, in fact—it was that our backup quarterback was run over and injured by a golf cart driven by the Tennessee Titans' mascot.

How the hell does something like that happen? Aren't these people supposed to be protected from nonsense like that? I mean, when the Saints play the Falcons, can we send Whistle Monster or Holy Moses down to give Michael Vick a pregame wedgie or something?

Anyway.

Reggie's run was no Miracle on Ice or Hail Mary Pass or Immaculate Reception. (Please note the overtly religious overtones of great moments in sports history, for it is well documented that Jesus was mad for all sports, with the exception of bowling.)

But I don't think it's a stretch to suggest that those 44 yards— the first glimpse of the potential of this guy Reggie—were fraught with implication, both real and imagined.

The first point is: it gave us something to talk about that was completely unrelated to The Thing—if anything that happens around here can be said to occur outside the all-consuming context of The Thing, which I doubt it can, but let's go with it anyway.

I watched part of the game in a loud and crowded Bourbon Street bar Saturday night and was amazed at how I witnessed a single run from scrimmage play a small part in making some people whole again. Right before my very eyes.

I heard at least two conversations in which the term "playoffs" was bandied about, and I thought: Wow, I miss that playful delusion that everyone around here used to have. That completely illogical yet congenital attachment to schemes that don't work and if there was ever—historically speaking—a scheme that doesn't work, it's the Saints.

Now, truth is, I'm not a Saints fan in the conventional sense. I watch every game and listen to the postgame shows and all that, but I have always been fascinated by the Saints more as a sociological phenomenon than as a mere sports team.

We could dig deep into the well of New Orleans clichés about how we don't do anything the way they do it in other places and our relationship with our football team is certainly up there on that list. Their performance seems to have such a profound influence on the mood of this community and never more so than this year and I know that sounds superficial and, in fact, it is superficial.

Only a game, right?

Not anymore. Not here. Not now.

We need a real juggernaut to lift us up, and it turns out that a big fireworks display and masquerade ball, as our mayor suggested, to commemorate the drowning of New Orleans wasn't quite the answer.

But a winning football team? Ah, that would be something.

In fact, I'm worried that if the team doesn't deliver, it could deal a devastating blow to the psyche of the city. More than anything else Saturday night, I was hoping and praying not that Reggie would play well but that he simply wouldn't get injured—by an opposing team's linebacker or a middle-aged man wearing a big furry costume.

If Reggie goes down, I told a friend on the phone Saturday afternoon, it could be the proverbial straw that breaks this camel's back.

Levee failures, looting, death, destruction, murder, corruption, depression, suicide, bankruptcy—those we can handle.

But another losing season? Oh, the horror.

So mark it in your memory lockbox—that 44-yard run—just like remembering where you were and what you were doing when you heard that Kennedy was shot or O. J. Simpson was on the run or a man had walked on the moon.

That was one small step for Reggie Bush, one giant leap for New Orleans.

Say What's So, Joe
9/24/06

Dear Joe,

Welcome back to New Orleans. As you have probably noticed, a lot of the city looks like it did when you were last here, whenever that may have been, in our pre-Katrina state.

Admittedly, all those windows blown out of the Hyatt downtown have an ominous look about them, a jarring reminder of what went down here a year ago. And since they loom over the Superdome, they'll make for good TV images, and that's why I am writing to you.

I am offering you some unsolicited and perhaps unwelcome comments on how you should do your job Monday night.

Joe, I hate when strangers give me unsolicited advice on how to do my job. But you and me, Joe, we've got history together.

I grew up in Washington, D.C., and was a young man when you came to the Redskins and gave us a new attitude and our first Super Bowl win. That was a night to remember.

It was 1982, before the era when "fans" of NFL and NBA teams began that wonderful tradition of looting their downtown stores and burning cars to celebrate winning the championship.

Ah, the old days.

And by the time L.T. busted your leg on *Monday Night Football* all those years later, I was living here in New Orleans and watched the game with some friends in a bar in Kenner and I want you to know, Joe: I was there with you.

It hurt me as much as it hurt you.

Well, maybe not.

But I'm straying from the point. The point is, I don't know much about all the other sports guys who are in town this weekend telling America our story. But it worries me that they won't get it right, so I wanted to write to you to ask you to get it right.

There's that guy on Fox Sports named Chris Rose—he does that *Best Damn Sports Show* thing—and I suppose maybe he's the guy I should be talking to but I don't know Chris Rose and the whole idea of talking to a guy named Chris Rose is a little weird to me.

But I know you, Joe. When you're in New Orleans, you hang out at my neighborhood bar, Monkey Hill. Hell, Joe—we're practically family.

So here's the deal: I know you like to talk a lot, a whole lot—and that's okay because it's your job—but I'm like a lot of people around here, very sensitive about what people say about us these days.

Maybe too sensitive, I don't know.

I'm afraid our circumstances will end up being cast in sports metaphors, and somehow I get the feeling that we'll be portrayed as the '76 Buccaneers or the 2003 Detroit Tigers—teams without hope or redemption—when the way we really see ourselves is as the '69 Miracle Mets.

Sad-sack underdogs. The odds stacked against us. Backs against the wall, all that cliché stuff. And then—the great story line—pulling together and overcoming the odds and winning the big game!

Of course, I'm talking about the city of New Orleans and our neighboring communities, Joe. Not the Saints.

We've got bigger issues than the Falcons to deal with. We've got life. And a lot of our life depends on what all you sports guys tell the world about us and my guess is that you'll all go to our really great restaurants on your expense accounts and rave about the survival of New Orleans cuisine, so that one takes care of itself.

But there are other pressing matters at hand that might come up during your conversation with ten to fifteen million Americans tomorrow night, so I'd like to offer you some talking points.

The first is this: I'm assuming you had the professional curiosity and courtesy to drive around town and take a look at it for yourself. If you did, you now understand what we mean when we say you have to see it to believe it and you'll understand why we kind of freak out when the message that goes out is that a tiny and interesting place called the Lower 9th Ward got wiped out but everything else is okay.

And if you haven't seen the Lower 9th—or Gentilly or Lakeview or Chalmette or any area of the devastation, which is roughly the size of Great Britain—then please, don't even talk about it because you won't know what you're talking about.

Here's the message you need to give America, Joe, and this part gets a little confusing: Tell everyone that the city is rocking, it's alive and kicking with music and food and all that good-timing crazy stuff that Americans have come to expect when they visit here.

The fact is, you can spend a week downtown and in the Quarter and the Marigny and Garden District and Uptown—the small, old part of the city to which tourists usually confine themselves—and hardly see any manifestations of the storm, the flood, and its damages.

Tell people that, Joe. Tell them that New Orleans is still the best city in America. Tell them to come see for themselves, that we're happy, hopeful, joyful, and celebratory still.

Then tell them this: New Orleans is a broken, suffering mess, weakened and scared. We're not ashamed to say it, Joe: We're afraid.

Because what tourists never see is the other 80 percent of the city and that's the part where businesses, homes, and churches were wiped off the map and that's where despair and sorrow have set in like incurable viruses. Depression, divorce, and suicide are the trifecta in this town now.

Tell them that, Joe. Tell them that New Orleans is also the

worst place in America, dysfunctional and angry, victimized by looters, predators, insurance companies, utilities, and even government.

Got that? It's simple: Everything is fine here. But it's not fine. I'm not sure why people get so confused when we tell them that.

Anyway, Joe, tell them we don't want a handout. Tell them we just want a fair shake.

The Feds built crappy levees, Joe, weaker than the Packers' secondary, more porous than the Browns' offensive line, and tens of thousands of people lost their homes and possessions and all physical manifestations of their youth in the flood.

Imagine if you had no photos of your grandparents anymore, Joe, or of your Little League football team or your best friend from high school or the letters your dad wrote to you from Vietnam or the diaries you kept all your life or your wedding album or your collection of jazz 78s, baseball cards, or some other stupid thing that was really, *really* important to you.

Imagine if you had lost one of your parents to a slow and unbelievably agonizing death in a dank attic last year.

All right, I'll stop there with the gloom.

I'm just trying to say, Joe, that we're a proud people around here and we're held tighter together through age, race, and social class than the outside world has been led to believe and we are resilient and determined to save our city and our culture and I guess sometimes we hear out-of-towners say stupid things and we get all in a tizzy about it because we think no one understands us.

Then again, we don't understand ourselves. That's why we all find one another so interesting.

So have a good time while you're here, Joe, live the good life and loosen your tie and say hello to strangers and talk a good game tonight and remember that even if we can't stop Michael Vick, in the end, we're going to kick Katrina's ass.

It's third and long—real long—but there's still a lot of time on the clock and although our front office is a joke and the game plan is shaky at best, we've got the guts, the courage, and the tenacity to persevere and nobody works as hard as we do day after day because nobody else has to.

Remember that feeling, Joe? It's almost rapturous: when everyone thought you'd be a pushover? That you'd just lie down and quit in the face of insurmountable odds? And then you showed them what you were made of?

That's us, Joe. We're *The Bad News Bears*, man. We're *Angels in the Outfield, Brian's Song, The Longest Yard, Remember the Titans.* We're *Rocky*, dammit. And we're gonna rise up. Tell the world.

A Night to Remember
9/27/06

How do you dress your kids for school on the day the Saints play *Monday Night Football* if you don't have any Reggie Bush jerseys in their size?

It was a dilemma that none of my self-help parenting books addressed Monday morning as the ritualistic battle over what my kids would wear took on a different tenor than usual.

To send them to school in anything but black and gold—as the administration had urged parents to do in a show of school spirit and city unity—would have been akin to sending my children out trick-or-treating on Halloween without a costume.

Basic black we've got plenty of in my house, but here's the rub: who, besides Paris Hilton and Elton John, actually owns gold clothes?

There was much give-and-take, and I finally convinced my kids by heavily referencing Mardi Gras that yellow actually is gold, at least in New Orleans.

"Yellow," I told my daughter, "is the color of kings and Saints." This seemed to satisfy her.

At the parent/teacher/student assembly at my kids' school Monday morning, the only "educational" item on the agenda was whether face painting would be allowed that day.

This had actually been discussed in administrative meetings that morning.

Alas, it would not be allowed. There were groans. Principals can be so exasperating at times. The many children who had arrived with fleurs-de-lis already in place on cheeks and noses would have to turn themselves in for a scrubbing before reporting to class.

Then the music teacher stepped forward and began pounding out a melody on his chest with his hand, and he asked the parents to follow his lead and chant, over and over, "Saints go marching in, Saints go marching in . . .," which we did, maybe two hundred of us, in group baritone.

Then he led the children into a high-pitched, squealy version of the song over our jungle beat and it was beautiful, poetic, and touching.

And very strange, really, when you think about it. I looked around and thought: What the hell is going on around here?

Funny: as the meeting broke up and the kids went off to classes, many parents and teachers and kids all hugged one another before parting as if it were the last day of school, as if there would be some sort of transformation and personal growth before we all saw one another again—the next morning. You knew then that, well . . . Monday would be a day like no other.

And you keep telling yourself: It's only a game.

Who dat?

I had instructed my children that they were to respond to any questions asked by their teachers Monday with one answer: "The Deuce is loose!" and I was kind of kidding but kind of not and when my son Jack greeted his kindergarten teacher with this as he entered the classroom, she looked at me as if I were crazy and maybe I am but it's nothing a little tweaking of my medication can't cure.

What happened after that, I don't know, but I do admit—now that I've had time to consider the implications of the matter—to a little apprehension about all this.

I have witnessed, firsthand, the long-term health effects of being a Saints fan. It's not pretty. It's a meat grinder, truth be told.

You have to ask yourself, after all our children have been through around here—you know, that death and destruction thing—do you really want them to enter a culture that leaves scars worse than fire?

Ah, why not?

As I got to the Superdome about 2 P.M., I could see that what I had witnessed in a microcosm Uptown had layered itself over the city.

Through the fog of a thousand kettledrum grills and Webers smoldering under the interstate overpasses, in the cacophony of hundreds of minivans and pickups with their doors flung open, blasting "Hey Pocky A-Way" and "Yellow Moon," and under portable tents set up in parking lots and on neutral grounds, jammed full of rebels without a care, it smelled, sounded, and felt like a new day, a beautiful day.

And a choir of angels did sing from on high, "Who dat? Who dat?"

Or did I just imagine that part?

Clearly, no one went to work; either that, or the term "business casual" has taken on new meaning around here.

It seemed as though all the adults in town just dropped the kids off at school and hoped some teenager to whom we paid nine bucks an hour would pick them up after school and would feed and bathe them because we had more important matters to attend to: rebirthing a city. Or at least a step in the right direction.

Now, of course, there were naysayers out there in the Great Elsewhere. All that money, they said, that could have been used to fix people's houses. All that effort that could have gone somewhere else. All this fuss—about a game?

The simple answer is that, for the city's economy to survive, the Convention Center and the Dome had to be fixed—first and fast—because they are the bread and the butter.

A more nuanced answer is this: Better a Saints game to rechristen the building than a boat show or a gun show, for the irony of that would have been simply too much, even here in the city whose chief export in the post-Katrina age is, in fact, irony. By the ton.

Bobby, my best friend from first grade, called me from Kansas City on Monday afternoon to say everyone in his office was watching the pregame stuff on ESPN and some were grumbling about our misplaced priorities, but I asked him, "Then why is everyone watching TV at your office when they're supposed to be working?"

Obviously, people care about this.

And what can you tell them? That the Saints are family around here and you're stuck with that just like you're stuck with, well . . . family?

The Saints are our crazy Uncle Frank, prone to off-color remarks and broken promises and he's certainly not the guy you send to car pool to pick up your kids when you're stuck at the doctor's office, but you have to admit: holiday gatherings just aren't as much fun without him.

And every now and then he delivers a nice present when you least expect it.

Outside the Dome before the game, the "family" swelled into the tens of thousands and the crunch of bodies on the concourses around the building was, in fact, chaotic and probably dangerous.

Crowd control was an oxymoron. I wound up pinned in, unable to move in any direction while the Goo Goo Dolls were playing and I was smooshed up against a sweaty, shirtless, moose-jawed guy whose face paint was melting in the sun and we looked at each other and we found the same spiritual impulse overcome us at the same time.

We hugged.

I hugged a sweaty, moose-faced guy and it just felt right, dammit. So go ahead, judge me.

The Goo Goo Dolls' lead singer—he of the famously pasted hair and impossibly east European name—yelled to the crowd, "Thank you for letting us be a part of this. You're amazing."

And yes, we are.

All the stages fell silent in the minutes preceding the opening of the Superdome doors, silent in that kind of "Star-Spangled

Banner" way, and a guy onstage counted backward from ten as if it were New Year's and the crowd joined in and confetti cannons blasted a storm into the air as the doors swung open and little bits of colored paper—and you know what colors—floated across the expanse and people just stood there—tens of thousands of them—silent with their arms raised in the air like it was the Rapture.

And it was.

This building, this monument to our shame, our disgrace, and our sorrow, will always be so, but it always has been and always will be more than that. Neither Katrina nor Tom Benson has been able to make the Superdome go away.

Its durability is our durability.

Untold hundreds, maybe thousands, of people were reentering the building Monday night for the first time since they had walked out of it last September—as evacuees, employees, police, and rescuers.

They will never forget. We will never forget. But we will also never surrender.

There was a game to play, but, before that, rock stars and ex-presidents, Hall of Famers and celebrities, cheerleaders and first responders and pomp, circumstance, and glory and it was too much, really—all for a game—but then again everything around here is too much, all day, every day, so why not too much here and now?

All the meanderers in the hallways and bathrooms were running into old friends, hugging the ticket takers just because, tipping like madmen, yelling incoherent cries of pride and defiance.

And the drunkest of them yelling, "Super Bowl!"

Funny, just about everyone in the visiting media made Super Bowl references—that was what it felt like—but they failed to realize that Super Bowls have no home teams. There is no sense of desire, longing, and need at a Super Bowl.

Irma sang the national anthem. Jesus wept and I died. Then and there. Died over and over. Live, die, rise up. Live, die, rise up. Over and over.

I was exhausted. I was ready to go home. And the game hadn't even started.

The game. When they blocked the punt and scored the first touchdown, something inside me that I didn't know was there broke loose. I let out a yell so loud that my throat still hurts today.

I fell into a human scrum that consisted of a tall skinny guy, a short woman, a cop, and a beer vendor. Every layer of authority and sociology was stripped away. We literally fell on top of each other. I have never experienced a flash point of sudden emotion unloosed so fast.

No drug, religion, or meditation has ever taken me there. And I don't know: maybe people in cities with great teams do that all the time, but this was a crazy good thing. Love Potion No. 9. I started hugging everyone in sight.

And, well, you know what happened after that. After the game, I thought about going to the Quarter or finding all my friends and waking the dead but, in the end, I turned to my wife and said, "I've given everything I've got."

I remember being all worked up in the daze leading up to the game, worried about the message we were sending America, and worried about what the guys in the broadcast booth were going to say, but the fact is, I don't know what they said or how it all looked because I was acting a fool and hugging strangers and too busy making seventy thousand new friends to give a hoot what everybody else thinks.

It is superficial and meaningless and a sign of total loss of perspective, but I stand before you and I declare: It is good to feel like a winner.

And out my window today as I write this—my open window, oh, glorious day—I hear the same sounds I hear every day—chain saws and hammers and drills—and it would be foolish to suggest that the workers have more pep in their step today and that everything is going to be easier now because, well . . . because it's not.

It's a long road home no matter what colored glasses you're wearing today, but there is something about waking up in a community that is thinking the same thing, that is feeling—if only for a moment—as if we had all just accomplished something together—when actually it was a bunch of millionaires whose names we hardly know.

Ah, but let us live it, just for today, because who around here hasn't felt as though we've had a big *L* stamped on our foreheads for the past year and I, for one, am ready to wipe it off, like all those silly kids had to do at Lusher Elementary the other day when the principal brought the hammer down.

Only a game, you say?

Like hell it was.

Eternal Dome Nation
10/3/06

My euphoria over the Saints dissipated this weekend, but it was long before their loss to the Carolina Panthers.

Though I'm still inspired by the team and their determination, it must be remembered that they are merely an enjoyable diversion from the massive challenges at hand—challenges for which the nation's goodwill and assistance are most vital.

But I have come to the discomfiting conclusion that all the hoopla and feel-good that we displayed to the country leading up to and during the *Monday Night Football* game did not translate in the American Heartland the way we might have hoped.

I was under the impression that we would win back America's love and admiration for our steely reserve and equanimity in the face of adversity and our ability to come together in communal celebration despite personal lives shrouded in sorrow.

Despite ESPN's sensitive handling of the tricky "New Orleans is back/New Orleans is definitely not back" message that we needed to send out, it seems that lots of folks did not buy into the Superdome extravaganza as a good thing at all.

This became clear to me as I read the letters to the editor in the weekend edition of *USA Today*. And while I am somewhat loath to let *USA Today* set the tone of dialogue on south Louisiana's recovery, there can be no getting around the unanimity of views of the six letters published on this topic.

To summarize their words: We—we being anyone who cheered for the Saints or greeted the Dome's reopening as a forward step in recovery—are wrong.

Let me offer a sampling from each letter.

Ravi Mangla of Fairport, New York, wrote:

Using the New Orleans Saints' home game at the Superdome as a metaphor for a city returning to normalcy after a horrific disaster is such arrant dreck. I found myself frustrated Monday, hearing reports describing how "inspiring" and "uplifting" it was for New Orleans' citizens to finally get their team back. What would be more inspiring and uplifting, in my opinion, would be seeing all the people of New Orleans finally getting their homes back.

Mark Washington of Omaha, Nebraska, wrote:

As an African-American, I was disturbed about things I saw on TV: Thousands of mostly white faces in the stands being sere-naded by white rock musicians. It wasn't exactly a vision of a re-turning New Orleans.

I highly doubt that the vast majority of former New Orleans residents, who happen to be African-Americans, would have se-lected U2 or Green Day as their preferred entertainment.

Jack Wood of Fort Wayne, Indiana, wrote:

Federal funding contributed hugely to the $185 million it cost to renovate the Superdome in New Orleans? Where are our priori-ties? With garbage still clogging the streets and people still home-less, what could that money have done to correct those conditions? This appears to be just another example of badly placed priorities by Americans. We should all be ashamed to put a football game ahead of human suffering.

Mark Van Patten of Bowling Green, Kentucky, wrote:

The restored Superdome is an ugly concrete monument plopped
down between interstate highway loops. It reflects the difference
in the classes in New Orleans.

When it was convenient, the poor were inhumanely herded
there to await rescue. Now, the Superdome is ready for business,
but the poor will not be welcome because they don't have the
money for admission or they have been relocated to another
city.

Ira Lacher of Des Moines, Iowa, wrote:

How many of the thousands of displaced New Orleanians could
have rebuilt their homes with the $185 million that was squan-
dered on restoring the Superdome for the use of overpaid professional athletes?

And Donald and Anna Mulligan of Upper Black Eddy, Pennsylvania, weighed in:

Very few hospitals and schools have opened in the city. And most
business owners are still out of luck. But the city says, "Let the
games begin."

As we've always said, when you have a city that prides itself on
booze, food, gambling and parades, what can we expect?

May God help us all.

All righty then. Thank you, America, for your comments. Now,
before I respond, let me pause here while you, the reader, go
refill your coffee cup. Or your big glass of bourbon or while you
take a break from the blackjack table or between lap dances or
while you rest between bites of an overstuffed alligator and hogs-
head cheese po-boy.

Where to begin? They don't give me enough space in the
paper to say all I want to say, but here we go.

Let's start with this: If we did not open the Superdome for

Saints games, presumably we could not then open it for the Bayou Classic, the Sugar Bowl, Tulane football, the state high school football championships, the Essence Music Festival, rock concerts, religious revivals, car shows, home and garden shows, or anything else that happens there in the course of a normal year and that generates massive spending, jobs, and activity in the community.

No Super Bowls, no NCAA championships, and no chance at the national political conventions. And, worst of all, no monster trucks.

I'm guessing those opposed to repairing and renovating the Dome for $185 million wouldn't buy into the concept of building a new stadium from scratch for about five times that amount. And therefore the logical extension is that all of the above events be moved to Houston, Atlanta, or somewhere else and Tulane can just play their games at Muss Bertolino Stadium in Kenner and this community can just muddle along without the perverse spectacle of "games" in a building that housed sorrow and despair.

The Saints? Send them to San Antonio. The Sugar Bowl? Please, don't trifle around while there is still garbage to be picked up.

The arguments posited in *USA Today* seem to suggest that there be no compartmentalization of funding for recovery. In other words, that repairing the Dome prevents homes' being rebuilt in the 9th Ward. Or that patching potholes on Bourbon Street is keeping hospitals from opening. Or that reopening the Aquarium of the Americas—or doing anything with federal dollars that rebuilds our economic engines rather than homes—keeps people homeless.

Pardon my plagiarism, but that is arrant dreck.

That people were "herded" into the Dome during Katrina is an interesting word choice. Here's some numbers for you provided by the Dome's administrative office:

Prior to the levees breaking and the water pouring into the city, there were approximately 10,000 evacuees inside the Dome. After the flood waters rose and trapped a population across the region, 20,000 more were delivered to the Dome by air and boat and bus.

I ask you—and those twenty thousand people: Better to be at the Dome or trapped on your roof or in your attic for those four days?

The fact is, the Dome, for all its squalor and misery, saved lives. It wasn't Abu Ghraib. The toilets didn't flush and there was no cold drinking water and not enough medicine, but toilets didn't flush anywhere and there was no ice or medicine anywhere and it's crazy to think that only folks who were at the Dome or the Convention Center have a lock on the misery that befell the Gulf Coast in early September 2005.

Everyone's got a story in this town, in this region, and not one I've heard is a day at the park.

While we're at it, let me toss this gasoline on the fire, a snippet from an editorial in the current issue of *The Nation*:

> The reality of refugee apartheid is hardly a memory. The game was held hostage to the awkward fact that the folks starring in ESPN's video montages of last year's "cesspool" were almost entirely black and the football fans in the stands were overwhelmingly white. But recognizing this would contradict the infomercial for the new Big Easy that was designed to appeal to the typical family, which finds gumbo too spicy and thinks of soul as something consumed with tartar sauce.

A guy named Dave Zirin wrote this; another guy who wasn't there telling me how white it was. Zirin also took umbrage with U2 and Green Day playing instead of the Neville or Marsalis families.

Well, I would have liked that, too, but guess what? The Neville Brothers won't play in New Orleans. And the Marsalises? I don't know, except that I saw Branford on the sidelines joshing around with Spike Lee, whose enthusiasm for the evening was palpable, so add his name to the roster of folks who just don't get it.

Not to suggest that Zirin is a conspiracy theorist or anything, but he also said that ESPN blocked out the live sound from the

Dome and played fake cheers on the air when former president Bush was introduced because the sound of booing was so resounding in the Dome, and again—why are people who weren't there talking about things that didn't happen?

That is utter nonsense.

Why are we having this discussion still? Why are people from other places spending so much effort to tell us that, as a community, we are wrong, misguided, amoral, and racist? Why are they making things up?

I mean, I can't really fathom how to craft a sensible response to a black man from Omaha who was offended by the appearance of U2. I mean, is this really an issue?

No African Americans on the Saints roster or in Southern University's band or in the attendant media or Dome employees or security staffs or Irma Thomas or Allen Toussaint or the first responders who were honored or African-American season ticket holders chose to boycott the game, and maybe that's because they don't get it.

If there weren't thousands and thousands of black folks in the seats Monday night, then I am blind. And it might be worth noting—just because I'm feeling ornery—that when you incorporate surrounding parishes and trace a map from southern Mississippi up through central Louisiana, the demographic makeup of the Saints' potential fan base is not an African-American majority.

In fact, it's not even close—but acknowledging this would weaken the demagogic arguments of outsiders who keep hammering home just what a cesspool of humanity we've turned out to be here in south Louisiana. Human dreck. Unworthy.

Let me ask you something, Omaha: If you get your ass kicked by a tornado, are you going to tell the College World Series to permanently relocate somewhere else so you can get your priorities in order?

Hey, Bowling Green: If Louisville or Lexington gets whacked with a dirty bomb and has to rebuild from scratch, where will the Kentucky Derby and Wildcats basketball fit into the recovery? Disposable entities, last on the list?

Hey, Upper Black Eddy, Pennsylvania . . . oh, never mind.

I called the editorial-page editor of *USA Today* to ask if he thought those letters were representative of American thought on the matter, but he didn't return my call.

Unlike some of that newspaper's correspondents, I don't speak for black people. And I don't speak for other white people. I speak for me, and I'll take the grenade on this one if my priorities are so misplaced as to think that the opening of the Dome was, above all else, an enormous boost to our economy—to say nothing of our spirits.

But then again, maybe I'm just fat, lazy, drunk, and stupid and don't get it and never will.

Just throw me something, mister, and I'll be content to mind my own business and ignore all the suffering around me while I wave my foam finger in the air and scream into America's living rooms, "Who dat say?"

Me dat say. Dat's who.

Falling Down

On the Inside Looking Out
6/16/06

I was in Washington, D.C., recently, talking to a very educated
man who was making reference to another man he knows who
does restaurant consulting work in New Orleans.

The man, a school administrator, said to me, "I don't know
what he thinks he's doing there. There are no restaurants in New
Orleans anymore."

Cue the ominous sound effect between scenes in *Law &
Order*.

I was recently working with an out-of-town TV news producer
who was looking to set up a shot of neighborhood desolation
and he asked me if I thought it would be hard to find any concentration of damaged and abandoned houses in New Orleans.

Cue the ominous sound effect between scenes in *Law &
Order*.

I was in Portland, Oregon, this week and I heard a guy in a
bar hold court with stories about New Orleans. He said, "The
police on Bourbon Street, they come around at night with a big
cart—like a hot dog cart—and they pile up all the drunk and
passed-out people on it and wheel them off to jail."

Cue the buzzer, the gong, the cowbell.

A hot dog cart?

Obviously, the range of opinions and "knowledge" about New

Orleans out in the Great Elsewhere is staggering. Said a documentary filmmaker from Indianapolis to me the other day, "Speaking for central Indiana, it's not that people don't care about New Orleans. It's more that they're oblivious to what happened. They just don't know."

And so some folks think New Orleans is a fine and peachy place, where finding footage of wrecked houses would be a challenge all these months later. And some folks think there are no restaurants open.

And some folks, it seems, got so pie-eyed when they visited Bourbon Street that they hallucinated some bizarre vision that married the cops and the Lucky Dog guys into a harmoniously cartoonish image of civic peacekeeping.

I've been traveling a lot lately. "How is New Orleans doing?" people ask all along the way, and they do care—really, really care—you can tell. But how do you answer that question?

Unless they have two days to listen to you talk about the unraveling of the social fabric, the menace of crime, the absence of leadership, the palpable fear of another hurricane, and the fact that fifteen of your closest friends are making plans to move away—joining the other fifteen of your closest friends who already have moved away—what do you tell them?

My wife and I recently made the circuit of journalism awards banquets in the Northeast, and I watched my media colleagues and peers fall into easy shoptalk at these events, but somehow Kelly and I always stood off to the side, wondering who all these people were and what they were talking about.

We were guests at many of these events and—in some cases—honorees, as I have had the privilege of picking up several awards that *The Times-Picayune* has won for its coverage of this unholy mess.

And people are warm and gracious and concerned, but at each event I asked my wife, "Did you ever go to a wedding where you didn't know the bride or the groom?"

That's kind of what it's like to be from New Orleans as you travel around the country these days. You just can't find the rhythm of the outside. Of the other.

I am on a plane bound for Salt Lake City as I write this, and I look around and realize how disconnected my life is from those of the folks who sit around me.

Not that they don't have troubles and sorrows and issues, too, but they don't necessarily look lost in a fog of war. I look around at the sleepy faces and the faces buried in books and newspapers and the bobbing heads of folks plugged into iPods and I wonder when I'll ever get back to the place where they are.

A City on Hold
8/27/06

I think I speak for most everyone in the room when I say: I am ready for August 30, 2006.

I am ready to get on with the next phase of all of this, whatever joys or traumas, comedy or tragedy, successes or setbacks it may bring.

It seems as if we folks in and around New Orleans have been stuck in that netherworld so aptly described in Dr. Seuss's immortal reflection in the pages of *Oh, the Places You'll Go!*.

He called it "The Waiting Place."

Waiting for the fish to bite
or waiting for wind to fly a kite
or waiting around for Friday night
or waiting, perhaps, for their Uncle Jake
or a pot to boil, or a Better Break
or a string of pearls, or a pair of pants
or a wig with curls, or Another Chance.

Sound familiar? Sound like your life?

Substitute "insurance settlement," "FEMA trailer," and "contractor to call," and bingo: Oh, the places you'll go.

Waiting for three cycles of the light to change on Causeway.

Waiting three hours to get a new driver's license. Waiting to see who comes back and who moves away. Waiting to hear what our mayor will say next.

Waiting to feel better. Waiting to get worse. Waiting for a Better Break or Another Chance. Does that day ever come?

Yeah, you're right. And waiting for the next hurricane.

Therein lies the rub. Even more than suffering from anniversary anxiety—the cauldron of agony and memory that we are boiling in—it seems as though much of our communal psyche is caught up in the strange and fruitless wait for the next big storm to come our way to see how we handle it—physically, civically, emotionally.

It's as if we want to know if we can take the hit and get back up again. It's like being a star quarterback or running back who gets injured and waits a whole season to play again and going into that first game thinking: Just get the first hit over with.

Like being a boxer stepping into a ring with a feared competitor. Just hit me and let's get on with this thing.

Let me get by Tuesday without succumbing to all the bad stuff that emanates from the newspaper, the radio, television, and every conversation with every friend and family member.

Let me remember the good stuff: people reaching out, helping. People coming together.

I remember: 9/11 was on a Tuesday. On Wednesday, about midday, I turned off the TV and told my wife, "I don't ever want to watch those buildings fall down again for as long as I live."

And I have never seen them fall again. Not once. It's an image television has largely shielded us from, though I suspect that in the coming weeks, that might change.

So sometimes I wonder how much I need to see and hear about last year, here.

Those people standing on rooftops with signs that say, HELP Us. Do you remember the horror of that first vision—for most of us, from the relative comfort of a hotel room or the home of a far-flung family member—and the dread that gripped you when you asked, "My God, what is happening down there? This can't be happening."

It happened, all right.

The whole damn city underwater, rooftops peeking out like alligator heads all in a row. Thousands trapped in hell. The Convention Center. That dead woman in a wheelchair with a blanket thrown over her. Wal-Mart. The looters.

We're going to see all of it plenty on TV's endless loop of sorrow. And I guess we must tune in because we must never forget.

Then again, how could we? What a disgrace, the whole damn thing, and there are so many to blame, but that seems beside the point now or, at least, not the main point anymore.

Our mayor keeps pointing fingers—all this time later—but everyone knows what went down and how it went down so, what the hell. What do we do now?

Just hit me.

Let's pick up the pieces still. Put it back together more. Let life ramble on in the new New Orleans, where everything is different and everyone is upside down in The Waiting Place.

My friend Jenni noticed that folks around here start conversations differently now. "Instead of asking 'Where did you go to school?' people ask, 'What medications are you taking?'"

Try that for an icebreaker with a stranger. The next time you're waiting in line.

A Tough Nut to Crack
3/28/06

A high school student from New Jersey interviewed me over the weekend for a school project and asked me, "Has Katrina changed your life and, if so, how?"

Well. Interesting question.

How much time do we have?

I gave the kid a pat answer about how this whole thing has shaken us to our very core as individuals and a community and left it at that, but it did give me pause.

Forgive my navel gazing, but I honestly cannot think of a single aspect of my life—as a writer, a father, a husband, a son, a person—that is not different from the way it was before.

For instance, I haven't played golf since The Thing, and that's all wrong.

And I have lost weight. Maybe too much. All of my pants are falling down.

When people comment on this to me, I dismiss it by telling them that my dramatic weight loss is actually a political statement, a living art installation, if you will, an anthropomorphic representation of the disappearing Louisiana wetlands.

This usually prompts a quizzical stare, then a comment like "Well, okay, I was just wondering if you wanted to share my sandwich."

And since I don't eat anymore—because eating is just a smug affectation of the bourgeoisie—feeding my kids has become a minor annoyance. Sometimes I get frustrated with their neediness. I ask my wife, "Why can't they just get by on cocktail peanuts and cigarettes like the rest of us?"

We pamper our kids too much today.

I have written extensively in this space about my personal trials of survival and adaptation in our post-Katrina world and, as a result, have been flooded with e-mails from psychotherapists and other mental health professionals who tell me that my sudden irrationality and irritability, coupled with my loss of former interests and hobbies, all paint a classic portrait of the post-traumatic stress syndrome sufferer.

I reflect on my current life and my actions, and I think: You needed to go to Harvard to come up with that?

In many ways, I feel as if I have become the New Orleans poster boy for posttraumatic stress, chronicling my descent into madness for everyone to read.

A psychologist from Lafayette, Heidi Perryman, sent me this: "You have chosen (or been chosen) to bear the cross of 'witness' to this tragedy and, like the Holocaust survivors before you who held their lives together on the notion of telling the story of what happened, you have saved yourself from disintegration and simultaneously exposed your readers to its threat."

And I thought it was just another day at the office. I thought it was the flood. I thought it was the looting and the burning and dead people.

I thought it was the refrigerators.

I got this from a woman in Tangipahoa Parish: "This mirror you've shown us reflects who we have become and where we'll go if we allow ourselves to become covered with darkness and despair."

This e-mail was signed "Deputy Susie." Now, correct me if my memory fails me, but isn't Deputy Susie a little kids' TV show personality?

Let me get this straight: Now I've got someone who teaches

children the difference between "good touch" and "bad touch" telling me I am "covered with darkness and despair"?

It has come to this? This can't be a good thing.

It makes me feel as though I—with the notable exception of Kimberly Williamson Butler—have performed the most public crack-up in a city full of people cracking up.

The triumph of this phenomenon was the recent delivery of a complimentary issue of *Grief Digest,* sent to me by a publishing company called the Centering Corporation, accompanied by a note that said, "We thought you might be interested in this."

And that's my journey—from *Golf Digest* to *Grief Digest* in twenty-eight short weeks. And "Lose Weight While You Go Crazy!" Operators are standing by.

In the Philippines. Or wherever.

Speaking of that. I was recently trying to track down a FedEx package that was late arriving to my house, and I got an operator on the line and she told me, "Sir, it seems there's a problem with the weather."

Then she paused, clicked away at her computer keyboard, and asked, "Was there a hurricane?"

Count to ten. Take a breath. Think: Has Katrina changed your life and, if so, how?

"Well," I told her. "Yes. Yes, there was a hurricane. It was seven months ago. The roads are clear now. The rebel forces have been defeated. Could you please tell me where my package is?"

And tell me: How is the weather in Malaysia these days?

And anyone wonders why we're all nuts?

I was part of a recent public forum on the mental health crisis here in town. The first presentation was on how to recognize the signs of post-traumatic stress syndrome, and when the doctor showed a list of the symptoms on his PowerPoint, everyone in the auditorium just started laughing.

I mean, they howled. Gut-busting hoo-has. Turns out, everyone in the room had every symptom and you don't need me to list them here because you're probably just curled into the fetal position on your kitchen floor, lying in a pool of hot coffee and reading the same sentence over and over and over again anyway, so you don't need me to tell you that the sensation of spiders crawling all over your face is perfectly normal.

The second presenter, one of those social-worker women who are cheerful to the point of annoying, then got up and offered ways to battle the darkness.

She listed exercise and proper diet and all that hooey. Then she got all New Agey and said that when times are bad, you should hug yourself.

Well, that's fine advice for those with more self-restraint than me, because every time I hug myself I wind up making promises I can't keep and spending more than I can afford on dinner and a movie and for what, I ask you?

I'd rather go it alone, thank you. Me and all the voices in my head telling me everything is going to be okay.

Hell and Back
10/22/06

I pulled into the Shell station on Magazine Street, my car running on fumes. I turned off the engine. Then I just sat there.

There were other people pumping gas at the island I had pulled into and I didn't want them to see me, didn't want to see them, didn't want to nod hello, didn't want to interact in any fashion.

Outside the window, they looked like characters in a movie. But not my movie.

I tried to wait them out, but others would follow, get out of their cars and pump and pay and drive off, always followed by more cars, more people. How can they do this, like everything is normal, I wondered. Where do they go? What do they do?

It was early August, and two minutes in my car with the windows up and the air conditioner off were insufferable. I was trapped, in my car and in my head.

So I drove off with an empty tank rather than face strangers at a gas station.

Before I continue this story, I should make a confession: for all of my adult life, when I gave it thought—which wasn't very often—I regarded the concepts of depression and anxiety as pretty much a load of hooey.

I never accorded any credibility to the idea that such conditions were medical in nature. Nothing scientific about it. You get sick, get fired, fall in love, get laid, buy a new pair of shoes, join a gym, get religion, seasons change—whatever; you go with the flow, dust yourself off, get back in the game. I thought antidepressants were for desperate housewives and fragile poets.

I no longer feel that way. Not since I fell down the rabbit hole myself and enough hands reached down to pull me out.

One of those hands belonged to a psychiatrist holding a prescription for antidepressants. I took it. And it changed my life.

Maybe saved my life.

This is the story of one journey—my journey—to the edge of the post-Katrina abyss and back again. It is a story with a happy ending—at least so far.

I had already stopped going to the grocery store weeks before the Shell station meltdown. I had made every excuse possible to avoid going to my office because I didn't want to see anyone, didn't want to engage in small talk, Hey, how's the family?

My hands shook. I had to look down when I walked down the steps, holding the banister to keep steady. I was at risk every time I got behind the wheel of a car; I couldn't pay attention.

I lost fifteen pounds, and it's safe to say I didn't have a lot to give. I stopped talking to Kelly, my wife. She loathed me, my silences, my distance, my inertia.

I stopped walking my dog, so she hated me, too. The grass and weeds in my yard just grew and grew.

I stopped talking to my family and my friends. I stopped answering phone calls and e-mails. I maintained limited communication with my editors to keep my job, but I started missing deadlines anyway.

My editors, they were kind. They cut me slack. There's a lot of slack being cut in this town now. A lot of legroom, empathy, and forgiveness.

I tried to keep an open line of communication with my kids to keep my sanity, but it was still slipping away. My two oldest, seven and five, began asking "What are you looking at, Daddy?"

The thousand-yard stare. I couldn't shake it. Boring holes into the house behind my backyard. Daddy is a zombie. That was my movie: Night of the Living Dead. Followed by Morning of the Living Dead, followed by Afternoon . . .

My own darkness first became visible last fall. As the days of covering the Aftermath turned into weeks that turned into months, I began taking long walks, miles and miles, late at night, one arm pinned to my side, the other waving in stride. I became one of those guys you see coming down the street and you cross over to get out of the way.

I had crying jags and fetal positionings and other "episodes." One day last fall, while the city was still mostly abandoned, I passed out on the job, fell face-first into a tree, snapped my glasses in half, gouged a hole in my forehead, and lay unconscious on the side of the road for an entire afternoon.

You might think that would have been a wake-up call, but it wasn't. Instead, like everything else happening to me, I wrote a column about it, trying to make it all sound so funny.

It probably didn't help that my wife and kids spent the last four months of 2005 at my parents' home in Maryland. Until Christmas I worked, and lived, completely alone.

Even when my family finally returned, I spent the next several months driving endlessly through bombed-out neighborhoods. I met legions of people who appeared to be dying from sadness, and I wrote about them.

I was receiving thousands of e-mails in reaction to my stories in the paper, and most of them were more accounts of death, destruction, and despondency by people from around south Louisiana. I am pretty sure I possess the largest archive of personal Katrina stories, little histories that would break your heart.

I guess they broke mine.

I am an audience for other people's pain. But I never considered seeking treatment. I was afraid that medication would alter my emotions to a point of insensitivity, lower my antennae to where I would no longer feel the acute grip that Katrina and the flood have on the city's psyche.

I thought, I must bleed into the pages for my art. Talk about "embedded" journalism; this was the real deal.

Worse than chronicling a region's lamentation, I thought, would be walking around like an ambassador from Happy Town telling everybody that everything is just fine, carry on, chin up, let a smile be your umbrella.

As time wore on, the toll at home worsened. I declined all dinner invitations that my wife wanted desperately to accept, something to get me out of the house, get my feet moving. I let the lawn and weeds overgrow and didn't pick up my dog's waste. I rarely shaved or even bathed. I stayed in bed as long as I could, as often as I could. What a charmer I had become.

I don't drink anymore, so the nightly self-narcolepsy that so many in this community employ was not an option. And I don't watch TV. So I developed an infinite capacity to just sit and stare. I'd noodle around on the piano, read weightless fiction, and reach for my kids, always, trying to hold them, touch them, kiss them.

Tell them I was still here.

But I was disappearing fast, slogging through winter and spring and grinding to a halt by summer. I was a dead man walking.

I had never been so scared in my life.

Early this summer, with the darkness clinging to me like my own personal humidity, my stories in the newspaper moved from gray to brown to black. Readers wanted stories of hope, inspiration, and triumph, something to cling to; I gave them anger and sadness and gloom. They started e-mailing me, telling me I was bringing them down when they were already down enough.

This one, August 21, from a reader named Molly: "I recently became worried about you. I read your column and you seemed so sad. And not in a fakey-columnist kind of way."

This one, August 19, from Debbie Koppman: "I'm a big fan. But I gotta tell ya—I can't read your columns anymore. They are depressing. I wish you'd write about something positive."

There were scores of e-mails like this, maybe hundreds. I lost count. Most were kind—solicitous, even; strangers invited me over for a warm meal.

But this one, on August 14, from a reader named Johnny Culpepper, stuck out: "Your stories are played out Rose. Why don't you just leave the city, you're not happy, you bitch and moan all the time. Just leave or pull the trigger and get it over with."

I'm sure he didn't mean it literally—or maybe he did, I don't know—but truthfully, I thought it was funny. I showed it around to my wife and editors.

Three friends of mine have, in fact, killed themselves in the past year, and I have wondered what that was like. I rejected it. But for the first time, I understood why they had done it.

Hopeless, helpless, and unable to function. A mind shutting down and taking the body with it. A pain not physical but not of my comprehension and always there, a buzzing fluorescent light that you can't turn off.

No way out, I thought. Except there was.

I don't need to replay the early days of trauma for you here. You know what I'm talking about.

Whether you were in south Louisiana or somewhere far away, in a shelter or at your sister's house, whether you lost everything or nothing, you know what I mean.

My case might be more extreme than some because I immersed myself fully into the horror and became a full-time chronicler of sorrowful tales. I live it every day, and there is no such thing as leaving it behind at the office when a whole city takes the dive.

Then again, my case is less extreme than the first responders, the doctors and nurses and EMTs, and certainly anyone who got trapped in the Dome or the Convention Center or worse—in the water, in their attics, and on their rooftops. In some cases, stuck in trees.

I've got nothing on them. How the hell do they sleep at night?

So none of this made sense. My personality has always been marked by insouciance and laughter, the seeking of adventure and new experiences. I am the class clown, the life of the party, the bon vivant.

I have always felt as if I was more alert and alive than anyone in the room.

In the measure of how one made out in the storm, my life was cake. My house, my job, and my family were all fine. My career was gangbusters; all manner of prestigious awards and attention. A book with great reviews and stunning sales, full auditoriums everywhere I was invited to speak, appearances on TV and radio, and the overwhelming support of readers, who left gifts, flowers, and cards on my doorstep, thanking me for my stories.

I had become a star of a bizarre constellation. No doubt about it, disasters are great career moves for a man in my line of work. So why the hell was I so miserable? This is the time of my life, I told myself. I am a success. I have done good things.

To no avail.

I changed the message on my phone to say, "This is Chris Rose. I am emotionally unavailable at the moment. Please leave a message."

I thought this was hilarious. Most of my friends picked it up as a classic cry for help.

My editor, my wife, my dad, my friends, and just strangers on the street who recognized me from my picture in the paper had been telling me for a long time: You need to get help.

I didn't want help. I didn't want medicine. And I sure as hell didn't want to sit on a couch and tell some guy with glasses, a beard, and a psych degree from Dartmouth all about my troubles.

Everybody's got troubles. I needed to stay the course, keep on writing, keep on telling the story of this city. I needed to do what I had to do, the consequences be damned, and what I had to do was dig further and further into what has happened around here—to the people, my friends, my city, the region.

Lord, what an insufferable mess it all is.

I'm not going to get better, I thought. I'm in too deep.

In his book *Darkness Visible: A Memoir of Madness*—the best literary guide to the disease that I have found—the writer William

Styron recounted his own descent into and recovery from depression, and one of the biggest obstacles, he said, was the term itself, which he calls "a true wimp of a word."

He traces the medical use of the word "depression" to a Swiss psychiatrist named Adolf Meyer, who, Styron said, "had a tin ear for the finer rhythms of English and therefore was unaware of the damage he had inflicted by offering 'depression' as a descriptive noun for such a dreadful and raging disease.

Nonetheless, for over 75 years the word has slithered innocuously through the language like a slug, leaving little trace of its intrinsic malevolence and preventing, by its very insipidity, a general awareness of the horrible intensity of the disease when out of control.

He continued:

As one who has suffered from the malady in extremis yet returned to tell the tale, I would lobby for a truly arresting designation. "Brainstorm," for instance, has unfortunately been preempted to describe, somewhat jocularly, intellectual inspiration. But something along these lines is needed.

Told that someone's mood disorder has evolved into a storm— a veritable howling tempest in the brain, which is indeed what a clinical depression resembles like nothing else—even the uninformed layman might display sympathy rather than the standard reaction that "depression" evokes, something akin to "So what?" or "You'll pull out of it" or "We all have bad days."

Styron is a helluva writer. His words were my life. I was having one serious brainstorm. Hell, it was a brain hurricane, Category 5. But what happens when your own personal despair starts bleeding over into the lives of those around you?

What happens when you can't get out of your car at the gas station even when you're out of gas? Man, talk about the perfect metaphor.

Then this summer, a colleague of mine at the newspaper took a bad mix of medications and went on a violent driving spree

Uptown, an episode that ended with his pleading with the cops who surrounded him with guns drawn to shoot him.

He had gone over the cliff. And I thought to myself: If I don't do something, I'm next.

My psychiatrist asked me not to identify him in this story, and I am abiding by that request.

I was referred to him by my family doctor. My first visit was August 15. I told him I had doubts about his ability to make me feel better. I pled guilty to skepticism about the confessional applications of his profession and its dependency medications.

I'm no Tom Cruise; psychiatry is fine, I thought. For other people.

My very first exchange with my doctor had a morbidly comic element to it; at least I thought so, but my sense of humor was in delicate balance, to be sure.

While approaching his office, I noticed a dead cat in his yard. Freshly dead, with flies just beginning to gather around the eyes. My initial worry was that some kid who loves this cat might see it, so I said to him, "Before we start, do you know about the cat?"

Yes, he told me. It was being taken care of. Then he paused and said, "Well, you're still noticing the environment around you. That's a good sign."

The analyst in him had already kicked in. But the patient in me was still resisting. In my lifelong habit of dampening down any serious discussion with sarcasm, I said to him, "Yeah, but what if the dead cat was the *only* thing I saw? What if I didn't see or hear the traffic or the trees or the birds or anything else?"

I crack myself up. I see dead things. Get it?

Yeah, neither did he.

We talked for an hour that first appointment. He told me he wanted to talk to me three or four times before he made a diagnosis and prescribed an antidote. When I came home from that first visit without a prescription, my wife was despondent and my editor enraged. To them, it was plain to see I needed something, anything, and fast.

Unbeknown to me, my wife immediately wrote a letter to my doctor, pleading with him to put me on medication. Midway through my second session, I must have convinced him as well, because he reached into a drawer and pulled out some samples of a drug called Cymbalta.

He said it could take a few weeks to kick in. Best case, he said, would be four days. He also said that its reaction time would depend on how much body fat I had; the more I had, the longer it would take. That was a good sign for me. By August, far from putting on the Katrina 15, I had become a skeletal version of my pre-K self.

Before I left that second session, he told me to change the message on my phone, that "emotionally unavailable" thing. Not funny, he said.

I began taking Cymbalta on August 24, a Thursday. As I had practically no body fat to speak of, the drug kicked in immediately. That whole weekend, I felt as if I were in the throes of a drug rush. Mildly euphoric, but also leery of what was happening inside of me. I felt off balance. But I felt better, too.

I told my wife this, but she was guarded. I've always heard that everyone else notices changes in a person who takes an antidepressant before the patient does, but that was not the case with me.

"I feel better," I told Kelly but my long-standing gloom had cast such a pall over our relationship that she took a wait-and-see attitude.

By Monday, I was settled in. The dark curtain had lifted almost entirely. The despondency and incapacitation vanished, just like that, and I was who I used to be: energetic, sarcastic, playful, affectionate, and alive.

I started talking to Kelly about plans—a word lacking from my vocabulary for months. Plans for the kids at school, extracurricular activities, weekend vacations. I had not realized until that moment that while stuck in my malaise, I had had no vision of the future whatsoever.

I han't been planning anything. It was almost like not living.

Kelly came around to believing. We became husband and wife again. We became friends.

It all felt like a Come to Jesus experience. It felt like a miracle. But it was just medicine, plain and simple.

I asked my doctor to tell me exactly what was wrong with me so I could explain it in this story. I will be candid and tell you I still don't really understand it, the science of depression, the actions of synapses, transmitters, blockers, and stimulants.

I've never been much at science. I guess I'm just a fragile poet after all.

The diagnoses and treatments for depression and anxiety are still a developing science. The *Diagnostic and Statistical Manual of Mental Disorders* — psychiatry's chief handbook — practically doubles in size every time it's reprinted, filled with newer and clearer clinical trials, research, and explanations.

Does that mean more people are getting depressed? Or that science is just compiling more data? I don't know.

Measuring depression is not like measuring blood sugar. You don't hit a specified danger level on a test and then you're pronounced depressed. It is nuance and interpretation and there is still a lot of guesswork involved.

But here's my doctor's take: The amount of cortisol in my brain had increased to dangerous levels. The overproduction, in turn, was blocking the transmission of serotonin and norepinephrine.

Some definitions: Cortisol is the hormone produced in response to chronic stress. Serotonin and norepinephrine are neurotransmitters — chemical messengers — that mediate messages between nerves in the brain, and this communication system is the basic source of all mood and behavior.

The chemistry department at the University of Bristol in England has a massive Web database for serotonin, titled, appropriately, "A Molecule of Happiness."

And I wasn't getting enough. My brain was literally shorting out. The cells were not communicating properly. Chemical imbalances, likely caused by increased stress hormones — cortisol, to be precise — were dogging the work of my neurotransmitters, my electrical wiring. A real and true physiological deterioration had begun.

I had a disease.

This I was willing to accept. Grudgingly, for it ran against my lifelong philosophy of self-determination.

I pressed my doctor: What is the difference between sad and depressed? How do you know when you've crossed over?

"Post-traumatic stress disorder is bandied about as a common diagnosis in this community, but I think that's probably not the case," he told me. "What people are suffering from here is what I call Katrina Syndrome, marked by sleep disturbance, recent memory impairment, and increased irritability.

"Much of this is totally normal. Sadness is normal. The people around here who are bouncing around and giddy, saying that everything is all right—they have more of a mental illness than someone who says, 'I'm pretty washed out.'

"But when you have the thousand-yard stare, when your ability to function is impaired, then you have gone from 'discomfort' to 'pathologic.' If you don't feel like you can go anywhere or do anything—or sometimes, even move—then you are sick."

That was me.

If that is you, let me offer some unsolicited advice, something you've already been told a thousand times by people who love you, something you really ought to consider listening to this time: Get help.

I hate being dependent on a drug. Hate it more than I can say. But if the alternative is a proud stoicism in the face of sorrow accompanied by prolonged and unspeakable despair—well, I'll take dependency.

I can live with it. I can live with anything, I guess. For now.

Cymbalta is a new generation of antidepressant, a combination of selective serotonin and norepinephrine reuptake inhibitors—SSRIs and SNRIs—the two common drugs for anxiety and depression.

I asked my doctor why he selected it over, say, Prozac or Wellbutrin or any of the myriad antidepressants whose brand names have become as familiar as aspirin in our community.

He replied, "It's a roll of the dice." He listened to my story, observed me, and made an educated guess. If it didn't work, he said, we'd try something else.

But it worked.

Today I can take my kids to school in the morning and mingle effortlessly with the other parents. Crowds don't freak me out. I'm not tired all day, every day. I love going to the grocery store. I can pump gas. I notice the smell of night-blooming jasmine and I play with my kids and I clean up after my dog and the simplest things, man—how had they ever gotten so hard?

The only effect I have noticed on my writing is that the darkness lifted. I can still channel anger, humor, and irony—the three speeds I need on my editorial stick shift.

And I'm not the only one who senses the change. Everyone tells me they can see the difference, even readers. I'm not gaunt. I make eye contact. I can talk about the weather, the Saints, whatever; it doesn't have to be so dire, every word and motion.

Strange thing is this: I never cry anymore. Ever.

I tell you truthfully that I cried every day from August 29 last year until August 24 this year, 360 days straight. And then I stopped. I guess the extremes of emotion have been smoothed over, but, truthfully, I have shed enough tears for two lifetimes.

Even at the Saints' *Monday Night Football* game, a moment that weeks earlier would have sent me reeling into spasms of open weeping, I held it together. A lump in my throat, to be sure, but no prostration anymore.

The warning labels on antidepressants are loaded with ominous portent, everything from nausea to sexual dysfunction, and, without going into more detail than I have already poured out here, let's just say that I'm doing quite well, thank you.

It's my movie now. I am part of the flow of humanity that clogs our streets and sidewalks, taking part in and being part of the community and its growth. I have clarity, and oh, what a vision it is.

I am not cured, not by any means. Clinical trials show that Cymbalta has an 80 percent success rate after six months, and I'm just two months in. I felt a backward tilt recently—the long.

stare, the pacing, it crept in one weekend—and it scared me so badly that I went to my doctor and we immediately agreed to increase the strength of my medication.

Before Katrina, I would have called somebody like me a wuss. Not to my face. But it's what I would have thought, this talk of mood swings and loss of control, all this psychobabble and hope-dope.

What a load of crap. Get a grip, I would have said.

And that's exactly what I did, through a door that was hidden from me but that I was finally able to see.

I have a disease. Medicine saved me. I am living proof.

Emphasis on *living*.

Letters from the Edge
10/29/06

Life is full of stunning moments of revelation; couldn't every one of us title our memoirs "Little Epiphanies"?

Certainly my world took a tilt this past Sunday—my privacy and worldview ripped wide open and exposed—when I wrote what I suppose is the most personal story I've ever laid down in print, a story about my yearlong bout with depression.

That term "bout with depression" just makes me cringe. I never would have read such an article had I not written it myself, all maudlin and self-helpy. But that's what it has been. A bout. With depression.

The response has been, to say the least, overwhelming. If you are one of the roughly 1,000 people who e-mailed or called me to say thank you or welcome to the club or hang in there, I want to acknowledge that with gratitude here because the odds of my actually getting an opportunity to respond to all of my recent correspondence are slim. I was already backlogged a few thousand e-mails and phone calls from the past few months, the period in which I sank into an incapacitating abyss.

I mean it. I feel the love, from so many readers, and I appreciate that more than I can say. And answering 1,000 e-mails definitely constitutes more than I can say.

Even to those who suggested I substitute yoga, Jesus, or Saint-

John's-wort for my antidepressant medication, I thank you and will take your recommendations under advisement but stick with my doctor's prescribed remedy for now.

There are two correspondences that particularly shook me, one of which I answered and the other I could not. One was from someone in our community who has already attempted suicide and had been in possession of a prescription for antidepressants for weeks but had not gotten it filled.

Maybe he or she would refill it now, the correspondent wrote. But it was expensive. But, after food, I don't know of a better use for money for one who is suicidal than medicine to make you not be.

So, whoever you are . . . please.

The other communication was a letter—unsigned—from someone who told me they were experiencing the same symptoms and despair that I had written about but were seeking an alternative solution.

I had written about three friends who had killed themselves, and this person wrote, "I will not be your fourth friend to die. I am only an acquaintance, so I will be your first, second, third or fourth or fifth to die. My rabbit hole is becoming deeper, more comfortable, more desirable. Your pain and fear is as valid as mine, your depression is as valid as mine. The only difference is that I will stop my pain differently than you."

Unfortunately, I don't think the writer was referring to yoga, Jesus, or Saint-John's-wort. Do I detect a cry for help? Do I detect a community in crisis, at wit's end? Hell yes, I do. (These were only among the extreme letters I got; there are hundreds that are mere Category 4s.)

Here's a funny thing: In my article about fighting depression, I listed, as one example of the weight that took me down, all the thousands of e-mails I have received over the past year from readers spilling out their own stories of misery and funk. I wasn't assigning blame, mind you, just listing the circumstances that preyed upon me from time to time.

So I have to believe that some readers would have taken this as a mild plea not to burden me anymore with their stories, and still—I got more than a thousand responses from folks telling me that they, too, have felt hope and purpose slipping away as they try to rebuild or even just get back to New Orleans.

How many wanted to write but didn't because they thought they might send me into a tailspin? I don't know. But I'm glad people did write to me because I have accumulated a mind-boggling compilation of stories that capture the emotional land-scape of life after the flood and I don't know what the hell I'll do with it but someday, someone smarter than me can take a look at it all and tell us just what happened here.

It boggles the mind to think of how many among us are hold-ing on by frayed threads, just barely, and trying to hide it as I was for so many months.

There is no cavalry on its way to save us. Other than putting vast stocks of serotonin and norepinephrine—the happy mole-cules in your brain—into the water system, I don't know what we can do to turn this thing around.

It is up to us. We need to start looking for red flags even where there don't appear to be any. I loathe even intimating that our community is weak, unable to face the challenge and devastation on our hands, but there's no question that a lot of folks are treading on thin ice or no ice at all.

It's simple stuff to look for and think about. It may be the guy next door whom you've never even spoken to because his yard is a mess or the woman you just honked your horn at and gave the finger to because she was befuddled at the intersection or the mail carrier you just chewed out because your *Sports Illustrated* didn't get delivered once again or the guy who was rude to you in the checkout line at Walgreens and not because he's a jerk but because he can't even see straight.

He probably didn't even know you were there. Didn't see you, didn't hear you. All he knows about is the scream in his head.

I was having a conversation the other day with a New Yorker who talked about how everybody was all touchy-feely in the months after 9/11 but that, in due time, everyone just went back to being New Yorkers.

She said she sees that here, now, that maybe all the goodwill and kindness and togetherness is fracturing as the slog goes into year two and everyone's kind of fed up with one another's neediness.

I was leaving my therapist's office Wednesday morning and encountered a guy in the waiting room who wore the mask of complete surrender. I have never seen in a man's eyes so much pain, someone just so damn spun around by what has happened that he can't even get his shoes on without full concentration.

I felt powerless in this man's presence. He was able to lift up his head to make eye contact only because his brother was pointing me out to him. I'm famous now. I'm the guy who's got depression, the New Orleans poster boy for all the sorrow in the world.

All I could muster for the guy was "Good luck." How lame. What else could I have done?

The poet Rick Danko used to sing, "Twilight is the loneliest time of day," and it is haunting and beautiful and I think about it a lot because we're in permanent twilight around here.

When you look into someone's eyes and see a cave with nobody living inside, say hello in there. I don't mean to get all Oprah on you here, but if you see the opportunity, help a guy get his shoes on, because sometimes it's harder than you know.

Find some way to shine a light. Together, maybe we'll find our way out of this.

Where We Go
From Here

Children of the Storm,
It's Time to Represent
5/14/06

I was asked to give the commencement speech at Ursuline Academy last night.

I have faced many personal challenges in the days since last August, but making an inspirational speech to a couple hundred restless Catholic schoolgirls—and their parents—strikes me as the most daunting yet.

For what it's worth, this is what I came up with:

Good evening. As you look at me, I know what you're thinking. Just what you need: another old man who doesn't understand you, giving you advice, rendering forth the wisdom of the ages like some geezer sage from the Paleozoic Era here to utter inspirational platitudes from Dear Abby and that fine self-help manual *All I Really Need to Know I Learned in Kindergarten.*

Or worse: *Oh, the Places You'll Go!*.

Those are all great books; don't get me wrong. But in kindergarten, they didn't teach you how to siphon gas during a natural disaster, how to send a distress signal with a flashlight, and how to decontaminate a refrigerator—to say nothing of how to properly open, season, and heat a National Guard–issued MRE without burning your hands.

We in New Orleans were always different from folks else-where. Now we're real different. I wager that you learned more about life, death, and everything in between this past year than in the rest of your life combined.

You are survivors. The Katrina Kids. The Children of the Storm.

And yes, I am middle-aged. Eisenhower was in office when I was born.

Eisenhower was a president. Of this country. Anyway . . .

Yes, I am from the past. I do not own an iPod. I do not text-message. I don't have a tattoo on my lower back. I think skate-boarding is dangerous. I think ketchup should be red and only red. Energy drinks give me the shakes. I don't know who the lead singer of Maroon 5 is. I think Bruce Springsteen is cool.

For those of you still awake . . .

I have an advantage that commencement speakers didn't have when I was your age: the Internet. Yes, there was a time before the Internet. It was a long time ago. It sucked.

My kids marvel when I tell them that television was once just in black and white. And that no matter how many channels you tuned into, you couldn't find Hilary Duff on any of them.

They don't believe me.

So I checked out some Web sites for tips about making a grad-uation speech, but I came up wanting. Most said to lean heavily on inspirational quotes from famous people, but if Ursuline Academy wanted Einstein or Mark Twain to give you a speech, I suppose they would have arranged for Einstein or Twain to be here today.

With the digital technology available today, I suppose that's almost possible.

And I found out that I could even purchase an audience-tested motivational commencement speech online for only $25—a much higher fee than the going rate for college term papers; I suppose they are mindful of the budgetary constraints of students as opposed to, say . . . someone who gives a gradua-tion speech.

One Web site pointed out that nobody listens to the gradua-tion speaker anyway because everyone is distracted and preoc-cupied, but if you make a winking reference to alcohol, you'll catch everyone's attention.

But I'm not going to do that. That would be a cheap gimmick.

And now that I have your attention, let me lay some heavy on you.

There are commencement exercises all over this country today, but you and your fellow graduates from the Gulf Coast are different, very different. Particularly here in New Orleans.

The water, it came to your school. The gasoline, chemicals, sewage, and blood came to your doorstep. It settled into the ground of this courtyard where we now gather.

Not a pleasant notion to consider on this joyous occasion, but there you are: the elephant is out of its cage again.

You must never forget what happened here. You must take that experience with you into the world.

You must, as they say, represent New Orleans.

I can tell you from my years of work and travel that to be from New Orleans has always been an interesting proposition. Histor-ically, if you were, say, in Europe, and you told someone you were from the United States, generally they would shrug. But if you told them you were from New Orleans, they would want you to pull up a chair at their table, they would want to know more about you and your city.

On our domestic shores, historically, when New Orleanians check into college dormitories their freshman year of college, they are an immediate attraction, and not just because everyone assumes their partying credentials are higher than everyone else's.

You are interesting because where you come from is interest-ing, unique, colorful, diverse, and tolerant. People have always wanted to know about it, to see it for themselves, to touch the magic here if by no other means than by the picture painted by your words, your stories.

Tell them what happened here.

I'm not going to offer you the language to describe it or the politics to color it; use your own words and thoughts.

But I'll give you an example:

My daughter was asked to write about her experiences over the past year when she came back to school in New Orleans in January, and this is what she wrote: "There was a Hurricane. Some people died. Some of them were kids."

My daughter was six when she wrote that. It just doesn't strike me as what you would wish for your child to write in her first-grade journal, but there it is.

You—all of us—are marked for life by what happened here, and if you go out into the world and you shrug it off—if you are soooo over the Katrina thing—then you are doing a disservice to yourself and to the community that gave you your spirit and identity.

Like it or not, this storm, these circumstances, have marked you. My belief is that your generation and those who come after you in this town will be extraordinarily resilient. That is a good quality to carry with you. You have seen and have suffered loss.

For those of you who fall into that huge swath of our community known as "lost everything," people try to tell you it was just stuff, get over it, at least you're alive, and what you lost was just stuff.

Yeah, well. It was your stuff. It took seventeen years to get that stuff. And if it all disappeared in one day, then, hell yeah, it's all right to be mad about that.

But move on. Make the anger work for you.

Perhaps the most valuable lesson we have learned as a community is humility. The great equalizer. We have been targeted by our circumstances as the recipients of the greatest outpouring of donations, charity, and volunteer help in American history.

People from elsewhere, people we don't know, saved us. They gave us their money and their time and they cleared our streets and protected our homes and, funny thing, most of us don't even know who they were. Or are.

They expected—and in most cases received—nothing in return.

Are you ready to do the same for someone else when the time comes?

Think about it. Discuss amongst yourselves. And get ready. Because that time will come, many times over, in your lifetime.

Life is short. Now you know that. What happened here shows how it can all be gone tomorrow. So just do it. Seize the day. Carpe diem. I am Tiger Woods. Rise up. Make levees, not war. Vote for Pedro. Whatever.

Just do something important with your young life. Don't sit around and wait until you're fifty to suddenly understand how precious all of this is.

There's always the story of the bitter, angry old man who picks on little children and never says thank you to the waiter or waitress and doesn't say hello to the mailman.

And then one day the old guy gets cancer and a wake-up call, reality check, and he realizes how little time is left and suddenly he's volunteering at the oncology ward at Children's Hospital and he asks after the bank teller's mama and he stops and pets the neighbor's dog and he tells everyone that he can: I never knew how beautiful it all was.

Don't be that guy. Nobody likes that guy.

New Orleans got cancer this past year. We got our wake-up call, and if you're living an existence here that is without purpose and mission, then you are asleep.

Twice in my column in recent months I have invoked the words of a Magazine Street barber named Aidan Gill, whose call to arms is the most powerful I have heard since the storm.

He said, "A time will come when someone asks you, 'What were you doing about it?' You can't tell them, 'I was just watching it. I was just an innocent bystander.' Let me tell you something: there are no innocent bystanders in this."

No truer words have been spoken.

I can't tell you what, exactly, to do; how to engage in your community. I wouldn't be so presumptuous; the philosophy here is think for yourself and find your own way.

But if finding your own way involves putting on work boots and heavy gloves this summer and going into neighborhoods you've never seen in this city before, then all the better.

There are tens of thousands of people and institutions that

need help in this community, and not all of them are going to make it—but by God, it's not going to be because we didn't try. It's not going to be because we didn't give everything we had—our hearts, our souls, and our bodies—into saving this place and making it better than it ever was.

Your home.

There are no innocent bystanders. Not in this courtyard. Not in this neighborhood. Not in this city. Not now. Not ever.

One more thing, and this is important:

Be kind to your parents.

I will tell you something that they cannot or will not tell you, and it is this: They are consumed right now with a world of worry and doubt that is crushing in its weight.

Maybe you can see this at home or maybe they are good at hiding it from you because that's what parents do—spend most of our lives trying to shield our children from pain.

They won't tell you this, so I will: They're scared. They're terrified. We're all terrified.

Everything we know and love is at risk. So be kind to them.

It's like we're all in a big boat right now, paddling for our lives, and we've got to be together of one mind to get through this.

So get in the boat and grab a paddle and get ready for the ride of your lives.

Nothing is more rewarding than a purpose-driven life. And it is here, outside your door, every morning—or afternoon—when you wake up.

Don't miss the boat.

Thank You, Whoever You Are
11/23/06

I was browsing through a used-book store out of town recently and stumbled upon a book in the bargain bin that I had never heard of called *The Day the World Came to Town*.

It's a story about an isolated circumstance that occurred on September 11, 2001, a thousand miles away from New York City, the Pentagon, and Shanksville, Pennsylvania.

It opened my eyes to the vast world of ancillary actions, reactions, ripples, and far-flung effects of the 9/11 tragedy, just one story in the millions of stories that unfurled from that terrible day outside the periphery of what has become our collective memory of what happened.

The book, by former *Miami Herald* columnist Jim DeFede, takes the reader to a faraway place called Gander, Newfoundland, a fishing community of about ten thousand residents in the northeast corner of Canada.

Newfoundlanders have always had a proud and separatist mentality, living in harsh weather and rugged terrain, a place so singular and isolated that it operates in a time zone all its own — ninety minutes ahead of U.S. eastern standard time.

On September 11, when the World Trade Center was attacked, there were more than 4,500 airplanes over U.S. airspace, and every one of them was ordered to land immediately at the closest available airstrip to await further instruction. Most of the planes remained grounded for several days.

Planes headed to the United States from overseas were directed elsewhere, and that's how, on that fateful day five years ago, thirty-eight planes, most of them jumbos, carrying 6,595 passengers from all over the world, came rumbling down the old airstrip in Gander, waking the population there to a world of suspicion (are there more terrorists on those planes?) and challenge (what the hell are we going to do with 6,595 people?).

Sound familiar?

The story, as it unfolds in DeFede's book—which I highly recommend—is a compelling narrative of people of every shape, stripe, and color all thrown into an involuntary communion.

If you think the Pilgrims and Indians made for an odd dinner pairing on the first Thanksgiving, imagine the implications of a Nigerian princess, a world-renowned Italian fashion designer, and a group of Orthodox Jews all foraging for meals—and it goes without saying that kosher products run scarce in a place like Gander.

To say nothing of the many animals stored away in the cargo holds and exotic medical necessities of the elderly and add to this the fact that, for security reasons, the passengers were not allowed access to their luggage during their stay.

Suddenly, Gander, Newfoundland, needed 6,595 new toothbrushes. And it somehow found them.

The townsfolk and the visitors, most of whom wound up staying the better part of a week, meshed in magical, comical, heartwarming ways. The town gave everything it had to make the situation work, and the town's only barroom became an epicenter of cultural exchange—poetry, music, folktales, and even romance—and the whole damn thing makes you feel good about the fundamental nature of people, all people.

Well, most people. There were small clashes and difficulties and plenty of temper tantrums—how could there not be in this sudden and involuntary gumbo?—but, overall, the story just makes you stand up and cheer.

The Newfoundlanders opened their homes and bathrooms and cooked up massive meals and donated every article of clothing and bedding that they didn't need for themselves and collected all their toys, toiletries, and medicine and all the businesses in the area cleared off their shelves and asked for no remittance (doubtful that the local hardware store takes euros, shekels, or nairas anyway) and it all just feels like that old Coca-Cola TV ad about peace, love, harmony, and all that other squishy stuff that seems so hard to remember and embrace in the cold harsh light of the cultural conflict and ubiquitous greed of America in 2006.

And then, in the days after the disaster, the thirty-eight planes gradually reloaded and took off for their original destinations and all those people just filtered away from Gander and some folks made lasting friendships and still keep in touch but no doubt the majority—imagine all the language barriers, all the distractions, all the stuff of life that gets in the way—just went away and went on with their lives. And all that's left on them—both the visitors and the hosts—is the imprint of the triumph of the human spirit, that dependency on the kindness of strangers that is so much a part of the fabric of our own New Orleans culture.

And here's what this book got me thinking about—and you're probably ahead of me on this point: Isn't that, now fifteen months after Katrina, the way it goes around here? So many of us have tried to settle back into our old lives—well, new lives would be more accurate—and move on and up and away from time and memory, but I am stuck in my head with the mystery of how many stories like Gander unfolded for our own people, how many ancillary tales of generosity, how many ripples in faraway places unfolded that we may never gather into the collective consciousness of post-Katrina life simply because the story is so damn big and stretches across thousands of miles.

Maybe you've heard this story about Gander before, but I never had and no one I have talked to since I read this remarkable and uplifting book has, either.

So how will all of our own stories be collected for the final record of the storm? Will it take five years to figure out who did what for whom?

Will we ever know just how big a human enterprise it was, the dispersal of hundreds of thousands of Americans across this land, people arriving on distant shores with nothing but a grocery bag full of belongings and no home, no job, no traction, and a whole lot of fear, to be met by strangers who opened their hearts and their lives (and their wallets) and made everything work as best as it could under the circumstances?

There are thousands of stories we'll never know—a legion of mini-Ganders out there that tell a story of the day Louisiana and Mississippi came to town and that town—Anytown, USA—rose to the challenge.

Big Government failed and politics failed but the people rose up, giving us such an abundance of things to be thankful for that it boggles the mind. And the strange thing is that—outside of each of our own singular experiences (those who sheltered us, gave clothes or money or provided whatever needs were most urgent)—most of us don't even know who it is we're supposed to thank and what it is they did for us. But there are hundreds of thousands of them—no, millions!—who made sacrifices of time, money, travel, labor, and spirit to help the people of south Louisiana and Mississippi get back on their feet and become some small semblance of what we once were and of what we will become again someday.

So today, Thanksgiving, just who do we thank? All those people. But how do we tell them, the soldiers and doctors and Common Grounders and church groups and corporate groups and school groups and animal rescuers and the uncountable and unknowable masses who came to our city to clean us up, dust us off, give us a meal, and give us a hug before going back to their own homes forever changed, just as the folks in Gander will never be the same?

It's weird: I just feel like picking up the phone today and randomly dialing some small town somewhere and saying thank you for what you did for us because it's inevitable that they did something for us.

Maybe they took in evacuees or maybe the local elementary school collected a water jug of pennies or maybe a local corporation sent $5 million. It's hard to know who did what—as I said, this thing is so damn big—but I swear that it seems as though everyone I meet every time I travel did something.

So when you look around this town, this region, and see the small steps we have taken on our long road to recovery, realize that there have been guardian angels at our side every step of the way. And since we'll never take stock of who they all were, really the best way to thank them is to succeed here, to become a city and region better than we were, a place strong enough, unified enough—and good enough—to take in thirty-eight planes full of strangers when it's our turn to answer to the call of membership in the human race.

A New Dawn
12/31/06

I remember sitting down to write a year-in-review column last year at this time and how it all seemed so easily collected and categorized. The year 2005 essentially boiled down to just the final four months—the previous eight being filed under The Past, Life Before The Flood, The Land That Time Forgot, The City Before The Thing.

Man, we took a powdering; sometimes it's still impossible to wrap your head around it, all this time later.

Those final four months were a blur of activity and emotional upheaval, but they also were easily compressed into a thin file folder labeled Destruction & Sorrow, a time capsule of memories not so much buried as washed away, set adrift, not something we can dig up in a poignant ceremony one hundred years from now. Last year ended with everything so unsettled; just a million questions piled up on the curbside like so much debris, the answers just beginning to be formulated in our heads.

What the new year would hold was anybody's guess, and unfortunately it has indeed all seemed like guesswork, a roll of the dice, the handiwork of card readers on Jackson Square; the lack of a competent and cohesive plan seems to have been all but ignored by the powers that be. While elected officials and develop-

1 Dead in Attic   359

ers offer us golden towers and jazz monuments and glistening cities and rail lines drawn up on pretty paper, the true rebuilding has been left to the busy worker bees of the city, carrying physical and emotional burdens a hundred times their own weight while the queen bees abdicate their responsibility and turn circles and sideways in an endless buzz of blame.

They need to get out of their hives more often.

The official New Orleans government Web site is cityofno.com, and doesn't that just say it all? The City of No. No plan. No answers. No confidence. With government headquarters on Perdido Street, which is Spanish (perfect) for "lost," it's all just perfect symbolism.

Ah, but let's move on to this year, the 365 days of transition that will define the next thousand days, two thousands days, ad infinitum.

Trying to wrangle all the events and emotions of 2006 into one narrative is a whole 'nuther kind of challenge, the ups and downs, highs and lows, triumphs and disappointments reaching such extremes that they set the head spinning, all summations amounting to a hill of beans.

It's just one small step at a time, small triumphs of family and community—the aquarium reopens, City Park gets a scrubbing, the Crescent City Steak House and Brocato's reopen, residents dribble home, the sound of children's voices brings life to once-darkened streets, a grocery store opens in Gentilly, a playground gets rehabbed in the east, flowers grow on a front stoop in the Lower 9, your in-laws finally move out of your house in Slidell, back to their rehabbed cottage in Mid-City.

Who says there's no good news?

There are a million little things, small victories, signs of life, signs of living, manifestations of love for a city, desperate reaches to regain a sense of place, our place, our home, our time. The Saints mantra is now transcribed as a city motto: Just wait until next year! But only a fool would try to predict what 2007 holds for New Orleans and its environs. For what it's worth, forecasters at the nation's preeminent hurricane study center—Colorado State University—announced this month that 2007 would be a busier-than-average storm season with at least three "intense" hurricanes.

Use that information for any planning purposes you wish, but without a companion prediction on whether the levees will hold in the case of rising water, I don't know what good it is. It's all just a numbers game, trivia, the means by which we as a civilization try to make sense of things that don't make sense.

They said 2006 would be a busy storm season and look what happened. (Still, I recommend keeping that generator and the extra red gas cans on hand, just in case "they" are right this time.)

'Tis the dawn of a new day. Just to show how brave the new world is, *Forbes* business magazine recently rated "America's Drunkest Cities," which may or may not be indicative of our nation's current business climate, but the results might surprise you. Based on "availability of data and geographic diversity," *Forbes* rated Milwaukee as America's drunkest city, Minneapolis–St. Paul second, on and on down the list until you get to New Orleans at No. 24. Yes, 24. The Saints are in the playoffs. White voters re-elected Ray Nagin and William Jefferson. *GQ* magazine says New Orleans restaurants suck. The city has just one assessor. Britney Spears is, well . . . ah, never mind.

Hell has indeed frozen over.

It shows that anything can change anytime, and it probably will. It's in our own hands. Let the queen bees buzz over their pots of honey. We've got work to do and a life to celebrate.

At Aidan Gill's fancy men's barbershop on Magazine Street, the proprietor recently hosted a fund-raiser for a peer across town, a man named Chill the Barber, whose shop got wiped out in the flood. Gill charged forty bucks at the door and gave away top-shelf drinks and smokes, and folks mingled, and Chill sat in a leather barber chair soaking in a plan to rebuild his life and business, courtesy of an Irish barber on the other side of town. Presumably their paths—Gill and Chill—rarely crossed before the storm, but now one whose business survived (but house did not) helps raise capital for the other to begin anew, a gesture born of nothing more than a sense of community, because it's the right thing to do, lend a helping hand, brother can you spare a dime.

I have quoted Aidan Gill several times in other columns, and I will quote him again here—and perhaps at the beginning of every new year—for his words are the call we must live by: "A time will come when someone asks you, 'What were you doing about it?' You can't tell them, 'I was just watching it. I was just an innocent bystander.' Let me tell you something: There are no innocent bystanders in this."

So what are you doing about it? What's your plan for 2007, other than getting sucked into the Saints's vortex? Joining a playground cleanup crew in 2006 and writing a check to Habitat for Humanity were fine things, but that's last year's news. We must keep working for the common good.

What survives here in the crucible of the old city is the historic architecture: the mighty fortresses of the Garden District, the impenetrably walled blocks of the French Quarter. They are as good a symbol as any of the unbreakable (and unfloodable) determination of the city's remaining residents—and those who still break their backs trying to get back here—to raise up a great city, a great region, from ruin, defy the odds and the naysayers (and the forgetters), and live life to its richest possibilities, which was always the best thing about New Orleans anyway. The infinite possibilities of the night for those who chase dreams and dreamers. We choose to be in that number. To go marching on.

Acknowledgments

Acknowledgments strike me as a grand gesture of omission, so let me keep it short and necessary: Thanks to my editors at *The Times-Picayune*—James O'Byrne, Mark Lorando, and Ann Maloney—for letting me find my way through this mess.

To the Warriors of Laurel Street, my newspaper brothers and sisters, who fought in the trenches with me.

Thanks to the readers who gave me purpose, a mission, and my reward.

To my family—my heroes—for taking care of me and my kids during our homeless days.

To Katherine, Jack, and James, for giving me a reason to stay alive, keep writing, keep moving, keep getting up, day after day when, truth is, for a long time, I didn't want to.

To Kelly, for the journey. It was a race worth running.

To the doctors, therapists, and counselors who have tried so valiantly to put me back together again.

To Katherine Fausset, my agent at Curtis Brown, Ltd.; Colin Fox, my editor at Simon & Schuster; and his colleague Michele Bové, for believing in this story, this book, these words—and giving them a national audience.

And to New Orleans, my sweet, bedeviling mistress; cunning, baffling, powerful.

Never surrender.